TRAVELS OF FAH-HIAN AND SUNG-YUN,

BUDDHIST PILGRIMS, FROM CHINA TO INDIA (400 AD AND 518 AD)

TRAVELS OF FAH-HIAN AND SUNG-YUN,

BUDDHIST PILGRIMS, FROM CHINA TO INDIA

(400 AD AND 518 AD)

SAMUEL BEAL

TRANSLATED FROM THE CHINESE

GYAN

Published by

GYAN

Gyan Publishing House
5, Ansari Road
Daryaganj, New Delhi-110002
Phone: 011-47034999, 9811692060
E-mail: books@gyanbooks.com

Distribution Network
gyanbooks.com
India, USA, Canada, UK, Australia, France

ISBN : 978-81-212-4159-5 (PB)
First Published, London, 1869

2nd Impression 2020

Printed at: Gyan Press, Delhi.

Travels of Fah-Hian and Sung-Yun
Buddhist Pilgrims from
China to India
(AD 400 and ad 518)
Translated by: Samuel Beal

TRAVELS

OF

FAH-HIAN AND SUNG-YUN,

BUDDHIST PILGRIMS,

FROM

CHINA TO INDIA

(400 A.D. AND 518 A.D.)

TRANSLATED FROM THE CHINESE.

BY

SAMUEL BEAL,

(B.A. TRIN. COLL. CAMB.)

A CHAPLAIN IN H.M.'S FLEET; MEMBER OF THE ROYAL ASIATIC SOCIETY; AND AUTHOR OF A TRANSLATION OF THE PRATIMÔKSHA AND THE AMITHÂBA SÛTRA FROM THE CHINESE.

LONDON:
TRÜBNER AND CO., 60, PATERNOSTER ROW.

1869.

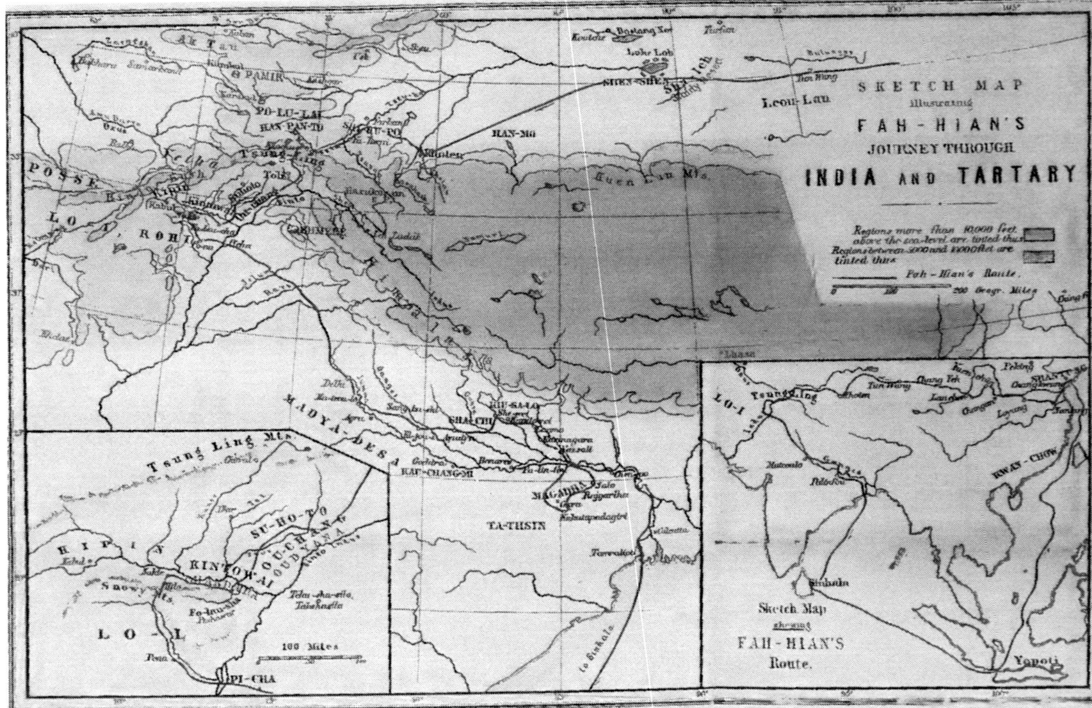

SKETCH MAP
illustrating
FAH-HIAN'S
JOURNEY THROUGH
INDIA AND TARTARY
Regions more than 10,000 feet above the sea-level are tinted thus
Regions between 3000 and 10000 feet are tinted thus
Fah-Hian's Route
Leou-Lan
HAN-MO
Kuen Lun Mts.
POSSE
LO-I
ROHI
PAMIR
PO-LU-LAI
HAN-PAN-TO
Tsung Ling
MADYA-DESA
KAU-CHANG-MI
MAGADHA
TA-THSIN
Tsung Ling Mts.
SU-HO-TO
OUDYANA
KIPIN
KIN-TO-WAI
Snowy Mts.
LO-I
100 Miles
PI-CHA
LO-I
Tsung Ling
KWAN-CHOW
Yepoti
Sinhala
Sketch Map
shewing
FAH-HIAN'S
Route.

TO

MY FATHER:

DUTY, AFFECTION, GRATITUDE.

"It is not a little surprising that we should have to acknowledge the fact that the voyages of two Chinese travellers, undertaken in the fifth and seventh century of our era, have done more to elucidate the history and geography of Buddhism in India, than all that has hitherto been found in the Sanskrit and Pali books of India and the neighbouring countries." —*Life of Gaudama*, p. 291, *n.* By Right Rev. P. Bigandet, Vicar-Apostolic of Ava and Pegu. 1868.

PREFACE.

THE present work contains two Translations from the Chinese—(1) The Travels of Fah-Hian (400–415 A.D.), and (2) The Mission of Sung-Yun; both Buddhist pilgrims from China to India.

A translation of Fah-Hian's Pilgrimage, by M. Abel-Rémusat, was published in Paris (1836), under the well-known title, Fo-koue-ki.

Of this work, M. Stanislas Julien has said that, although it is "très-recommandable pour l' époque ou il a été publié, il n'est pas sans dangers pour les personnes qui ne sont pas en ètat de vèrifier ses traductions" (Vie de Hiouen-Thsang, p. xi. n).

It was, in fact, published at a period when little was known in Europe of Chinese-Buddhist literature, and without having received the last revision of its lamented author.

That period has now passed by, and, owing to the labours of M. Abel-Rémusat's successors in the same field, and especially to the works of M. Stanislas Julien, we are able to approach the subject with some degree of confidence.

To shew the faulty character of the translations found in the Fo-koue-ki, it may be as well to select any chapter in the book, and consider a few of them in detail.

Let us take the 20th chapter as an example.

In that chapter (line 5) we read—"on y est très-affectionné à la loi," as a translation of 大愛道 but this phrase is, in fact (as we learn from Jul. iii. 495), the Chinese form of the name of Mahâprajâpatî, the aunt of Buddha.

Again, in the words immediately following the above—"aussi dans l'enceinte du temple"—we have a translation of 故精舍處 but, in truth, this clause ought to be joined with the previous one, and the whole rendered, "in the spot where stands the old Vihâra of Mahâprajâpatî," (the use of the symbol 故' (because), for '古 (old or antique) is of very frequent occurrence in the present work).

Following the same sentence, we read—"au lieu où etait le mur du puits du vieillard Siu-tha," 須達長者井壁處 but the expression 井壁

is a phrase denoting the foundation walls of a building, and probably refers here to the foundation walls of Sudatta's house.

Further down (line 15) we read—"à douze cents pas à l'orient de la route," as though it were 道東 whereas the text is really 道西 "to the westward of the road."

Towards the bottom of the page we read—"c'est là ce qu'on appelle le Temple de Tchi-houan" 即所謂祇洹 which Mr. Laidlay translates—"there too is the temple called Tchi-houan," as though this temple were distinct from the one previously described; whereas the sense of the passage is, that the account he had just given applies to and is descriptive of that, and all such Vihâras, commonly known as (tsih sho wei) Chi-ün temples. And so we read in the history of the Sañghârâmas of Lo-Yang, that in the neighbourhood of various temples belonging to that city (*e.gr.* the White Horse Temple) the founders had laid out "Chi-ün" grounds, *i.e.* elaborate gardens—gardens, in fact, corresponding to those which were, in the first instance, attached to this Chi-ün Vihâra at Sravâsti.

On page 172 (line 2) we have the expression 即刻牛頭栴檀佛像 rendered, "il fit en conséquence sculpter une tête de bœuf en bois de santal,"—but, in truth, the phrase 牛頭栴檀 is equivalent to "the sandal wood called Gosira," so that the whole sentence would be, "he caused a figure of Buddha to be carved out of (a peculiar sort) of sandal wood, called Gosira (*i.e.* ox-head)."

Again (page 173, line 22), we find—"la mére de Pi che-khiu fit bâtir un temple," where the expression 毗舍佉毋 is the same as the Singhalese Wisâkhâ-Mâtâwî, (although, in reality, it ought to be Migâra-mâtâwî), *i.e.* "Mother Vâisaka"—because she was the mother or chief of Upâsikhâwas, or female disciples of Buddha." (Manual of Buddhism, p. 226.)

On the same page (line 23), it is written—"cet endroit est dans une étroite dépendance du temple de Tchi-houan," corresponding to the Chinese 此處故在 which, in fact, means "the ruins of this place still exist." In this passage, Abel-Rémusat has evidently mistaken the division of the sentence (we must remember that the Chinese is unpunctuated), and included the next phrase 祇洹精舍 in the connection of the previous one; and hence the mistake found in the sentence immediately following the above—"le bourg a deux portes," the rendering of

祇洹精舍大𢮦落有二門 The complete translation of the passage is this—with regard to the former part of it, referring to the Vihâra of Mother Vâisakha, the remark is (as before stated), "the ruins of this place still exist;" and then he goes on to say—"the great garden enclosure (大𢮦落 for 大園落) of the Chi-ün Vihâra has two gates;" but Abel-Rémusat has taken it as if Fah-Hian referred to the gates of the city of Sravâsti, which is certainly not to be gathered from the original. But as the above is an important passage, perhaps it may be as well to state at greater length on what considerations I ground my translation. The phrase, "ta yuen loh," (大𢮦落) as it stands, has no meaning. From M. Abel-Rémusat's translation, I should judge that he had considered it equivalent to "ta tsu loh" (大聚落) which is a common phrase (as in Chap. 28) to signify a great village or town; but I have no hesitation in proposing "ta yuen loh' (大園落) as the correct reading—(1) because the characters 𢮦 and 園 are homophonous, and therefore might have been easily interchanged; but (2) because in the following sentence Fah-Hian uses this very word 園 in reference to the same place—he says, 此園卽須達長者布金

鏤買地處 that is, "this garden is the same as the place which the nobleman (Signor) Sudatta covered with gold coins and bought as a site." It seems almost certain, therefore, that the proposed reading is the correct one; and if so, then the expression 園 落 is undoubtedly properly translated the "garden enclosure."

Without citing any more passages, it will be seen from the above, that M. Julien's remark, respecting the untrustworthiness of the Fo-koue-ki, was not made without reason, and that, therefore, a more careful translation of the book was to be desired.

Whether the present work will meet the want or not, is a question for those best able to examine it, to determine. The only regret we must all feel, is, that M. Stanislas Julien himself has not been able to carry out his original design (Vie de Hiouen Thsang, lxxix.) to include both Fah-Hian and Sung-Yun in the number of Buddhist pilgrims, the account of whose travels he proposed to translate.

With reference to the foot-notes in the present volume, I have tried to include in them, in a small space, the best information bearing on the subject I could glean from works within my reach—especially from the Si-yu-ki of M. Stanislas Julien, the Manual of Buddhism by Rev. Spence Hardy, and the Archæological Surveys of India (1861–5) by General Cunningham.

It now only remains for me to express my gratitude to Vice-Admiral the Hon. C. G. B. Elliott, C.B., for the constant encouragement he afforded me in pursuing these studies during the five years I served (in China and Japan) as Chaplain of Her Majesty's ship "Sybille," under his command; and for his kindness on several occasions in securing books for me, and giving me opportunities of gaining information respecting various subjects of inquiry. Also to Major-General George Alexander, C.B., to whom I am indebted for my copy of Fah-Hian,[1] and who, by his own knowledge of the Chinese language, frequently assisted me in the work of translation.

To Dr. Rost also, and Mr. Laidlay, I desire to offer my thanks for the use of many books, and especially the English version of the Fo-koue-ki, which I could not have procured without their assistance.

[1] This copy, and also that of the Loyang Temples, from which I have translated an account of the mission of Sung-Yun, are parts of the seventh series of a large Miscellany called Hioh-tsin-t'au-Yuen.

INTRODUCTION.

I. Buddhism, which had arisen in India (500-600 B.C.)[1] under the form of a reaction against the material worship and the intolerant claims of the Brahmans, in time (260 B.C.)[2] became the adopted religion of the country. Missionaries, proceeding from the various centres of religious influence, carried a knowledge of their doctrines and discipline north and south—until, from Balkh to Ceylon and from Pattala on the Indus, to Tamluc on the Húgli, the vast territory was leavened by their teaching, and the priestly power of the Brahman began to pale.

During this period, there was occurring an equally important movement in the eastern portions of Central Asia. This vast territory (that portion of it commonly known as Chinese Tartary) had been long occupied by conflicting races of people, who, from early times, descended from the northern steppes of Mongolia and the country watered by the Amûr and its branches, towards the more tempting territory bordering on China. During

[1] The conventional date of Buddha's death is 543 B.C.

[2] That is, about the time of Asôka.

the Chow dynasty, which ruled the empire from 1122 to 250 B.C., China was divided into a number of petty states or nations—at one time amounting to 125, and at another to 41—each of which was governed by its own Prince, who paid but a limited obedience to the monarchs of the reigning dynasty. In knowledge of this disunion, the empire was repeatedly attacked by the migratory bands of northern barbarians, who hovered on its frontier, until Che Hwangti, the first universal monarch of the world (as he boasted) (250 B.C.), built the Great Wall to repel further aggression, and burnt all the books and records he could find in the country, to obliterate the recollection of any one event or person before himself.

The Yuchi were the most formidable of these Tartar hordes. They were a branch of the people known as the Tungnu or Eastern Tartars.

Just[1] before 200 B.C. they had been defeated and driven from their territories by Mothe, chief of the Hiungnu (Huns), who finally extended his conquests from the frontier provinces of China on the east, to the Volga on the west. The increasing power of this Prince alarmed the Chinese. Accordingly, during the reign of Kaoutsu, the first emperor of the Han dynasty (202–194 B.C.), they marched an army against him, but were obliged to escape by a ruse from his overwhelming forces. The victorious career of the Hiungnu continued unchecked

[1] For this part of the narrative I am indebted to General Cunningham's Arch. Surv. of India (*passim*).

during the following half century. The Yuchi then separated, the smaller division called the Little Yuchi proceeding southwards into Thibet, and the larger division, called the Great Yuchi, advancing westward to the banks of the Ili. Finally, the Great Yuchi (163 B.C.) moved still further to the W. and S. and occupied the provinces now called Yarkand and Kashgar, driving out the original inhabitants, whom the Chinese name Sakas or Sus.

In 139 B.C. the Emperor Woo-ti of the Han dynasty, wishing to humble the power of the Hiungnu, sent an embassy to the Great Yuchi to obtain assistance from them against their common enemy. The Chinese ambassador, however, was captured, and only after ten years' imprisonment managed to effect his escape. The Yuchi at this time were being pressed further westward by the Usun, whilst they themselves were pushing the Sus or Sakas out of Sogdiana and Tahia (the country of the Dahœ), across the Oxus and the mountains, into the territory watered by the Cophes (Cabul R.), commonly called Kipin or Cophene. The Yuchi, in this expedition, were accompanied by Chang-Kian (the Chinese ambassador above referred to), who, after thirteen years' absence, returned to his country with two companions out of 100 who had originally composed his suite. In consequence of the knowledge of Western Nations which Chang-Kian had gained during this expedition, he was elevated to an important post, and served (123

–121 B.C.) on various occasions against the Hioung-nu. Finally he was reduced to the ranks on account of his ill success against these barbarians. It was during this war with the Hioung-nu that Hou Kiu-ping, the Chinese general, first saw a golden statue of Buddha, to which the King of Hieou-to[1] (Kartchou?) paid worship, and which accurately corresponded with the reports of Chang-Kian respecting the worship of Feou-to (Buddha) in Thian (India). This statue was taken and brought to the emperor 121 A.D., and was the origin of the statues of Buddha, that were afterwards in use.

Thus, whilst the missionary zeal of the Buddhist church had spread their doctrines to the borders of the great country of the conflicting tribes, the warlike spirit of the Chinese, under the Han dynasty, had caused their arms to extend to the same point, and the knowledge of Buddha and of his doctrine was carried back to the seat of government as a seed ready to germinate in due season.

The events on the Indian frontier which followed this first intercourse of the two civilizations were rapid and most interesting.

The Emperor Wu-ti, although at first unsuccessful, was yet in the end able to check and humble the power of the Hioung-nu; and his successor, Chaou-Ti, signally defeated them. This reverse was followed by civil war,

[1] I suppose Hieou-to be be a corrupt form of Khie-p'an-to, *i.e.* Kartchou—a kingdom in the midst of the Tsung-ling mountains.

plague, and famine—till, in 60 B.C., they became subject to the Chinese Empire.

The Great Yuchi (who had been driven by their enemies towards the northern frontier of India), being thus relieved from pressure, were able to consolidate their power, so that about 100 years after Chang-Kian's embassy, *i.e.* about 30 B.C., the five tribes into which they had separated were united under Khieu-tsiu-ki, the chief of the Gushan (Kuei-shang) horde; and, thus united, proceeded to advance further south to the conquest of Kashmir and Cabul. It is conjectured that the chief, Khieu-tsiu-ki, who thus consolidated the power of the Yuchi, is the same as Hyrkodes of the coins, who probably effected his conquests about 50 B.C., and died 35 B.C., at 84 years of age. This chieftain left the throne to his son, Yen-kao-ching, to whom the Chinese assign the conquest of India to the west of the Jumna. He has been identified with Hima Kadphises of the coins. His successor was Kanishka (about 15B.C.) to whom frequent allusion is made in the following memoirs. His conversion to Buddhism by the example and instruction of a little boy, is a commonly received legend in Chinese works. Whatever may have been the immediate cause of his conversion, however, there is no doubt that it led to the still wider diffusion of Buddhist doctrine through the Tocharian (Tartar) dominion. From the Raja Tarangini (Hist. of Kashmir) we learn that Kanishka and his two brothers, Hushka and Jushka, ruled over Kashmir for 60 years. During this period (15 B.C.–45 A.D.), a great Buddhist Synod was held (in the Tâmasavana Convent, at the confluence of the Sutlej and Bëiah Rivers,) under the presidency of Vasoumitra,[1] and the large Tope, of which ample mention is made by Sung-Yun, was erected by the King at Peshâwar. At this time, also, was made the last authentic revision of the Buddhist Scriptures (according to Northern authorities).

We are now prepared to return to the effect produced in China by the knowledge of Buddhist worship conveyed there by the warlike expeditions against the Hioung-nu.

It was in the fourth year of the reign of Ming Ti (62[2] A.D.), the second emperor of the Eastern Han dynasty (so called from the selection of Lo-yang to be the (eastern) capital by his predecessor, Kwang-wu), that a remarkable vision appeared to him by night. He saw a golden image, 19 feet high (1 chang and $\frac{6}{10}$), resplendent as gold, and its head surrounded by a halo as bright as the sun, approach his palace and finally enter it. This dream was interpreted by the Literati to refer to Buddha, whose golden image had been rendered familiar to them through the information brought by Chang-Kian and Hou kiu-ping from the west.

Another account, however (Loyang Temples, iv. 4),

[1] Vasoumitra is otherwise named Devamitra (Theophilus) (Wassiljew Der Buddhismus, § 222).

[2] I have adopted throughout this sketch, the dates supplied in the Chinese Repository, vol. x. No. 3, March 1841.

states, that "The golden spirit, speaking to the Emperor, said, 'Buddha bids you send to the west countries to search for him, with a view to obtain books and images.' On which the Emperor despatched an embassy that returned and entered Loyang in company with a white horse, carrying the books and images—on which occasion the Temple of the White Horse was founded." The account further states that "these books still remain, and are reverenced and worshipped; and from the cover, in which they are wrapped, often proceeds a miraculous shining light."

But whether the dream be explained one way or the other, there appears to be no authority for the explanation given by some early Christian missionaries, that its interpretation was connected with the supposed saying of Confucius, that the "Holy man is in the West." It is generally believed no such saying exists in the works of the Sage.[1] The passage most like it occurs in the 29th Chap. of the Chung Yung, § 4: "The Ruler (kwan tsze), being prepared, without any misgivings, to wait for the rise of a Sage (holy man), even a hundred generations (shai) after his own time, shews that he knows men (or human affairs)." But this passage is too general to have any immediate connection with the doctrine of Buddha. Considering all

[1] Hardwick, Christ and other Masters, Vol. II., 81 n. [There can be little doubt, however, that the reference of the missionaries was to the mysterious sentence occurring in a chapter on Confucius by Lieh-tze, viz., "Si fang chih jên yeu shêng chê yeh," "The men of the West possess a Sage."] (*Vid.* Notes and Queries on China and Japan, April, 1868, p. 52.)

things, we may fairly connect the dream and its explanation with the golden statue of Buddha brought from the borders of India. Ming Ti immediately dispatched a mission to the country of the Great Yuchi and also to Central India. After eleven years his messengers returned. They were accompanied by the Indian Kâsyapa Matañga (or Kâsyamâtanga, Jul. I. xviii.), who translated the Sutra of 42 Sections, and died at Loyang. He was soon followed by Tsu-fah-lan, who worked conjointly with him in the task of translation. They had together brought five Buddhist works from India—amongst which was the Sutra above referred to, the Dasabhûmi Sutra, and the Lalita Vistara (Fo-pen-hing-king). These were translated by Imperial order, and their date may be fixed at about 76 A.D.

From this time Buddhism began to prevail in the country. In 150 A.D., An-shi-kau, a priest of An-sih,[1] a country in Eastern Persia, is noticed in the annals as an excellent translator. About[2] 170 A.D., Chi-tsin, a priest of the Yuchi, produced a translation of the Nirvâna Sutra. Sun-k'iuen, prince of Wu (one of the three kingdoms), who (some time after the embassy which Marcus Aurelius Antoninus sent to China) received at his court (226 A.D.), a Roman merchant (called, in the Liang History, Tsin-Lun), treated with equal regard an Indian priest who trans-

[1] An-si, according to Rémusat, a name for the Parthians: probably a corruption of Asvakas or Assakas (Ἱππάσιοι).

[2] Edkins. I am indebted to this accurate scholar for most of the remarks in this part of the Text.

lated for him some of the books of Buddha. About 250 A.D. we find Chi-Meng, residing at Kao Tch'ang (Tourfan), translating the Seng-ki-liuh (Rules of the Priesthood), which he is said to have obtained at Hwa-chi, *i.e.* Kousoumapoura or Pâṭalipoutra (Patna). Shortly after this (260 A.D.), we read of a Shaman called Fa-hou (Dharmarakcha) reaching China and living under the dynasty of the Western Tsin. Subsequently he traversed the Western countries in every direction. and gained a knowledge of the dialects of 36 kingdoms, On his return he brought with him a large number of Buddhist and Brahman works, which he presented to the Imperial court. He finally took up his residence at Lo-Yang, and, from the year 265 A.D. to 308 A.D., translated, with the help of many Shamans, 165 Buddhist books; and amongst which was the second version of the Lalita Vistara (Pou-yao-king),[1] a corrected copy of the Nirvâna Sutra, and the Suvarṇa Prabhâsa Sûtra. About 300 A.D., a foreign priest named Chi-kung-ming translated the Wei-ma (Vimalakîrtti Sutra ?) and the Fa-hwa (Saddharma puṇḍarîka). Shortly after him (335 A.D.), the prince of the Chau kingdom (the modern Pei-chi-li, and Shan-si) first permitted his subjects to take Buddhist monastic vows. He was influenced to do this by an Indian named Bouddhasiñha (Fo-to-ching) who pretended to magical powers. Hitherto natives of India had been allowed to build temples in the large cities, but now, for the first time, the people of the country were permitted to be-

[1] Lalita Vist. xviii., *n.*

come Shamans; and, as a final proof of the rapid growth of the religion, we find that at Loyang alone (Honan-fu) there had been erected (350 A.D.) 42 pagodas, from three to nine stories high, richly painted and formed after Indian models.

It was at this time Chi Fah-Hian lived. He was apparently a native of Tchang'an, or, at any rate, a resident there. He was grieved to observe the imperfect rules of discipline of the monks in that city—the translations of Buddhist books as yet known in China were, in fact, to a great extent, erroneous. For this reason the Emperor Yao-hing (397–415) had sent an army to Koutché (a kingdom to the westward of Lake Lob) to bring back a learned Indian priest, Kumârajîva, who might supply correct versions of the chief books as yet known in the country. More than 800 priests were called to assist, and the king himself, an ardent disciple of the new faith, was present at the conference, whilst the Prince Yao-wang and the Count Yao-seng (of the town of Tchang'an) helped to transcribe the sheets of the new translations (Jul. i. 322). Whilst this task was proceeding, Fah-Hian was travelling through India in search of original copies of works not yet known to his countrymen. His success will be found mentioned in the following pages. Scarcely had he returned to his country (415 A.D.), when the Tsin dynasty was overturned (420) by the irruption of a powerful Tartar tribe known in history as the Northern Wei. A native dynasty, the Southern Sung, ruled in the southern provinces, and has been regarded by subsequent writers as the legitimate one. It was under this dynasty that the Fo-koue-ki was published, and therefore bears the name of the Sung on its title-page.

During the early period of the Sung and Wei dynasties, the Buddhist religion in China was persecuted, and image-making and building of temples forbidden. Shaou-ti, the second emperor of the Sung dynasty (423 A.D.), interdicted it; and in 426 A.D. an order was issued by the Prince of Wei to the same purpose. Books and images were destroyed, and many priests put to death. It was made a capital crime to construct idols of earth or brass, or to worship foreign divinities.

In 451 A.D., there was a relaxation of these severe rules. An edict was issued permitting one Buddhist temple in each city, and 40 or 50 of the inhabitants to become priests. The king himself performed the tonsure for some who took the monastic vows. A few years afterwards (458 A.D.), a conspiracy was discovered, in which a Buddhist priest was the chief party. A manifesto, issued by the emperor on this occasion, says: "Among the priests there are many men who have fled from justice and taken the monastic vows for safety. They take advantage of their assumed character to contrive new modes of mischief. The fresh troubles thus excited provoke the anger of gods and men. The constituted authorities, therefore, must examine narrowly into the conduct of monks. Those that are guilty must be put to death. Such as will not keep their vows of abstinence and self-denial must return to their families and previous occupations, and no Nuns are to be permitted to enter the Royal Palace, or converse with the emperor's wives."

The rapid progress of Buddhism excited much opposition from the Literati and followers of Lao-tseu. The latter affirmed that Sakya Buddha was but an incarnation of their own master, who had died 517 A.D., shortly after which date (it was said) Buddha was born. This slander was resented by the Buddhists, and they put back the date of their founder's birth in consequence—first, to 687 B.C., and afterwards to still earlier periods.[1]

The controversy between the Buddhists and the Literati (followers of Confucius,) may be understood from the following extract from the biographical section of the history of the Sung dynasty:[2]—"The instructions of Confucius, says the Buddhist assailant, include only the single life; they do not reach to the Future State, with its interminable results. His only motive to virtue, is the happiness of posterity. The only consequence of vice he names, is present suffering. The rewards of the good do not go beyond worldly honours; the recompense of guilt is nothing worse than present obscurity and poverty. Such ignorance is melancholy.

[1] Hae-kwo-to-chi- (45th Kieuen, p. 21).
[2] Notices of Buddhism in China (Edkins).

The aims of the doctrine of Sakya (Buddha), on the other hand, are illimitable. His religion removes care from the heart, and saves men from the greatest dangers. Its one sentiment is Mercy seeking to save. It speaks of Hell, to deter people from sin; it points to Heaven, that men may desire its happiness. It exhibits the Nirvâṇa as the spirit's final refuge, and tells us of a body (dharmakâya) to be possessed, under other conditions, long after our present body has passed away."

To this the Confucianist replies:—"To be urged to virtue by the desire of Heaven, cannot be compared to the motive supplied by the love of doing what is right for its own sake. To avoid wrong from fear of Hell, is not so good as to govern oneself from a sense of duty. Acts of worship performed for the sake of obtaining forgiveness of sins, do not spring from piety. A gift made for the purpose of securing a hundred-fold recompense, cannot result from sincerity. To praise the happiness of Nirvâṇa, promotes a lazy inactivity. To dwell upon that form of body which we may hereafter attain to, is calculated only to promote the love of the marvellous. Whilst you look for distant good, the desires of the animal nature remain unchecked, and it is false to say that any form of Being can be without such desires."

To this the Buddhist rejoins:—"Your conclusions are wrong. Motives derived from a consideration of the future are necessary to lead men to virtue. Else how could we adjust the evil of the present life? Men will not act spontaneously without something to hope for. The countryman ploughs his land because he hopes for a harvest. If he had no such hope, he would sit idle at home and perish."

From this extract we see that the discussion turns entirely on the advantage to be derived from a belief in the doctrine of a Future State as a motive to virtue. This question of another life, in fact, has ever been the great subject of contention between the two sects; for, as Confucius rarely alluded to the appointments of Heaven, and regarded his mission to be, not to declare new truths, but to preserve old ones—so he carefully avoided speaking about the future. "Whilst you know not life," he said to Ke Loo, "how can you know about death;" and "whilst you are not able to serve men, how can you serve their spirits (after death)" (Analects, xi. 11). In sharp contrast to this cautious spirit, was the bold speculation of the Buddhist; and on this question of the Future—its rewards, its punishments, its issue—the whole controversy turned.

Buddhism, though formerly persecuted and still controverted, rapidly prevailed in the Wei kingdom. In the year 467 A.D. the prince of that kingdom caused an image of Buddha to be constructed, 50 feet high. Five tons of brass and 6 cwt. of gold were used in its composition. This prince resigned his throne five years afterwards and became a monk. About this time, also, Ming Ti, the sixth of the Sung emperors, erected a magnificent Buddhist temple, for which he was severely rebuked by his Literati.

At the beginning of the sixth century the number of Indians in China was upwards of 3,000. The Buddhist temples had multiplied to 13,000. The prince of the Wei country discoursed publicly on the Sacred Books. The adverse government of the Liang, established in the South, was also eminently favourable to foreign priests. The first emperor of that dynasty (502–550 A.D.) three times assumed Buddhist vows and expounded the Sûtras to his assembled courtiers. In the 26th year of his reign, he entered the T'ung-Tae monastery in Nanking. As might be expected, this event calls forth much censure from the Confucian historian. The preface to the History of the Liang dynasty is occupied by a lamentation over the sad necessity of adverting to Buddhism at all, in the Imperial annals of the nation. In reference to the emperor becoming a priest, the critic says: "Not only would the man of common intelligence condemn such conduct in the Supreme Ruler of a commonwealth, but even men like Bodhidharma would withhold their approval." This Bodhidharma was the 28th Buddhist Patriarch. Having grown old in Southern India, he reached Canton by sea (526 A.D.). Persecution had probably caused him to abandon his country, as the successor of Setsi, the 24th Patriarch, had been forced to do before him.[1] His arrival in China is an im-

[1] Life of Buddha from the Chinese (Shing-Tau-ki), § 179.

portant epoch in its religious history. Hitherto the form of Buddhist doctrine most prevalent there, was that which taught the practice of Morality to be the means of deliverance. But now the mysticism which had developed itself gradually in India was imported full-blown into China. "Do nothing," was the creed of Bodhidharma; for in doing nothing, and abstracting the mind from every object, we arrive (so he taught) at a state of entire self-absorption; lust is suppressed and bliss attained. Bodhidharma, after a while, left Canton and the Liang kingdom, and came to Loyang, the Wei capital. Here he sat with his face to a wall for nine years. The people called him the Wall-gazing Brahman. His desire was to conquer all sensations—to arrive at the possession of mind without object—the same end as Kapila taught "the conclusive, incontrovertible, only knowledge" that "I am not, nor aught is mine" (Banerjea, Hindoo Philosophy, 264). Bodhidharma's example was not without effect. We read of one enthusiastic disciple arguing thus: "Bôdhisatwa[1] formerly broke off his bone, poured out his marrow, shed his blood, gave himself to the famishing tiger cubs—what can I do?" Accordingly, while snow was falling he exposed himself to it, till it had risen above his knees. The Patriarch, observing him, asked what he hoped to gain by such conduct. "I only desire," he said, "that Mercy may open a path to save the whole race of men." The Patriarch replied that his suffering could not be compared with that of

[1] That is, Buddha, during a previous existence.

Bôdhisatwa. Stung with the answer, the disciple took a knife and severed his arm, and placed it before his master. On this he was satisfied, and highly commended him, and subsequently appointed him his successor in China. Bodhidharma died of old age, and was buried in the Hiungrh mountains, between Honan and Shansi.

It was just before this (518 A.D.) that Sung-Yun (a native of Tun-wang, in Little Thibet) was sent by the Queen of the Wei country from Loyang to India to search for Buddhist books. He was accompanied by Hwui-Seng. He returned after three years with 175 volumes. After Bodhidharma's death, we are told, Sung-Yun inspected his remains. As he lay in his coffin, he held one shoe in his hand. Sung-Yun implored him to say where he was going. "To the Western Heaven, was the reply." The coffin was afterwards opened and found to be empty, except the shoe, which was for a long time preserved as a relic.

It will be seen from Sung-Yun's narrative (given in the present volume), that Buddhism in his time had become corrupted by the introduction into its code of the practice of magical arts. The use of charms, and the claim to magical powers, do not appear to have belonged to the original system. Buddhist teaching was, in the first instance, connected principally with Morals. After a few centuries, however, the simplicity of its doctrine was corrupted, and fabulous stories were invented and local superstitions permitted, to please the people and advance the power of the priests,—especially among the Tartar tribes, who, like all northern races, were particularly given to superstition. We read, therefore (515 A.D.), that several priests were put to death for practising magical arts. The account given of their leader in these arts, is, that he used wild music to win followers, taught them to dissolve all ties of kindred, and aimed only at murder and disturbance.

About this same time, the King of Siam sent to Wu-ti a letter offering to give him a hair of Buddha, 14 feet long. Priests were sent to meet it and bring it home. Three years before this, as the History of of the Liang Dynasty informs us, a similar relic had been discovered under an old Pagoda in Nankin—viz., a hair of a blue-lavender colour. This hair was so elastic, that when the priests pulled it, it lengthened indefinitely; and when let alone, it curled up in a spiral form. The historian quotes two Buddhist works in illustration—one of which says, that Buddha's hair was blue and fine; the other, that when Buddha lived in the palace of his father, his hair was 12 feet long, and, when curled, was of a spiral form. This description, it is added, agrees with the hair found by the Emperor.

Chinese intercourse with Siam had been preceded by by the arrival of many priests from Ceylon—so early as

460 A.D. five Buddhists had arrived from that country by the Thibetan route. They brought with them many images—to some of which miraculous properties are assigned.

We may gather from the records of the Sui dynasty (beginning 589 A.D.) that Buddhism was yet subject to persecution. The first of these emperors, Kaou-tsu, issued an edict, giving full toleration to the sect. Towards the close of his reign, he prohibited the destruction or disfigurement of images used in religious worship. "It was the weakness of age," says the Confucian historian, "giving way to superstition, that caused such an enactment." There were now 1950 distinct Buddhist works, says the same historian, translated into Chinese.

The period of the Tang dynasty (620-904) may be regarded as the Augustan age of Chinese literature. What the first Han dynasty had commenced (in restoring and re-editing the lost Books), was now brought to its highest perfection. As it has been observed, the darkest age of the West was the brightest of the East. Le-Yuen, of the house of Leang, who founded the dynasty, took the name of Kaou-Tsu on ascending the throne. He was induced by Fu-yih, one of his ministers, to call a council for deliberation on the mode of action to be adopted in regard to Buddhism. Fu-yih, a stern enemy of the new religion, proposed that the monks and nuns should be compelled to marry and bring up children. "The reason they adopt the ascetic life, he says, is to avoid contributing to the revenue. What they hold about the fate of men depending on the will of Buddha is false. Life and death are regulated by a self-governing fate. The retribution of vice and virtue is the province of the prince; riches and poverty are the result of our own actions. Buddhism, he proceeds to say, has caused the public manners to degenerate, whilst the theory of the metempsychosis is entirely fictitious. The monks are idle and unprofitable members of the commonwealth." To this Siau-ü, a friend of Buddhism, replied: "Buddha was a Sage (the term applied to Confucius); in speaking ill of a Sage, Fu-yih had been guilty of a great crime." To this his opponent answered, that loyalty and filial piety are the greatest virtues, and the monks, casting off as they did their prince and their parents, disregarded them both; and that Siau-ü, in defending their system, was equally guilty with themselves.

Siau-ü, joining his hands (the Buddhist mode of polite address), merely said that Hell was made for such men as his vilifier.

In the end the Confucianists gained their aim, and severe restrictions were imposed on the foreign faith, which were, however, almost immediately removed.

It was in the reign of the second emperor of this dynasty, (Tae-Tsung) that the celebrated Buddhist traveller, Hiouen-Thsang, set out for India (629 A.D.). The account of his journey is familiar to European scholars, through the translation of the Si-yu-ki, by M. Julien. The modern Chinese editor of the work complains of its author's superstition.[1] "Anxiety to detail every Buddhist wonder has been accompanied, by neglect of the physical features of the countries that come under review." Here, says the critic, he cannot be compared with Ngai-ju-lio (Giulio Aloni, one of the early Jesuits) in the Chih-fang-wai-ki (a well-known geographical work by that missionary). In truthfulness, he adds, he is not equal to Fah-Hian in his account of the Buddhist kingdoms, but his style is much more ornamental.

As the pilgrimage of Hiouen-Thsang is frequently alluded to in the following pages, it will be as well perhaps to indicate his track towards India until he crossed that of Fah-Hian. Passing from Liang-cheu at the north-western extremity of China, he advanced along a westerly route (to the south of the great Thian-shan range) through Khamil (celebrated for its melons), Tourfan, Karachar, Aksu, to the Ling-shan, or Ice-Range (called in our maps Muzart mountains), which extends from the transverse course of the Aksu river eastward to Kucha (Koutché), being covered with perpetual snows, which feed enormous glaciers. This range borders on Songaria, the great pasture country and transit between Mongolia and the lower plains bordering on the Jaxartes. Crossing these mountains, through the pass of

[1] Notices of Buddhism in China (Edkins).

glaciers (Djeparlé of Humboldt), the pilgrim skirted the lake Issikoul, and seems to have advanced, at first, along the valley of the Tchoui river, and afterwards along the rich pasture land watered by the affluents of the Talas river, at the foot of the northern slopes of the Alatau mountains. In this way he reached Taras or Turkestan (his furthest point north). Turning southward (S.S.W.), and keeping along the course of the Jaxartes, he arrived at Tchadj or Tashkend (mentioned by Ptolemy as on the route of caravans from India to Serica). Continuing in a south-easterly direction, he arrived at Khojend (the Alexandria of Arrian, and the furthest point north of Alexander's expedition). Westward of this he passed through Uratippa, near the Cyropolis of Alexander, and arrived at Samarkand (the scene of the murder of Clitus). South-west of this he arrived at Kesch, where Timour was born (the Nautika of Alexander); and advancing through the Iron Gates (the Durbund of Elphinstone (Cabul) and T'ieh Mun of the Chinese maps), he entered on Toukhâra, which includes the actual province of Balkh and the mountain provinces of Kunduz, Hissar, Vokhan, Bolor, and Badakshan. Crossing the Oxus at Termez, he probably intended to pass the Hindu Kush by the pass of Ghourbend or Anderâb, for he actually went as far as Ghoûr, but then returned to Balkh. Finally he arrived at Bamian by the pass Haji-yak, and proceeded to Kapisa (probably corresponding with the Nidjrow and Punjsheer valleys of Elphinstone). Then he advanced to Lampâka (the Laghman of the Turks and Lughman of Elphinstone), and afterwards to Nagrâk and Hiḍḍa. Beyond this point we will not follow his route, as it constantly intersects that of Fah-Hian. Having completed the tour of the Indian peninsula, he returned across the Indus, and, pursuing a course nearly identical with that of Fah-Hian's outward journey, he reached home in the sixteenth year after his departure—having occupied a few months more than Fah-Hian had done in his pilgrimage. Tae-Tsung, was still reigning when Hiouen-Thsang returned, and the pilgrim was summoned to the court at Lo-yang, to answer for his conduct in leaving his country and undertaking so perilous a journey without the Imperial permission. His apology consisted in the result of his undertaking, which is thus detailed: "Twenty-two horses, carrying 657 Buddhist works; 115 grains of relics; a gold statue of Buddha, 3ft. 3in. high, with a transparent pedestal; a second, 3ft. 5in. high; and many others of silver and sandal wood."

The emperor, after listening to the traveller's account of what he had seen, commanded him to write a history of the western countries, and the work called the Si-yu-ki (compiled chiefly from Sanscrit sources) was the result. After this Hiouen-Thsang lived nineteen years, and passed nearly the whole of that time in translating.

He completed 740 works in 1335 books. We are casually informed that the number of monasteries in China at this time was 3,716; at the request of Hiouen Thsang, the Emperor issued an edict that five new monks should be received in each of these, thus swelling the number by some 18,000 persons.

About this time the Nestorian Christians arrived in China—they called their doctrine the Illustrious Religion. A priest called Rabban (Olopuen) appears to have reached Tchang'an with books and images (736 A.D.). Tae-Tsung received him graciously, and ordered the authorities to build a church in the E-Ning way of Tchang'an, over which twenty-one priests were to preside. In the time of Kaou-tsung, the same Rabban was appointed "Great Conservator of Doctrine for the Preservation of the State," and orders were given for the erection of Illustrious churches in every province. The priests all shaved their crowns and preserved their beards; they had worship and praise seven times a day, and every seventh day they offered sacrifice.

These particulars are stated on the tablet discovered 1625 A.D., by the Chinese while digging for the foundation of a house at a village not far from Se-gan-foo, in the province of Shense (lat. 34° 16′ N., long. E. 108° 57′).

The Manicheans also arrived in the country about this time; the picture of Mani is still preserved; he is regarded by the Buddhists as one manifestation of Kwan Yin, the God of Mercy (so called).

Early in the eighth century, the Confucianists made another attempt to bring about a persecution of Buddhism (714 A.D.). In consequence of their efforts, more than 12,000 priests and nuns were obliged to return to their wordly pursuits; and the casting of images, writing sacred books, and building temples, were strictly forbidden.

But Su Tsung (760 A.D.) and his successor, Tae-Tsung (763 A.D.), were both firm adherents of the new faith—the latter, particularly, was a consistent patron of it: he maintained monks because he believed that, by propitiating the unseen powers, he could preserve his empire from danger at less cost than by expending blood and treasure on the battle-field.

The emperor, Hien-Tsung (819 A.D.), sent mandarins to escort a bone of Buddha to the capital; on which occasion Han-ü, one of his ministers (vice-president of the board of Punishments), presented a strongly-worded remonstrance to his master. "Why should a decayed bone—the filthy remains of a man long ago dead—be introduced to the Imperial residence. As for Buddha, he braved his vengeance, and defied his power to inflict punishment." The minister was banished to Chau-cheu, in the province of Canton, where, according to one account,[1] he was converted by Tai-Teen, the priest, and became a member of the religious sect he had so recently calumniated.

In the year 845 A.D., a third and very severe perse-

[1] Wu-tsing-tsze (Preface to the Prâjna-Paramita Hṛidaya Sûtra).

cution befel the Buddhists. By an edict of the emperor, Wu-Tsung, 4,600 monasteries were destroyed, and 40,000 smaller chapels; the property of the religious establishments was confiscated and used in the erection of public buildings. The copper images and bells were melted down and made into cash. More than 260,000 priests and nuns were secularized. But, as so frequently occurred, the successor of Wu-Tsung reversed his policy—the confiscated property was to a great extent restored, and unlimited permission given to all so disposed to enter the religious profession. The Confucian historian regrets such a short persecution, and comments, with ill-disguised feeling, on the fact that former emperors had continued their hostility to religion for many years, but, in this case, the persecution had lasted only a few months.

The emperor I-tsung (860 A.D.) was devoted to the study of Buddhist books. Priests were invited to discourse on their religion in the private apartments of his Palace, and he frequently visited the monasteries. The Literati protested in vain. The emperor went so far as to learn Sanskrit and practise the mode of chanting common in India. Nothing could have been more hateful to the rigid Confucianist than to hear such sounds proceeding from the Royal apartments. Another bone of Buddha was found and brought to the Palace. The emperor received it prostrate on the earth, weeping and worshipping it the while.

About this time we find foreign priests flocking to China from every quarter. From Corea and Japan frequent missions arrived to obtain books and conduct priests to the celebrated monasteries of those countries; whilst from India and the neighbourhood came a constant succession of wandering monks, who brought books and images to the Eastern capital (the present Honan-fu). We read that this city now possessed 1367 Buddhist temples, exclusive of those on the outskirts (Loyang Temples).

She-Tsung, the last emperor of the after Chow dynasty (955 A.D.), placed severe restrictions on Buddhism, and prohibited all temples, except those that had received an inscribed tablet from former emperors. More than 30,000 of these buildings were in consequence suppressed and only 2694 retained. This emperor also established a mint for the purpose of converting the copper and silver of the temples into coin. Shortly after this, the Emperor Tae-Tsung (the second of the Sung dynasty, 976 A.D.) stopped the examinations of candidates for monks' orders, which had been instituted under Fei-te (the last of the after Tang dynasty, 934 A.D.), and prohibited the building of any more temples; yet he himself ordered a pagoda to be erected, 380 feet high, which was finished in eight years, and relics shrined within it.

Perhaps no greater change had occurred in the character of Buddhism than the introduction into its code of a belief in the merit of self-destruction. The law of Buddha strictly forbids even the mention of the advantages of death, or any approach to a disposition to undervalue life—the third rule of the Parájiká section of the Pratimoksha runs thus: "If any priest shall wilfully take away the life from the body of a man, or if he procure for a man a weapon for the purpose, or if he speak of the advantages of death, or teach how death may be procured, saying, O man! what dost thou derive from this sinful life; death is more excellent for thee!—thus, thoughtful and designing, if he in various modes celebrate the advantages of death, or teach how death may be procured: let him be parájiká, excluded." We find in the narrative of Fah-Hian, however (Chap. xxx.), an account of a Shaman who, by self-destruction, arrived at the condition of a Rahat. His argument was, that though Buddha had forbidden self-murder, yet that rule did not forbid the destruction of lust, anger, ignorance—and it was against these he raised the knife and completed his own death. By some such argument, probably, the custom of priests committing themselves to the flames crept in, and became a common event in the history of later Buddhism. The frequent accounts we have of the patriarchs thus ending their career (Rémusat), may, I think, rather refer to their funeral obsequies, than to self-immolation; but there can be no doubt that the practice of burning alive was not unusual, even in China. On one occasion we read[1] that an inmate of the Tian-tae Monastery, near Ningpo, expressed to the Emperor his wish to commit himself to the flames when the erection of a certain temple was completed. His desire was granted, and an officer sent to see that the temple was finished, and the rash vow of the priest also carried into effect. The pile was made, and the priest was called upon to come forward. He excused himself; but in vain: he looked round on the assembled crowd for some one to save him; among the priests and people, however, no one offered to help the trembling victim of his own folly. The stern voice of the Imperial messenger bade him ascend the pile. He still lingered, and was at length seized by the attendants, placed forcibly on the pyre, and burnt. So common had these fanatical proceedings become, that the Emperor Tái-tsu, hearing that wood was being collected to form the pyre for a priest, prohibited any more temples being built, and set his face against all such delusions.

But the conduct of the Sung emperors (960–1278) towards Buddhism was as inconsistent as it well could be. We find Jin-tsung (1035) endeavouring to preserve in the empire a knowledge of Sanskrit by appointing fifty youths to study it. Shin-tsung (1068 A.D.) and Hwei-tsung (1101 A.D.) seem to have set their mind upon amalgamating Buddhism and Tauism, by changing all Indian titles used by the former, into

[1] Notices of Buddhism in China (Edkins).

native ones adopted by the latter. Kaou-tsung (1143 A.D.) withdrew the usual certificates given by the emperors to candidates who became Buddhist monks—a withdrawal, in fact, of State patronage, which strengthened rather than weakened the cause of religion—in consequence of which, the higher members of the Buddhist hierarchy undertook themselves to distribute the certificates of membership to all candidates for ordination, and thereby frustrated the aim of the Emperor.[1]

Kublai Khan (She Tsu), the first Mongol emperor (1280 A.D.), was strongly attached to Buddhism. The Confucian temples were converted to Buddhist uses, and Tauism was openly persecuted. Kublai, at first, refused to invade Japan on the ground that it was a Buddhist country; and it was only when the Japanese government neglected to send the customary tribute that he attempted to use force—how unsuccessfully, is generally known. In the reign of the second emperor of this dynasty, Ching Tsung (1295 A.D.), we read of 3,000 taéls of gold being set part to provide materials for writing Buddhist books in gilt letters, and other expenses for this religion on an equally extravagant scale. The aim of Kublai, in his prefer-

[1] When the neophyte visits the chief monk for initiation, by the new custom, an indentation is made on the top of the head by fire, and every successive grade in the priesthood is marked by a similar stigma, so that a priest is proud to shew these marks as testifying to his merit in attaining an advanced position in the monastery.

ence for Buddhism, was a politic one. Having become sovereign of a wild and extensive country, with an intractable and quarrelsome population, in order to give his native deserts a civilized appearance, and to soften down the natural roughness of his people and unite them in a compact body, he resolved to adopt the Chinese model of government, and to put the people under a Public Instructor. To this latter office he appointed a Buddhist monk, whose orders were to be received with the same respect as Imperial proclamations, and who was only second to the Chief Civil Mandarin in privileges and rank. It was in this way the mild character of the Buddhist religion gradually leavened the mass of the Mongolian people and produced amongst them some degree of order and love of peace.

Towards the end of the thirteenth century a census of the Buddhist temples and monks in China was taken by Imperial command. Of the former there were reported 42,318; of the latter, 213,148. Three years after, at the close of Kublai's reign, a priest came from Thibet to be appointed National Instructor; the Emperor regretting that he could not converse with him, ordered Kalutanasi, a Mongolian, to learn the Thibetan language from him. This task was accomplished in a year, and the complete translation of the Buddhist Sutras and Shastras from Thibetan and Sanscrit into Mongolian (written in the Ouighour character), was presented to Kublai in the year of his death, 1294 A.D. He ordered the whole to be cut in blocks and distributed among the kings and great chiefs of his nation.[1]

Chinese pilgrims still visited India. In 965 A.D. a Buddhist priest (Tai-yuen) returned from a journey to the Western countries with relics and Sanscrit copies of Buddhist books written on palm leaves (peito), in number forty volumes. The next year, 157 Chinese priests set out together, with the Emperor's permission, to visit India and obtain books. They passed through Varousha (Jul. ii. 122) and Kashmir; but nothing is said of their further proceedings. Early in the Yuen dynasty, a priest named Tau-wu was excited, by reading the account of Fah-Hian, to try his fortune in a similar way—a contingency that Fah-Hian himself appears to have foreseen and wished to prevent (Chap. xl.). He passed the Sandy Desert, through the kingdoms of Kui-tsi (Koutché?) and Sha-la (also mentioned by Sung-Yun) to Kipin (Cophene). He there learned the original language of Buddhist books; and, turning westward, proceeded through the country of the Getæ into India. He returned by sea to Canton. This is the last record, however, of any such pilgrimage.

There was no violent re-action against Buddhism during the early period of the Ming dynasty (1368–1628 A.D.). Monks from the countries west of China were still welcomed at Court, and decrees were issued

[1] Edkins, *ut suprà*.

in favour of the benevolent aims of their system. But, as happened elsewhere, the ruling class became alarmed in view of the increasing real property of the monastic establishments. In 1450 A.D. it was forbidden for any monastery to possess more than 6,000 square feet of land; and whatever they possessed in excess of this, was given to the poor to cultivate, taxes being paid to the Emperor.

In the reign of She-tsung (1530 A.D.) some attempts were made to renew the persecution against Buddhists; but all that was effected was the destruction of the Chapel belonging to the Palace. High titles were still conferred on western priests; the term Shang-si, "superior teacher," being substituted for Ti-si, "imperial teacher," which had been the usual title under the Yuens.

The Christian missionaries who arrived in China towards the end of the sixteenth century loudly protested against Buddhist idolatry. Matthew Ricci had a controversy with a noted Buddhist priest residing at Hang-cheu. Su-kwang-ki, Ricci's most illustrious convert, wrote a short tract against Buddhism, and also against ancestral worship; but no great change appears to have been produced in the national feeling on these subjects.

The early Manchu emperors dealt equally with all religious systems. Shun-chi (1644 A.D.), however, favoured Buddhism, and wrote prefaces to some of the works of the followers of Bodhidharma. But Kang-he, his son, opposed all sects except the Confucian, and, in the sacred Edict, recorded his sentiments for the instruction of the people. In this manifesto, the Buddhists are condemned for fabricating groundless tales of future happiness and misery. They are charged with doing this only for gain, and encouraging, for the same object, large gatherings of the country population at the temples, ostensibly to burn incense, but really to promote mischief. These opinions are extensively approved of at the present time. One of the sixteen lectures comprising this Edict is read at the period of each new or full moon, in the "Ching hwang meaou," or temple of the Patron God belonging to every Chinese city. The town clerk, the local officers of government, and a few rustic people, compose the audience. The Buddhist priests are denounced as drones of society—creatures like moths and mischievous insects, that thrive on the industry of others, whilst they do no work themselves. The people are warned not to go to their temples, nor take part in their village festivals. In this way a strong feeling is kept up antagonistic to the advance of Buddhist worship. Yet the common people are much engrossed by it; the better class affect to despise it, but secretly adhere to it; the temples, though said to be falling to decay, are not more neglected than other religious buildings, and, in some cases (as *e.gr.* the Fei-lai-sse at Canton), are the most gorgeous structures to be met with in the country. It is the opinion of one well able to judge (Dr. Legge, Chinese Classics I., Prolog. Chap. v. § 2), "that the faith of the nation in Confucius will speedily and extensively pass away;" and it is possible that in the general decay of the religious sentiment, Buddhism will also lose its hold on the minds of the people. In the disappearance of old forms of belief, we may, perhaps, look for our opportunity to bring to their notice that which is better than the old.

II.—Buddhism, as it existed in India, we have remarked, may be regarded as a protest against the intolerable claims and corrupt worship of the Brahmans. This protest was directed principally against four particulars. 1. That the Gods, whom the Brahmans reverenced, were proper objects for the Supreme worship of men. 2. That the enjoyment of Heaven, *i.e.* the Heaven of the popular belief, was the highest happiness to which men could attain. 3. That religion consisted in ceremonial observances. 4. That its advantages could be confined to any particular caste. The four principles, therefore, involved in the existence of Buddhism are these: 1. That man may become superior to the Gods. 2. That Nirvâna is the Supreme good. 3. That religion consists in a right preparation of heart (suppression of evil desire—practice of self-denial, active benevolence). 4. That men of all castes, and women, may enjoy the benefits of a religious life.

Of the founder of this system (Sâkya, the son of Suddhôdana Raja), we know comparatively little. The trifling particulars contained in the ordinary records of his life, may be considered fabulous. They tend, in fact, to shake our belief in the more probable statements respecting him. But from the general agreement of all the schools, we may conclude—(1) That Sâkya is an historical character. (2) That his natural temperament, combined with certain accidental occurrences, induced him to adopt a religious life. (3) That he was led—how we can hardly tell—after years of painful preparation, to the apprehension of what he regarded as Vital Truth. (4) That he assumed the character of an inspired teacher, and founded a community (sañgha) of religious men and women, who professed belief in his law (Dharma). Buddha's law or Dharma was first of all conveyed under the form of four truths (Ârya satyâni). 1. That sorrow is inseparable from sentient existence. 2. That evil-desire is the cause of the progressive accumulation of sorrow. 3. That there is a way for arriving at the extinction of desire, and therefore of sorrow. 4. That this way is to be found in the use of means (entering the paths).

Such was the primitive doctrine of Buddhism as it came from the hands of its founder.

In process of time (the Shamans having now assembled themselves into fixed communities and adopted conventual life) the friendly discussions in which the members of the Sañgha had formerly indulged (during the Season of the Rains) developed into a confirmed practice of religious controversy. This led to a love of philosophical speculation. The great monasteries from this time became seats for polemical discussions rather than religious instruction. The people and their rulers were led to consider the possession of dialectical skill as the chief excellence of a teacher. If the superiors of the various monasteries were not equal in this particular to their rivals, the people lost confidence in them, and their establishments passed into other hands. As an instance of this, we read of a monastery in Paṭâliputra being closed for ten years, in consequence of the defeat of its occupants in controversy with the heretics (Jul. ii. 432). In the Life of Hiouen-Thsang, also, we find that he established for himself a high renown, by his skill in controversy. In Fah-Hian, again, we have an account of a learned doctor at Patna (Artha Svamin), who was invincible in argument, and had mightily promoted the cause of religion in the kingdom. But, as a matter of necessity, these discussions weakened the position occupied by the Buddhists, as a religious community. For, besides the chance of defeat, two evils were thereby entailed on the system. 1. Internal discord. 2. Neglect of fundamental principles. And these causes, combined with persecution from without, led to the overthrow of the system in India.

The case was otherwise in China. Here Buddhism has exhibited a vitality which has enabled it to survive persecution and triumph over every obstacle. This may be attributed to three circumstances. 1. The character of this religion. The system of Confucius, highly moral and truthful within its province, cannot be considered as a religious system in the true meaning of the phrase. As we have observed before, its scope does not extend beyond the present life. It acknowledges no argument drawn from the hope of Heaven, or the fear of Hell. It does not profess to speak of man's future destiny, or the consequences of death. "Confucius was practical in his tendencies, and had no liking for the subtleties of metaphysics" (Edkins, Relig. in China, 200). Buddhism, therefore, supplied a want felt by the people, when it brought to their notice the subject of a future life—its rewards and punishments—and the possible destiny of the soul, in arriving at the Supreme good, known as Nirvâna. 2. Buddhism in China owes its success and continuance also, to the character of the Chinese people. Their tendency is to approve of that which is moral. This national preference results, no doubt, from the teaching of Confucius. Hence the doctrine of Buddha, founded on a rigid morality, recommended itself to their notice. The corrupt (Sakti) worship, which, under a symbolized form, found its way into the northern schools of Buddhism in India, and developed itself still further in Thibet, would not be tolerated by the better classes of the Chinese. In the Lama temples near Pekin may be found traces of this impure symbolism; but it is confined to them. The great majority of monastic establishments throughout China, however ignorant the priests may be, are, at least, free from any taint of this sort. It is contrary, in fact, to the genius of the people. On this account, Buddhism in China has retained something of its natural vigor, and is still (however imperfectly so) a living witness in favour of virtue and purity of life. But a third reason for this may be found in the absence of the scholastic element in Chinese Buddhism. Even if the priests were inclined to scholasticism, the fact of their religion being a foreign one, and the language of its books unknown to them, would forbid the indulgence of such a taste. Not that the Chinese are incapable of appreciating subtle scholastic enquiries. On the contrary; there is no Buddhist Sûtra so popular amongst them as the "Ling-yen-king" (Surañgama Sûtra), and this is perhaps the most scholastic of all the latest productions of the Mahâyâna system. They appreciate, however, the subtleties of the book without enlarging upon them. Their commentators confine themselves to a bare explanation of terms, and indulge in no original speculation. In India, as we have seen, the fate of a monastery, nay! of many together, often depended on the ability of a favourite champion of the faith to defend a thesis or maintain a point in dialectics, against every opponent. But in China no such necessity could occur. The question between the Literati and the priests was not one of logic, but of morals, and of fact. What was the right motive to a virtuous life? Is there a Heaven for the good, or a Hell for the bad? These were the questions raised, the answers to which, in the very nature of the case, come within the province of dogma rather than scholasticism.

Passing by other subjects, we now come to consider the motive which induced Fah-Hian to undertake his perilous journey to India.

His professed object was to seek for correct copies of the various portions of the Vinaya Pitaka. The rules of religious discipline (comprised in this Piṭaka) were not in his time commonly known in China. The books already translated were of a mixed character. There had been no arrangement in their translation. The early pilgrims had returned with a miscellaneous collection of works, just as they procured them, and they were translated without discrimination. In the first consignment brought by Matañga and Tsu-fah-lan, we find two works, at least, of a very opposite character, viz. the Sûtra of 42 Sections, which, from internal evidence, appears to be of a primitive type; and the Dasabhûmi Sûtra, belonging to the development known as the

Mahâyâna or Great Vehicle, and therefore of a comparatively late date. These two books, however, were impartially translated and regarded with the same reverence. Hence arose the confusion of which Fah-Hian complains; he was induced therefore to set out on his pilgrimage, with a view to obtain books of a uniform character—viz., those belonging to the Rules of Discipline, and of the development known as the Little Vehicle.

The Little Vehicle (Hînayâna) may be conveniently regarded as the original form of Buddhist doctrine. It was called so in after years, when this system was regarded as an imperfect or unfinished method for the "conveyance" of man through the troubles of life to the blessedness of Nirvâṇa. It concerned itself principally with morals and the rules for ascetic or conventual life. It allowed the existence of matter, but affirmed that man was merely an aggregate of qualities. Being so, when these qualities or constituent parts are broken up, logically speaking, nothing should remain. The *man* disappears as much as the thing named a chariot would disappear, if the wheels, and the pole, and remaining portions were separated and scattered. In other words, Buddha declared, according to this school, that there is no such thing as individual soul. When the parts of the body are separated by death, there is an end of the subject. Yet, by a stretch of imagination, we are required to suppose that there exists a sort of intangible destiny or Karma which has a power of reproducing the subject under another form —the same subject and yet not the same; for there was nothing left to reproduce. The aim of the disciple, under this development, was, by entering on a course of means (the paths), to destroy Karma, so that there could be no appearance even of reproduction. The subject, then, would be blown out; or (if Nirvâṇa has the meaning attributed to it by Colebrooke and Hodgson) it would be unmoved, passive, without possibility of again becoming active, which is the same as extinction.

The problem of Deliverance, therefore, resolved itself into this—What is the *cause* of the continued existence of Karma? The first theory on this point, as we have observed above, was, that such continued existence results from Desire.[1] Desire, therefore, must be overcome, crushed entirely out, and then existence would terminate. This theory lasted awhile, but gave way in time to another, of a more recondite order. It was this—that existence results from the connection of cause and effect. "On account of ignorance, merit and demerit are produced; on account of these, consciousness; on account of this, body and mind; on account of these, the six organs of sense; on account of these, touch or contact; on account of this, desire; on account of this, sensation; on account of this, cleaving to existence; on account of this, reproduc-

[1] That is, concupiscence, (φρόνημα σαρκὸς).

tion; on account of this, birth; and on account of birth, decay and sorrow." In this theory there is an appearance of a regular deduction without any reality; for, in the absence of any description of ignorance (Avidyâ), the Nidânas, as they are called (*i.e.* causes), fall to the ground like so many unsupported links of a chain. A further advance was then made, and the proposition resolved thus—there is *no cause*, but all things exist "of themselves" (tsze in). This theory is stated by Chinese authorities to belong to the southern school, and is treated fully in the Lañkâvatâra, or the Sûtra delivered by Buddha at Lañkâ, in Ceylon. We find it also combatted by Nagardjuna, in the Shaster known by the name of "One Sloka." It appears to have finally resolved itself into the form of belief maintained by the Svâbâvika school, which yet exists in Nipal, and is opposed to that known as the Aishvârika, or Theistic School. These three divisions belong distinctively to the Little Vehicle.

We now come to a period marked by the removal of the old basis of belief—viz., that man is nothing but a connection of parts, and the substitution of another, that there is a soul[1] both within man and in the universe. To arrive at Nirvâṇa, was now, to bring ourselves into union with the universal soul. There is no more usual phrase in the liturgical books common in

[1] The Chinese word is "heart" (sin), but this undoubtedly corresponds with the Sanscrit "Âtma."

China than this—to worship with "one heart"—to pray with "one heart"—to adore and supplicate with "one heart"—which, in fact, points to the supposition that there is a union possible between the soul of the worshipper and the soul of the universe; and in the perfection of this, consists the Pari-Nirvâṇa. It was now this phrase—Pari-Nirvâṇa—was introduced, signifying the complete or final Nirvâṇa, which, in fact, corresponds as nearly as possible to absorption. This theory marks the rise of the Great Vehicle (Mahâyâna). A question, however, similar to the one which arose in the former stage, presented itself here again. The former question was, "What is the cause of the continuation of existence?"—the question now is, "What is the cause of material existence?"—in other words, of all which is not the soul. This question, which is as wide almost as philosophical speculation itself, caused many divisions in the Buddhist community. Finally, however, the formula was adopted, which is the most commonly met with in all Buddhist books—that all things which exist result from the heart (yih tsai wei sin sho tso).[1] In other words, that all things are just what the mind represents them to be. That there is no substance (tai) except mind, or, to use the Buddhist phrase, "all things (*i.e.* material things) are empty." We may further illustrate this

[1] This phrase occurs on the great Ningpo Bell, which faces the visitor to the British Museum as he ascends the principal staircase.

question by turning to the account given us of the conversion of Vasoubhandou. He lived about the time of the Christian era, or, at, any rate, he preceded Vasumitra, who was a contemporary of Kanishka, for we are distinctly told that Vasumitra commented on the Abhidharma Kosha, which was composed by Vasoubhandou (Burnouf, I. B. 566–7; Jul. ii. 223). His elder brother, Asañgha, pretended to have received his inspiration from visiting Mâitrêya, the future Buddha, in the heaven called the Tusitas. This was a common fiction in those days, and helps to denote the period of any great transition in thought; just as Nagardjuna, in starting the Pâramita class of books, declared he had received the copies of them from the Dragons. Asañgha, who had been brought up in the school of the Mahîsâsakas, belonging to the Little Vehicle, now professed his conversion to the Mahâyâna system. His brother Vasoubhandou had also been trained in the principles of the Little Vehicle. Asañgha desired his conversion. Vasoubhandou was now coming from North India towards Ayôdhyâ (Oude). Asañgha therefore, dispatched one of his disciples to meet him. They encountered each other at a choultry or hostel not far from Oude. Vasoubhandhou, having retired to rest, was awakened in the middle of the night by the voice of the strange priest, whom he had met. He was reciting the lines of a religious book. We are told it was the Dasabhûmi Sûtra (Jul. ii. 273). The Chinese account informs us of the exact words (Shing To, § 185). They were these: "The man who desires to understand thoroughly (the doctrine, or the nature) of the Buddhas of the three ages, must consider (kwan) that they are the only existing substance of the universe, and that all (other) things are just what the mind reports them (to consciousness)." The last line in this verse is the one to which we alluded above, and which is generally used to formulate the distinctive principles of the school in question. Vasoubhandou, when he heard this gâtha, was convinced of the imperfect character of his knowledge, and became one of the principal promoters of the new doctrine. He afterwards composed numerous works in support of his creed, which were principally directed against the Vâibashîka school (belonging to the Little Vehicle) dominant in North India (Gandhâra), where he had been himself brought up.

The last development of the Mahâyâna school is one fully exhibited in the later expanded Sûtras. It adopts the theory, that sensible phenomena are not merely the capricious forms which the mind reports them to be, but that we see all things in the soul, or, to use the Chinese exposition of the doctrine, that mind and matter are one—that there is no difference between phenomena (siang) and substance (sing)—that cause and effect are not different—that variety is the same as unity, and unity as variety, etc.;—in fact, in this development we see the end or the madness of all philosophy, which aims at the elucidation of questions beyond the province of consciousness—an idealistic pantheism of the grossest character.

Such, in brief, is the account the Chinese give us of their own creed. Fah-Hian alludes very seldom to these theories, yet it is plain that, as he recited the Ling Yen Sûtra (Surañgama) at the cave near Rajagriha, he lived himself some time after the latest development, and we have, therefore, thought it advisable to allude to it.

III.—From the preceding remarks we gather that in Fah-Hian's time Buddhism in India had arrived at a stage of development that foreshadowed its approaching decline and overthrow. It had flourished under varying circumstances during 800 years and more, boldly asserting and maintaining its distinctive principles against all opposition. But now the folly of a so-called philosophy was hastening it to its end.

There is no proof that Tantric worship (use of magical charms) had been largely introduced into the system in Fah-Hian's time. But it followed, in natural order, on the steps of the last stage of thought to which we have referred. We may regard, indeed, this belief in the virtue of magical processes in religion as the mark of the infancy as well as the decay of man's inventive power in such matters. Hence we observe that it distinguishes both extremes of thought in the case under consideration; for whilst the earliest worship of the majority of the northern nations, who now profess Buddhism, was nothing less than the use of certain magical words and acts in the worship of devils or fetishes: so, after their conversion to the principles of this religion, they were led, by the uncertain light of false speculation, back to the very principles from which they had started, and once more adopted charms, magic, and a purely mechanical method of worship, in the religious reverence they paid to the idea they had conceived of an all-pervading and universal Soul.

We find no reference in Fah-Hian to the various works mentioned by Hiouen-Thsang on Yôga (*e.gr.* the Yôga shâster, the Yôgâtchâryabhûmi Shâster, etc.), and on which he dwells with such pleasure (Jul. i. 144). We may suppose therefore that the two centuries which followed Fah-Hian marked the last stage of Buddhist history. The system gradually degenerated from the high platform it had assumed to the level of Sivite worship and a corrupt popular taste. And so it was in a position to be absorbed by the dominant creed. The people reverted to their idols. The priests were banished or slain. The temples were destroyed and burned.

It now remains to exhibit in a few words what little special information we may collect from the incidental remarks of Fah-Hian in his records.

There is very little in his account which tends to settle the vexed question of the date of Buddha's Nirvâṇa. He alludes to the Council held at Vâisâli (chap. xxv. p. 100) one hundred years after that event, and mentions a tower erected there to commemorate the fact. His account, both as to the number of priests composing the assembly, and the "ten particulars" in which the Vinaya had been violated by the heretical Shamans, agrees with the southern tradition (Mahawanso, cap. v.). So, also (chap. xxx), he mentions the convocation held immediately after the Nirvâṇa by 500 priests, to arrange the collection of the sacred books, in the Sattapani cave, near Rajagriha. It is singular, therefore, when he comes to speak of Pâtaliputra, that he makes no allusion to the Council of the thousand Rahats held there under the presidency of the Thero Tisso, during the reign of Dharmâsôka, 118 years after the convocation at Vâisâli. His allusions, indeed, to Asôka are plain and frequent. His extensive charity—erection of pagodas—and the religiousness of his son, are all referred to. And these are circumstances equally commemorated in the southern schools. But there is no mention made of the king under his name Dharmâsoka. This appellation, in fact, is wholly unknown in Chinese records. It is strange, too, that in the Dípawanso, the reign and name of Kalâsoka, is altogether omitted, and the Nandos made the brothers of Susanago, who is elsewhere called Maha-

Nandi (Turnour, Ex. of Pali Buddhist Annals, No. 4, *passim*). Can it be supposed, however, that Fah-Hian resided for three years at Pâtaliputra, learning the Sanscrit language, and that, too, during the very time when Buddhagosha was engaged in compiling the Attakathá of the Pittakattya in Ceylon, without having heard of the famous Council of 1000 Rahats, or even the name of the monarch under whose auspices it was assembled in that city? Or, if he had heard of it, would he have failed to record the fact?

But the truth is, the circumstances connected with this supposed council, are generally of an incredible character. The conception of Tisso (Mogalliputto), who descended from the Brahma Loka world on purpose to preside over the assembly—an event resting on a prophecy of the Theros composing the Vâisâli convocation, 118 years before—is a manifest invention, which throws discredit on the whole history. The improbability of seventeen schisms having occurred in one century, viz. between the time of Kalâsoka and Dharmâsoka (Mahawanso, chap. v.), is equally against the record. Whereas there is no improbability that so many divisions should have incurred in the interval between the date of the former monarch and the time of Kanishka, according to northern accounts (Burnouf, Introduct. 579). It is true, indeed, that Fah-Hian does not allude to any council held by Kanishka either, but that may be explained on the ground that he did not visit the Tamâsavana Convent where it was held, under the presidency of Vasumitra. But then, on the other hand, Hiouen-Thsang, who says nothing about the convocation of the 1000 priests at Pâtaliputra, does mention, at some length, the one assembled by Kanishka (Jul. ii. 119). It is as well here, perhaps, to refer to the statement "that the Northern Buddhists know but one council besides the assembly following immediately on the death of Buddha, viz. the Council of Pâtaliputra under Dharmâsoka, 110 years after Buddha" (Sanscrit Lit. p. 272). The Chinese and Thibetan records, however, fully describe the Council under Kanishka (Burnouf, Introd. 579, and Jul. ii. 119); nor can there be found, I believe, in those records, any mention of a "Council of Pâtaliputra;" the usual statement is, as Burnouf gives it, "the second revision of the sacred books took place 110 years after the death of Sâkya, in the time of Asôka, who *reigned* at Pâtaliputra" (Introd. *ut supra*); but the council was held at Vâisâli (the Thibetan accounts give Allahabâd by mistake) according to the statement of the Mahawanso and the express declaration of Fah-Hian.

These difficulties are increased by the assertion of Fah-Hian, that, when in Ceylon, he heard a proclamation made by royal mandate, stating that since Buddha's death 1497 years had already elapsed (Chap. xxxviii. p. 156). Supposing the year of his visit to have been about 410 A.D., this would place

Buddha's Nirvâṇa 1087 B.C.—an impossible date for many reasons, but yet, according to our author, one received in Ceylon at the time of his visit. We are necessarily forced to suppose some mistake here; but then, on the other hand, is it possible, if the conventional date of 543 B.C. for Buddha's death was so well known and acknowledged in the great temples of Ceylon at this time—temples, be it remembered, in which Fah-Hian passed two entire years—that he would have returned to his own country without being prepared to stand by this Buddhistical era, resting, as it is said, on "incontrovertible evidence" (Turnour, No. 2, p. 10)—for the benefit of his own countrymen and the rectification of all previous errors? Whereas we find no reference to it.

Duly weighing the facts on both sides, there seems to be some ground for suspecting the accuracy of the records of the Mahawanso and the Attakathâ of Buddhagosha, in reference to the period between the second and the (so-called) third convocation. It is as well to remember that the Sâutrântika school, generally followed in Ceylon, whose text-book is the Agama, is root and branch opposed to the Vâibâshikas of the north of India, whose text-book is the Vâibâsha; both these great sects belong to the Hînayâna or primitive system of Buddhism, but they embody two distinct streams of tradition. It was in the north, where the Vâibâsha was principally followed, that the Council of

Kanishka was held. Was this council disowned by the Sâutrântika school? and, if so, was it purposely omitted in the Ceylonese records, and the absent third council supplied by the invention of Kâlâsoka, and the exaggerated accounts of the 1000 Theros who assembled at Patâliputra? At least, I believe that more weight ought to be attached to the unanimous verdict of the northern schools, and the undesigned coincidences found in their numerous records, than is generally allowed.

There is no difficulty in tracing Fah-Hian's route as far as Khoten. The position of this town has been fixed by astronomical observation as follows:[1] lat. 37° 37′ N., long. 78° 57′ E. of London. From Khoten he advanced towards the country of Tseu-ho, *i.e.* the Yarkand river. The position of Yarkand (lat. from observation, long. by dead reckoning) is as follows, according to Capt. Montgomery: lat. 38° 20′ N., long. 77° 30′ E. According to the Jesuits it is: lat. 38° 19′ N., long. 76° 16′ E. Fah-Hian then proceeds through the country of Yu-hwui towards Ki'a-Cha. The former place cannot be Ladak (as Klaproth supposes), but most probably corresponds to a district in the neighbourhood of the Chiltung Pass, on the very borders of the Tsung-ling mountains. Ki'a-cha is certainly Kartchou, to the east of which flows the Mang-tsin river (*vid.* p. 183). Kartchou is placed on all maps to the

[1] Ravenstein.

S.W. of Yarkand. Kiepert (1867) places it 88 miles in that direction; the same author, on a map accompanying Ritter's Geography of Asia (1852), places it 108 miles to the S.W. Vivien de St. Martin (1857) assigns its distance at 100 miles in the same direction. No doubt it was approached by a difficult and circuitous route, which may account for the long time (25 days) employed on the journey from Yu-hwui. This kingdom (Kartchou or Han-pan-to) appears to have been one of considerable importance in the early period of our era; and, in Fah-Hian's time, the inhabitants were all Buddhists, attached to the Little Vehicle. From Kartchou our pilgrim proceeds westwards across the Tsung-ling mountains, and, after a month's travel, reaches the frontiers of Northern India. Here, he says, there is a little kingdom called To-li. Judging from the time given, we may suppose that the distance from Kartchou to To-li was about equal to that from Yarkand to Kartchou, *i.e.* about 100 miles in a direct course. Taking the course to be S.W. or W.S.W., this would bring us into the neighbourhood of the head waters of the Gilgit river. We are fortunately able to identify To-li with the Tha-li-lo (Dhalila) of Hiouen-Thsang, for they both are connected with the enormous image of Mâitreya Buddha, and the Arhat Madhyântika (compare Jul. ii. 149 with Chap. vi. p. 20 of the present volume). In the notes appended to the Fo-koue-ki (p. 59) it is stated that the streamlet (ruisseau) Tha-li-lo is 1000 li to the N.E. of Meng-kie-li; I was led to assume therefore that To-li was the name of a small river as well as of a country, and hence to identify it with the River Tal (Chap. vi. n. 2). But on turning to M. Julien's more trustworthy version, I found Rémusat's "ruisseau" to be rendered "vallée." "To the N.E. of Moungali, after crossing a mountain and traversing a valley, and following up the course of the Sintou . . . . for about 1000 li, we arrive at the middle of the valley[1] of Tha-li-lo" (Jul. ii. 149). Now, according to a previous statement (Jul. ii. p. 133), the source of the Swêti river is about 260 li to the N.E. of the same town of Moungali; proceeding then still to the N.E. of the head waters of this river, until we strike the Indus, and then advancing along its course, or rather that of the Gilgit river, altogether 750 li, we ought to arrive at the valley of Tha-li-lo, or the To-li of our author. The course and distance above described would, I am inclined to think, bring us near the head of the western branch of the Gilgit river; and as the Dardu people (who may possibly correspond with the people of To-li, or Tha-li-lo) live in this neighbourhood, I have brought Fah-Hian across this river into Oudyâna. The latest and most accurate description of the Indus in this part of its course is found in Cunningham's Ladak, from which I extract the

[1] Probably the word in the original is ch'uen, which means a river, but more frequently a valley (*vid.* p. 61, *n*).

following: "From Skardo to Rongdo, and from Rongdo to Makpou-i-shang-rong, for upwards of 100 miles, the Indus sweeps sullen and dark through a mighty gorge in the mountains, which, for wild sublimity, is perhaps unequalled. Rongdo means the country of defiles . . . Between these points the Indus raves from side to side of the gloomy chasm, foaming and chafing with ungovernable fury. Yet even in these inaccessible places has daring and ingenious man triumphed over opposing Nature. The yawning abyss is spanned by frail rope bridges and the narrow ledges of rock are connected by ladders to form a giddy pathway overhanging the seething caldron below" (p. 89). "The Gilgit river is a mighty stream, perhaps not inferior to any of the mountain tributaries. From the junction of this river with the Indus, the course is S.W. and the distance to Attok 300 miles" (p. 80). On the whole, I am tolerably satisfied that Fah-Hian travelled about W.S.W. from Kartchou, and then S.W. to the Gilgit river (which he calls the Sintou), over which he passed by one of the frail bridges referred to above, into Northern India. Had he really passed over the Indus proper, he must have crossed it *twice* (in Klaproth's map illustrating his route, he is made to pass it four times) before he could have reached Oudyâna, of which we should doubtless have been apprised; his course, moreover, would in that case have been S.E. instead of west from Kartchou, which we cannot think possible.

After entering Oudyâna, he appears to have advanced southward towards the Swêti river (the word translated "descended" in the text (p. 28) is a mistake in the original, *vid.* Chap. x. p. 30, n. 1), and skirting its banks, along which many monasteries were built, he finally turned eastward towards Gandhâra and its capital, Pouroushapoura. Beyond this no great difficulty occurs in his route, which may now be followed by means of the notes appended to the text.

There is an interesting statement by Fah-Hian (Chap. xxix. p. 116) to the effect that when in the neighbourhood of Rajagriha, he proceeded to the "Hill of the Vulture Cave," and recited there the greater part of the Shau-leng-yan, or Surañgama Sûtra. In this work is contained the most complete list of Dharanis (invocations) found in any Chinese compilation. There are 426 distinct sections, containing the names (disguised in a Chinese form) of the different Buddhas and Hindu deities worshipped at the time of the composition of the Sûtra. Considering that Fah-Hian, in the early part of the fifth century, regarded this book with such reverence as to recite it throughout in the place where tradition stated it had been delivered, we may reasonably assign it to a period not later than the end of the first century A.D. Now, amongst the invocations (Kiouen vii. § 43 and 44), we find distinct reference to the Dhyani Buddhas, Vâirôchana, Akchôbya, Amitâbha, and the others, shewing that they were commonly recognized and worshipped even at that early date. There is no need therefore to suppose that the invention of Amitâbha belongs to a late period in Buddhist literature (*vid.* Notes and Queries on China and Japan, March, 1868). But whether his name of "boundless light" (Amîta + bhâ), or, as he is sometimes called, the Eternal (Amirta), with the fable that his son Avalokitêshwara, *i.e.* the manifested God, had entered into an inviolable covenant with him to save mankind—is a proof that even at such an early period an imperfect knowledge of Christian doctrine had extended thus far to the east; or whether all this is mere invention, or "the blank blasphemies of Chinese Buddhists" (Chips from a German Workshop, vol. i. p. 183), or a much later graft on an old stock, may be left for future investigation. At any rate, there is no foundation for the following strange assertion "that the Chinese so vividly expected the Messiah's advent—the great Saint, who, as Confucius says, 'was to appear in the west,'—that about 60 years after the birth of our Saviour they sent their envoys to hail their expected Redeemer. These envoys encountered on their way the missionaries of Buddhism coming from India; the latter, announcing an incarnate God, were taken to be the disciples of the true Christ, and were presented as such to their countrymen by the deluded ambassadors. Thus was the religion of Buddha introduced into China, and thus did this phantasmagoria of

Hell intercept the light of the Gospel" (Schlegel's Philos. of Hist., Bohn's Ed. p. 136, n.).

This story, which is said to rest on the authority of Du Halde, although without foundation in Buddhist records, seems to confirm what may be called a traditional belief, that the earliest Buddhist emissaries to India heard of and brought back some knowledge of an "incarnate God," and, so far as it is worth, strengthens the hypothesis, that much of what is true in the later Buddhist speculation owes its origin to events which occurred in the West about the time of that development.

RECORDS

OF

BUDDHIST COUNTRIES.

BY

CHI FAH HIAN OF THE SUNG DYNASTY.

[DATE 400 A.D.]

CHAPTER I.

FAH HIAN, when formerly resident at Tchang'an,[1] was grieved at noticing the fragmentary character of the Rules of the Buddhist Discipline[2] (as they were then known in China). Whereupon, in the second year of Hung Chi, the cyclical characters being Ki Hae,[3] he agreed with Hwui King, Tao Ching, Hwui Ying, and

[1] The former capital of the Province of Shense, now called Se-ngan.

[2] That is, of the Vinaya Pitaka. There are three Pitakas (boxes sc. for holding the several collections of Buddhist Sacred Books). The Vinaya Pitaka relates to Discipline and Morality. The Sûtra Pitaka contains the discourses of Buddha himself. The Abhidharma Pitaka includes all compositions explaining doctrine.

[3] There is an error here of one year. It should be the cyclical characters Kang tsze, *i.e.*, A.D. 400-1. (Ch. Ed.)

Hwui Wu, to go together to India to seek for complete copies of these Rules.

Setting out, therefore, from Tchang'an, they first of all crossed the Lung (Mountains),[1] and arrived at the country of Kon Kwei,[2] where they sojourned during the season of the Rains.[3] After this they pushed forward, and arrived at the country of Niu Tan;[4] then crossing the Yang Lau Hills they reached the great frontier station of Chang Yeh.[5] This place was in such an unsettled condition that the roads were unsafe for passengers. The Prince[6] of the country prevailed on them to remain there for some time, and himself afforded them[7] hospitality. It was here they fell in with Chi Yen, Hwui Kan, Sang Chau, Po Wan, and Sang King, and

[1] 35° N. lat. 10° W. long. from Pekin (R).

[2] This is the name of the Prince who ruled the country. The place itself is called Yuen Chün, and is in the western parts of the province of Shense.

[3] "This season extends from the 16th day of the fifth month to the 15th day of the 7th month." (Jul. ii., 62.) "It was an ordinance of Buddha that the priests, who were then supposed to dwell most commonly in the wilderness, should reside during the three months of the rainy season in a fixed habitation." (S.H.) "This season is called Varchavasana, and extends over the four months of the rainy season." (Burnouf, Introd., p. 285.)

[4] This also is the name of a prince, and not of a country. He ruled over a district called Ho Si, *i.e.*, "the country to the west of the (Yellow) River."

[5] Chang Yeh is still marked on the Chinese maps as a district city of the department Kan Chow, in the Province of Kansu. It is just within the north-west extremity of the Great Wall. At the time of Fah Hian's visit, it was under the rule of Tün-nieh of Liang Chow.

[6] Called Tün-nieh, who died A.D. 401. (Ch. Ed.)

[7] In the original it is "became their patron or benefactor (Dana pati)."

pleased to find they all had one common aim in view, they remained together during the season of rains.[1] After this they again set out and arrived at Tun Wang.[2] There are fortifications here extending about eighty li (i.e., about sixteen miles) east and west, and half that distance north and south. They all stopped here a month and some odd days, after which Fah Hian and his four companions[3] made arrangements to set out in advance of the others, and so they were again separated. The military governor of Tun Wang, Li Ho by name, provided them with all necessaries for crossing the Desert.[4] In this desert there are a great many evil demons, there are also sirocco winds, which kill all who encounter them. There are no birds or beasts to be seen; but so far as the eye can reach, the route is marked out by the bleached bones of men who have perished in the attempt to cross the desert. After

[1] This shows that nine months had elapsed since leaving Kon Kwei.

[2] Tun Wang, a frontier town of considerable military importance, 40° 12′ N. lat., 21° 37′ W. from Pekin (P), in the province of Tangut. It was first named Sha Chow during the early part of the tenth century (P). It is mentioned by Marco Polo under the name Sachion. This town was wrested from Tun-nieh in the third month of this year by Li Ho, or more properly Li Ko, who ruled it as the "illustrious warrior king of the Liang dynasty." (Ch. Ed.)

[3] Rémusat translates this "Fah Hian and five others." It should be "Fah Hian and his companions, being altogether five persons," or as we have rendered it in the text.

[4] This is the Gobi Desert, called by Marco Polo the desert of Lop. His account of the dangers encountered in crossing it agrees closely with that of Fah Hian. The desert extends, according to Dr. Halde, to 35° W. long. from Pekin.

travelling thus for seventeen days, a distance of about fifteen hundred li,[1] they arrived at the kingdom of Shen-Shen.[2]

[1] A li is the Chinese mile, it is commonly said that it represents a distance of 1898 English feet, or that $27\frac{4}{5}$ li are equal to 10 English miles (Williams' Chinese Dictionary). The geographical li is also said to be $\frac{1}{250}$ of a degree, or 1460·44 feet $\frac{1}{10}$ of a French astronomical league. But M. Vivien de Saint-Martin has satisfactorily shewn (Mémoire Analytique) that in the time of Hiouen Thsang (A.D. 629), and therefore probably in Fah Hian's time, the Chinese li was much less in valne. We shall nearly be correct in considering five li as equal to one English mile (Jul. iii. pp. 259-260).

[2] Shen-shen is the same as the Leou-lun of Hiouen Thsang, or as he likewise terms it, Na-po-po or Navapa. It is at present called the desert of Makhaï, about 150 miles S.W. of Tun Wong. Both Fah Hian and Hiouen Thsang left China at the same point, viz., through the Yuh Mun, or Gem Gate, just beyond Su-Chow. But Hiouen Thsang proceeded northward towards Kamil, whilst Fah Hian advanced S.W. towards Lake Lob. Hiouen Thsang returned from India by the outward route of Fah Hian, whilst Fah Hian returned by sea from Ceylon and Java.

CHAPTER II.

This land is rugged and barren. The people dress like the Chinese, except they wear garments made of felt and woollen stuff. The King of this country is well affected to the Law of Buddha. In his dominions are about four thousand priests, all of whom belong to the religious system[1] known as the Little Vehicle. The common people[2] and the Shamans[3] of this and the neighbouring kingdoms all follow the religious customs of India, only some more exactly than others. All the kingdoms westward from this, as a rule, have the same characteristics, except that

[1] In Sanscrit, Hîna Yâna. This may be called the elementary system of Buddhism.

[2] As distinguished from the priests. We may here observe that the word "priest" is used in an accommodated sense. Every member of the Buddhist fraternity is a priest. The word, in fact, means a member of the congregation or church (Sangha).

[3] The Chinese word Shaman represents phonetically the Sanscrit "Sramana," or the Pali "Samana." The Chinese word is defined to mean "diligent and laborious," to wit, in fulfilling religious duties. The Sanscrit root is "sram" श्रम to be fatigued. The following description of a Shaman is from the Sutra of 42 Sections: "The man who leaves his family, quits his house, enters on the study of Supreme Reason, searches out the deepest principles of his intelligent mind, so as to understand that there is a law which admits of no active exertion, this man is called a Shaman."

their languages differ,—each using its own dialect of the Tartar[1] language. All the followers of Buddha (prajarwikás),[2] however, practice themselves in reading Indian books, and conversing in that language. Remaining here one month and some days, they again set out in a north-westerly direction, and after journeying for fifteen days, arrived at the kingdom of the Ou-i.[3] This kingdom also has about four thousand priests, all professing the doctrines of the Little Vehicle. When Fah Tsih and Tsai Tch'ang, two Buddhist priests of the land of Thsin,[4] arrived at this country, they were unable to conform to some of the customs of the religious community. Fah Hian, therefore, having obtained a pass, proceeded to the palace (hall) of the reigning Prince, Kung Sün, where he remained two months and some days; after which, he returned to Po Wan and the rest (who had by this time arrived at the country); but as there was a general dissatisfaction with the want of politeness

[1] The original words translated Tartar language, signify generally the language of those wandering tribes that frequent the pasture lands of Mongolia. In a Chinese work, called "Fah kai lih to," it is referred to all languages except Sanscrit, in which Buddhist works are written.

[2] Those who have quitted their homes and families.

[3] The Ouigours, who from the second century B.C., had occupied the territory of Kamil, under the name of Kiu-sse (Jul. iii. 263).

[4] The land of Thsin,—alluding probably to one of the petty sovereignties established at this time in the west of China. The expression is also applied to China generally. The Shamans alluded to in the text were, in all probability, two who had lately returned, and whom Fah Hian had met at Tchán'gan. Rémusat translates this passage differently.

which the people of the country showed towards their guests, three of the pilgrims, viz., Chi Yan, Hwui Kan, and Hwui Wu, resolved immediately to retrace their steps towards Kao Tchang,[1] for the purpose of obtaining there the provisions necessary for their journey. Fah Hian and the others, in consequence of their possessing a pass, were furnished with all they needed by Kung Sün. After having provided themselves with these things, they immediately set forward in a southwesterly direction. On their route they found neither dwelling-houses or people. The miseries they endured in crossing the rivers, and in surmounting the natural difficulties of the road along which they had to journey, exceed all conception. After being on the road a month and five days, they at last arrived at Khoten[2] (Yu-tien).

[1] Otherwise written Ho-tien (Ch. Ed.) Derived from the Sanscrit Kustana (कु+स्तन) the earth's pap.

[2] Not far from the present Tourfan.

CHAPTER III.

This country is exceedingly prosperous; the people are very wealthy, and all of them, without exception, reverence the Law of Buddha, and take delight in attending to their religious duties. The body of priests may, perhaps, amount to ten thousand men,[1] and principally belong to the system of the Great Vehicle. They all partake of their meals in common. The people of the country build their houses in clusters.[2] Before the doors of their houses they erect small towers. The smallest are about twenty-two feet high.[3]

[1] I have so translated this passage; it may also be rendered "amount to several ten thousand." I prefer, however, taking "sho" as a verb. The writer of the preface of the Imperial Catalogue of Kien Lung ridicules the idea of Buddhism being so popular at Khoten. His words are: "It is well known that from very ancient time till now, Yu-tien, or as it is at present called, Ho-tien, has been much given to reverence the law of the Ui-Ui doctrine (*i.e.*, Mahomedanism), as is clearly proved in the famous work 'Khin-ting-si-yu-to-chi' (*i.e.*, Description and Maps of Western Countries, imperial edition); and yet Fah Hian speaks of fourteen temples and 10,000 Buddhist priests there. He is clearly in error," etc. This does not say much for the historical knowledge of the writer of it.

[2] This is a perplexing passage. Rémusat translates it, "determine their abode according to the stars." A very unlikely rendering. I have no doubt the same expression is used by Hiouen Thsang, in his description of the country of Tsiu-Kiu (Yerkiang), and which M. Julien translates "Les maisons du peuples sont trés rapprochées" (Jul. i. 460).

[3] Two chang. The chang is equal to 141 inches English.

They also construct apartments for foreign priests,[1] where they entertain them as guests, and provide them with all they require. The ruler of the country located Fah Hian and his companions in a Sañghârâma,[2] which was called Gômati.[3] The priests of this temple belong to the system known as the Great Vehicle.[4] At the sound of the gong,[5] three thousand priests assemble together to take their meal. Whilst entering the dining hall they observe the greatest decorum and propriety of conduct; one after another they take their seats. Silence is observed amongst them all; they make no noise with their rice-bowls, and when they require more food there is no chattering one with the other, but they simply make a sign with their fingers (and so are supplied).

Hwui King, Tao Ching, and Hwui Ta, set out in advance towards Ki'a-Cha (Kartchou),[6] whilst Fah

[1] "Priests from the four quarters." Rémusat prefers "Priests chambers of a square form." The phrase, however, is repeatedly used throughout the work in the former sense.

[2] The Chinese Seng-kia-lan is the equivalent of the Sanskrit Sañghârâma, *i.e.*, the garden of the priests (सङ्घ+आराम). The Sañghârâma includes the vihara or chapel, the various apartments of the priests, and the surrounding grounds. What we should call a college.

[3] Kiu-ma-ti.

[4] Mahâyâna.

[5] Kien, for Kien-ti, *i.e.*, Ghaṇṭâ or Gong.

[6] I have identified Kia-cha of Fah Hian, with the Khie-pan-to of Hiouen Thsang. In the 5th cap. Fah Hian states that this kingdom is in the midst of the Tsoung Ling Mountains. It cannot therefore be Kashgar; much less Cashmir. Its situation accurately corresponds with the Khie-pan-to of Hiouen Thsang, which has been happily determined as Kartchou, a name sufficiently like Kia-cha for identification.

Hian and the rest, wishing to witness the ceremony of the procession of images, halted here for a period of three months and some days. In this country there are fourteen large Sañghârâmas, without reckoning the smaller ones. On the first day of the fourth month, they begin within the city to sweep and water the roads, and to decorate the streets. Above the chief gate of the city they stretch out a large cloth screen, and ornament the covered space in every possible way, then the King and the court ladies, with their attendants, take their places there. The priests of the Gômati temple, belonging to the Greater Vehicle, being chiefly honoured by the King, first take their images in procession. They construct a four-wheeled image-car about three or four li from the city, its height is about thirty-five feet,[1] and in appearance like a moving royal pavilion. It is adorned with the seven precious substances, and adorned with silken streamers and flags and curtains. The chief image is then placed upright in the centre of the carriage, with two Bôdhisatwas[2] in attendance, and surrounded by all the Devas.[3] All

[1] Three chang, *i.e.*, 35 ft.

[2] A Bôdhisatwa is a being who has arrived at supreme wisdom (Bôdhi), and yet consents to remain as a creature (Satwa) for the good of men. Such are Avalôkitêsvara, Mañjusrî, Sarasvati, Mâitrêya, and others. The Bodhisatwa was originally a man of eminent piety, but under the later system they were imaginary beings, idealized under certain forms, and possessed of certain distinct attributes.

[3] The Devas are the gods of the Hindoos. The great offence of Buddhism in the eyes of the Brahman was, not that it denied the existence or the majesty of his gods, but that it subordinated them to Buddha and his viceregents.

are made of gold and silver, whilst glittering gems are hung suspended in the air. When the image is about one hundred paces from the city gate, the King removes his royal head-dress, and putting on new garments, with bare feet he proceeds from the city to meet the procession, holding flowers and incense in his hand, and followed by his suite. On meeting the car he bows down with his face to the ground in adoration, whilst he scatters the flowers and burns the incense. At the time when the image enters the city, the court ladies and their attendants throw down from the pavilion above the gate flowers in endless variety. Thus everything is sumptuously arranged. Each Sañghârâma has its own car, and its own day, for the procession. Beginning on the first day of the fourth month, they continue till the fourteenth day, after which they conclude, and the King and the ladies return to the palace. Seven or eight li to the west of this city is a Sañghârâma, called the Royal New Temple. During the last eighty years three kings have contributed towards its completion. It is about two hundred and ninety feet high. There are many inscribed plates of gold and silver within it. Jewels of every description combine to give a perfect finish (to the pinnacle) above the roof. There is a hall of Buddha[1] behind the main tower,

[1] Rémusat translates the word "heou" by "since," thus—"a chapel dedicated to Foe has since been erected," but the sense is best given as in the text.

which is perfectly adorned and very magnificent. The beams, pillars, doors, and windows are covered with gold plates. Besides this, there are priests, chambers elegantly finished and adorned, so that no words can adequately describe them. All the kings of the six kingdoms to the east of the great mountain range called (Tsung) Ling [1] send as religious offerings to this temple whatever most costly gems they have, and in such abundance that but few of them can be used.

[1] The Tsoung Ling mountains form the western portion of the Great Kuen-Lun range, and blend with the Bolor range. They comprise the Karakorum and Pamir ridges, and separate Little Thibet and the country of the Dardus from Badakshan. The name signifies Onion Mountains. In Hiouen Thsang, vol. iii. 194, it is said they are so called because the region produces many onions. But in the Fah-kai-lih-to the reason assigned for the name is that the mountains are covered with rocky boulders of a rounded shape.

CHAPTER IV.

The religious processions of the fourth month being over, one of the pilgrims, called Sang Chau, set out in company with a fellow disciple[1] belonging to the country of the Ouigours, towards Ki-pin[2] (Cophene); Fah Hian and the rest pressed on towards the country of Tseu-ho,[3] and after a journey of twenty-five days they arrived there. The king of this country, by the determined energy of his character,[4] has collected round him about one thousand priests, chiefly belonging to the system known as the Great Vehicle. The pilgrims rested in this country fifteen days, and then going to

1 A fellow disciple; in the original, Tao-jin, a man of reason (Bôdhi), a Buddhist. I need hardly observe that Rémusat's rendering of this expression throughout the present work is incorrect. He translates it either as a follower of Lao-tseu, *i.e.*, a Tauist, or as a traveller.

2 Ki-pin, *i.e.*, Cophene, the district through which runs the Cophes or Cabul river. The classical name of Cophes, given to this river, is a corruption of the old Vedic name of Koubhâ, from which also we derive our own Cabul. In its widest extent Ki-pin includes the whole of Ariana of the classical writers (Cunningham). The Chinese traded with this country B.C. 60.

3 Tseu-ho, corresponds with the Tcho-kiu-ka or Tchakouka of Hiouen Thsang and the Chu-kiu-pho of Klaproth (Foe-koue-ki, note). It is the ancient name of the town and district of Yarkiang (Jul. iii., 427). Klaproth places it 37.30 North, and 73 E. from London, but this is certainly too westerly. Probably, as Mr. Laidlay suggests, it should be 76° 20′ E. of London, or 74° E. of Paris.

4 This translation is doubtful. I prefer it, however, to Rémusat's.

the southward for four days, they entered the Tsung Ling mountains, and reached the country of Yu-hwui,[1] where they rested. After this, proceeding directly onwards for twenty-five days, they arrived at the country of Kie-cha (Kartchou, the Kie-pan-to of Hiouen Thsang), where they rejoined Hwui King and the others.

[1] Assuming that the country of Tseu-ho, alluded to above, extends from the meridan of Yolarik (77° E.) to Yanghi-hissar (75° 30′ E.) as Klaproth states (*n.* in loc.), I should be inclined to take Fah Hian by the same route as Benedict Göes followed, viz., South from Yanghi-hissar through the Chiltung Pass towards the country of Karchu. (*Vide* Yule's Map.) In this case the Yu-hwui of the text would correspond with the Tanghetar of Göes. (Yule, 563.)

CHAPTER V.

The king of this country holds the quinquennial assembly known as the Pan-che-yu-sse.[1] At the time of the assembly he invites the priests (Shamans) of the four quarters (of every country) to attend. A vast concourse of them having come together, they then proceed to decorate the priests' session-place with silken flags and canopies. (In the midst) they erect a draped throne[2] adorned with gold and silver lotus flowers, and behind it they arrange the seats for the priests. The king and his attendant ministers then proceed to make their religious offerings. It is principally in the spring time that the King convokes the assembly, either during the first, second, or third month. After it is over, the King again exhorts his ministers to prepare and present further religious offerings. This occupies from one to five days more. After this is all done, the

[1] I think Professor Wilson's derivation the most probable, viz., Pancha + Varsha, five years; or, according to the Pali inscription of Asoka's third edict, "Panchasu panchasu vasesu," five five years, *i.e.*, every five years or five yearly (L.). It refers to (or is supposed to refer to) the quinquennial expiation recommended by King Priyadarsi (Asoka) in the 12th year of his inauguration. Edict III. (*vide* Mrs. Spiers' Ancient India, p. 233).

[2] Corresponding, perhaps, with the Therásanan, or seat for the chief Thero, described by Turnour. Essays, July, 1837, p. 17.

King further makes an offering of the horse which he rides, with its trappings, whilst the chief minister (of the country), and the principal nobles and officers of the land, offer theirs also; moreover, they make presents of white woollen stuff and every kind of precious thing which the Shamans require. All these things are given as votive offerings by the various ministers of the King. But, after being thus publicly presented by vow, they are redeemed from the priests for a certain value.[1] These mountainous regions are so cold that they will produce no cereal but wheat. As soon as the ecclesiastics have gathered in their harvest (or, received their dues), the weather becomes cloudy and overcast. The King, therefore, usually supplicates the priests to allow all the wheat to ripen before they begin to gather in (or receive) theirs. In this country is a stone spitting-vessel[2] of Buddha; it is the same color as his alms-bowl. There is also one of Buddha's teeth, over which the inhabitants have raised a tower. There are about 1,000 or more priests here, all of them belonging to the system called the Little Vehicle. Everywhere to the eastward of these mountains the ordinary people wear coarse garments like those of China, with the exception of some woollen stuffs and felt, which are different. The variations and additions of the religious observances of the Shamans (of these different countries) I

[1] Just as Asôka gave the whole of Jambudwipa to the priests and then redeemed it for a sum of money

[2] A Pik-Dani.

am unable fully to record.[1] This country is reputed to be in the midst of the Tsung Ling Mountains. From these mountains onwards, the plants and fruits are, as a rule, different from those of China, except the bamboo, the pomegranate, and the sugar-cane.

[1] Or it may be rendered, "The various excellencies (chun chun shing) of the religious usages of the Shamans (of all these countries) I cannot hope to record within the present work." The version of Rémusat, "The Shamans conformably to the Law make use of wheels," is very unlikely.

CHAPTER VI.

From this country, proceeding westward[1] towards North India, after a journey of one month, we succeeded in passing the Tsoung Ling Mountains. These mountains are covered with snow both in winter and summer. They shelter venomous dragons also, which, if once provoked, spit out their poison (against travellers). Scarcely one person out of ten thousand survives after encountering the various difficulties which oppose their advance—the wind, and the rain, and the snow, and the driving sand and gravel. The men of these districts are also known as men of the Snowy Mountains. On passing this mountain chain we arrive in North India. On the confines of this region is a little kingdom called To-li,[2] in which, likewise, there is a congregation of priests, belonging to the Little Vehicle. In this kingdom there was, formerly, an

[1] From the direction here given, it would appear that Fah Hian crossed the Tsung Ling Mountains near the great Pamir plateau, and then instead of keeping along the Tengi Badakshan of Göes, that he pursued a more southerly route towards Kitaur or Chitral, according to a caravan route still laid down (vide Yule's map).

[2] Rémusat identifies this with Darada or Dardu, "the capital of the Dard country, situated among the mountains where the Indus takes its rise" (Wilson). But I would suggest the little town still known as Dhir, near the River Tal.

Arhat,[1] who, by his spiritual power,[2] transported a sculptor up to the Tushita Heavens,[3] to observe size,

[1] The Arhat or Arhan is a saint who has arrived at the fourth gradation of mind in the Buddhist scale of excellence. These successive steps are:—1. Srôtâpanna; 2. Sakradâgâmin; 3. Anâgâmin; 4. Arhan. There are two higher gradations, viz.:—5. Pratyêka Buddha; 6. Buddha. For the privileges and virtues of these various gradations, *vide* Spence Hardy, E. M. 289, 290, and Wassiljew, § 247, n. In the Sutra of 42 sections, § 2, we find the following:—Buddha said, "The Arhat is able to fly, change his appearance, fix the years of his life, shake heaven and earth. The successive steps towards this condition are—1. A-na-hom (Anâgâmin), which is the condition that allows a man after death to mount above the heavens and there attain the condition of an Arhat; 2. Sakrâdâgamin (Sz'-to-hom), in which, after one birth and death more, a man may become an Arhat; 3. Strotâpânna (Sü-to-hun), in which after seven births and deaths more a man may obtain the condition of an Arhat." The Arhat alluded to in the text was called Madhyântika (Jul. ii. 149).

[2] Irrdhi-pada. In the original, "the Divine foot," i.e. power of instant locomotion.

[3] The Tushita heaven (from the root "tush," तुष् to be joyous) is, according to the Buddhist system of the universe, the second heaven above Mount Sumeru. The Buddhists reckon three systems of heavens:—1. Those heavens in which there is still "desire" (Kama), six in number; 2. Those heavens in which there are still visible forms (Rupa), eighteen in number; 3. Those heavens in which there are no forms (Arupa), four in number. These systems have been frequently described (*vide* Spence Hardy and Burnouf particularly). I append the following account, forming a chapter in the Chinese work, "Far Kai lih to," headed "A consecutive account of the three worlds." . . In the midst of the inferior region of space is the great wind-circle, 1,600,000 yojanas in height. Then comes the water circle, 800,000 yojanas high, and 1,203,450 yojanas in breadth. By the power of the Karma (effective destiny) of all living creatures the water is not dispersed, just as food, not yet digested, is retained by physical energy, and not dispersed through the system. Next comes a circle of gold 320,000 yojanas high (the same breadth as the water circle). A wind constantly blowing over the surface of the water-circle forms this golden crust, just as cream is formed on the surface of milk. Then comes the earth circle, 68,000 yojanas in depth. The earth circle is surrounded by a mountain range, which contains the Salt

colour, and general appearance of Maitreya[1] Bodhisatwa, so that, on his return, he might carve a wooden image of him. Having first and last made three ascents for the purpose of correct observation, he finally completed the image. It was 94ft. high,[2] and the length of the foot of the image 9ft. 4in. On festival days it always emits an effulgent light. The princes of all the neighbouring countries vie with each other in making religious offerings to it. It still exists in this country.

Sea; then are seven other ranges of Golden Mountains, within which is the Fragrant Sea, and in the middle of which is Mount Sumeru. At the base of Sumeru, 10,000 yojanas high, is a range of mountains where dwells the Deva Vibâsha (Kin-shan, strong-hand), again ascending 10,000 yojanas is an encircling range of mountains 8,000 yojanas in width, the abode of the Deva Chi-fah-wan. Ascending 10,000 yojanas is an encircling range 4,000 yojanas in breadth; again ascending 10,000 yojanas is an encircling range where dwell the Sun, Moon, and Star Devas. Again ascending 10,000 yojanas is an encircling range, 4,000 yojanas round, where dwell the four kings. Again ascending 40,000 yojanas we arrive at the crest of Mount Sumeru, which is 40,000 yojanas round, and in the middle of which is the city Sudarsana (Shen-kin, beautiful to behold), 10,000 yojanas round. This is the abode of the thirty-three Devas (Triyastriñshas). Immediately above this, 40,000 yojanas high, is a region like the clouds for tenuity, but adorned and perfected with the seven precious substances like the great earth, this is where the Yama Devas reside. Again ascending 10,000 yojanas (others say 320,000) is a cloud-like earth, where the Tushita Devas live. Above this 10,000 yojanas come the Nirmânarati Devas. Above this 10,000 yojanas the Paranirmita Vasavartin Devas (Ta fah), and this is the termination of the Kama Rupa."

[1] Maitreya, possessed of love (root *maitra*, मैत्र love or charity), is to succeed the Buddha Sakya Muni (the present Buddha), after a lapse of time equal to 5,670,000,000 of years (R). The Bodhisatwa destined to become Buddha, is always supposed to reside in the Tushita heavens from the time of his predecessor's incarnation till his own advent.

[2] M. Julien has, by mistake, classed this calculation among the errors of M. Rémusat's translation (Jul. i. xi. n.).

CHAPTER VII.

Keeping along the incline of the Tsung Ling Mountains, in a south-westerly[1] direction, they travelled onwards for fifteen days. The road is difficult and fatiguing. Steep crags and precipices constantly intercept the way. These mountains are like walls of rock, standing up 10,000 ft. in height. On looking over the edge the sight becomes confused, and then, on advancing, the foot loses its hold and you are lost. At the base there is a stream called the Sin-to (Indus). Men of old days have cut away the cliff so as to make a passage, and have carved out against the rock steps for descent, amounting altogether to 700 in number. Having passed these, there is, suspended across the river, a bridge[2] of ropes, by which travellers pass over it. From one side of the river to the other is eighty paces. According to the records of Kau Yih,[3] neither Chang

[1] A south-easterly direction would be more likely, yet the difficulties of the road, and the windings of the mountains, would perhaps account for any uncertainty of the course.

[2] The jhula or swinging bridge (W).

[3] M. Rémusat suggests a correction in the text, and explains the expression Kau Yih, as referring to the office of the interpreters attached to the cabinet of foreign affairs under the Han dynasty. He is probably correct. Klaproth's suggestion is not so probable.

Kian[1] nor Kan Ying[2] of the Han[3] dynasty, reached so far as this. All the priests asked Fah Hian what he knew as to the time when the law of Buddha began to spread eastward from their country. Hian replied, "On enquiry, men of those lands agreed in saying, that, according to an ancient tradition, Shamans from India began to carry the sacred books of Buddha beyond the river, from the time when the image of Maitreya Bodhisatwa was set up." Now this image was set up 300 years or so after the Nirvana[4] of Buddha, which cor-

[1] Chang Kian was a Chinese general who lived in the reign of Wou-ti of the Han dynasty, B.C. 122. He conducted the first memorable expedition of his nation into Central Asia (vide Rémusat).

[2] Kan Ying lived in the year 97 A.D. He was sent as far as the Caspian Sea, to subjugate the Roman empire. As he heard, however, that with an unfavourable wind it would take two years to cross that sea, he returned without accomplishing his object (R).

[3] That is, the Eastern Han dynasty, which lasted from A.D. 25 to A.D. 190.

[4] The Nirvàna, that is the death, of Buddha occurred, according to the Pali Annals of Ceylon, B.C. 543. This is the only date which pretends to any historical accuracy. General Cunningham places the death of Buddha, 477 B.C., forming his opinion partly from an inscription he copied at Gaya, in Magadha. Professor Max Müller seems to agree in the probability of this date (Sanscrit Literature). Westergaard brings down the date to A.D. 370 (Schlagintweit). The Chinese are not at all agreed respecting it. Their dates range from 2000 B.C. downwards. The following is their own account of the matter:—"The followers of the sect of Reason (the Tauists) affirm that their master, Laou Tsze, having assumed the appearance of a Tartar after his death, was the one who attained perfect Reason (*i.e.* became Buddha). They say that Buddha was born in the second year of King Wang, of the Chow dynasty (517 B.C.). and that he did in the third year of Kaou Wang (B.C. 437), and that this was just after Laou Tsze died. The priests of Buddha, indignant at this slander, violently opposed it, and on that account they put back the date of Buddha's birth to the ninth year of the reign of Chwang Wang, of the

responds with the time of Pingwang,[1] of the Chau Family. Hence it may be said that the diffusion of the great doctrine may be attributed to the influence of

Chow dynasty (687 B.C.), which was the era of the falling stars. [This is according to the history of the sects of Buddha or Laou Tsze, published during the Wei dynasty, also according to the History of the Sacred Books published under the Sui dynasty.] Again, the priests put back the date still farther, to the time of Hwan Wang, of the Chow dynasty (719-696 B.C.) [According to works published in the Sung dynasty.] Again they put it further back, to the time of Ping Wang, of the same dynasty (770 B.C.) [This is according to the Fah ün chu lin.] Again they put it back to the the time of Mo Wang (1001 B.C.) [This according to a work called Tung Lih, which says Buddha entered Nirvana in the first year of Heaou Wang (909 B.C.)] Again they put it back to the time of Chau Wang (1052 B.C.) [This is according to works of the Tang dynasty. The "Fah ün chu lin" also, and various works of the Sung dynasty.] Again, others put it back to the end of the Yin dynasty (this was a part of the Shang dynasty, dating from 1401 B.C. downwards). [This is ascording to the work of Fah Hian, of the Tsin dynasty, called 'Foe kwo ki,' in which he says that Buddha entered Nirvana 1497 years before the reign of I Hi, of the Tsin dynasty; now this would take us back to the reign of Ching Wang, of the Chow dynasty, and therefore he should have been born in the reign of Woo Yeih, of the Yin dynasty (1198 B.C.)] Again they put it back to the time of the Hea dynasty (2205 B.C. to 1818 B.C.). [This is according to a work called 'General Records of Buddhist or Tauist priests of the Tang dynasty.' Also according to authorities in the Yuen dynasty.] Hiouen Thsang, of the Tang dynasty, in his Si yu ki, says 'that all the sects have different opinions respecting the time of Buddha's death, some say it took place 1200 years before the third year of the reign of Kaou Tsung (*i.e.*, 547 B.C.), others 1300 years before, others 1500 years before, whilst others said that not 1000 years had passed.' Of these only the first two are probably near the truth; now from the third year of the reign of Kaou Tsung (663 A.D.) to the reign of Hwan Wang, of the Chow dynasty, is 1265 years, and this date substantiates the prophecy of the (Nirvana) Sutra respecting the duration of the true law and image worship, and also tallies with the time of the falling stars. Others who think there is evidence to support the theory about the trans-

[1] 770 B.C.

this image. For apart from the power of the great teacher Maitrêya, following in the footsteps of Sakya, who would have been sufficient to cause the knowledge of the three precious ones[1] to be spread so far, that even men on the outskirts of the world acquired that

formation of Laou Tsze, reject all the preceding dates. Now this theory would make the date of Buddha's birth the second year of King Wang (517 B.C.), and consequently his death in the third year of Kaou Wang (B.C. 437). Considering all things, we would place the birth of Buddha in the reign of Chwang Wang, of the Chow dynasty (696 B.C.), for three reasons:—1st, because this agrees with the records concerning the prodigies which took place at the time of Buddha's birth; 2nd, because this agrees with the prophecy (of the Nirvana Sutra), that the true law should last 500 years and the law of images 1,000 years; 3rd, because it is declared in Indian records that the death of Buddha took place twelve or thirteen hundred years before the reign of Kaou Tsung, of the Tang dynasty. In this way we would reconcile the differences between the followers of Buddha and Laou Tsze, and also satisfy the doubts of old and modern writers." (Hoi-kwo To Chi, Vol. 45.) From the above extract it is evident that the chief cause of the remote period assigned for Buddha's death in China, is the jealousy existing between the two great sects, the Buddhists and Taouists. Taking every thing into consideration, it seems most likely that, in the earliest times, it was allowed that Buddha was not born till after the death of Laou Tsze, *i.e.* after 517 B.C., but how long after this is not easily decided. But if we compare with this other legends known in India, we incline to regard the latest date assigned to that event as the most probable one. Regarding, then, the Nirvana of Buddha as having taken place about 400 B.C., the legend in the text would date the diffusion of his doctrine, beyond the Indus, from about 100 B.C., a date which agrees very well with the Chinese records (*vide* Rémusat's note).

[1] The three precious ones, that is, Buddha, Dharma, Sañgha; or Buddha, the Law, and the Church. This triad is a remarkable one; it is acknowledged by all the schools of Buddhism, though they interpret the reference (of Dharma especially) differently. In Buddhist liturgical works there are found frequent ascriptions of praise to these three objects of adoration, "Namo Foe, Namo Fah, Namo Sang," or, as we should say, "Glory to Buddha, to Dharma, to Sañgha."

knowledge? We may conclude, therefore, with certainty, that the origin of this diffusion of the law of Buddha was no human work, but sprang from the same cause as the dream of Ming Ti.[1]

[1] Ming Ti, the second emperor of the Eastern Han dynasty, began to reign A.D. 58. In the fourth year of his reign he had a dream of this sort—he thought he saw a Divine Being with a body like gold, and of a vast height (70ft.), his head surrounded by a glory like the sun, fly down towards him and enter his palace. This dream was interpreted as referring to Buddha (Fo), and, consequently, an embassy was despatched to the country of the Tai-yue-chi (the Great Getæ), and to India, to seek diligently after the law of Buddha. After eleven years the members of this embassy returned, bringing with them Buddhist books and figures, and also several foreign Shamans. From this time Buddhism began to prevail in China. (*Vide* Rémusat in loc., also Translation of Sutra of 42 Sections, Transact. R. A. S.)

CHAPTER VIII.

Crossing the river we arrive at the country of Ou-chang.[1] This is the most northern part of India. The language of middle India is everywhere used. Middle India is that which is called the Middle Country (Madya Dêsa). The clothes and food of the ordinary people are, likewise, just the same as in the Middle Country. The law of Buddha is universally honoured. The names given to places where the priests take up their fixed abodes is Sañghârâma.[2] There are

[1] Ou-chang, that is, Oudyâna, a country well-known in Indian literature. It is the country watered, on the east, by the river Sweti or Swat, and on the west by the Indus, between Cashmir and Cabul; the present plains of Hashtnagger, peopled by the Yazofzais. The banks of the river Swat had been, at one time, lined with Buddhist monasteries; but, in the time of Sitsi, the 24th Buddhist patriarch, a fierce prosecution arose against them, under the auspices of king Mahirakula (the Mehrkul of the Ayeen Akberi). "Sitsi was murdered, the waves of the Swat river rose several feet owing to the numerous massacres of the priests, and so ended the transmission of the law in that country." Mahirakoula is placed about A.D. 500 (Cunningham). (*Vide* the above legend Jul. ii., 197, and Memorials of Sakya Buddha, § 179.)

[2] The term Sañghârâma, as before mentioned, signifies priests' garden. At first all the disciples of Buddha were accustomed to remain in solitary places during a great portion of the year, and occupy themselves in meditation. Afterwards they began to assemble in communities,—at first only during the rainy season (Varchâs), afterwards, when ground was bestowed on them, and Vihâras built by the faithful, in perpetuity. These places were then called Sañghârâmas, and the community, Bikshus. So they are termed in the Pratimôksha, or, the work treating on their internal discipline. The females are called Bikshuni.

altogether about 500 of these (in this country), all of which are attached to the system called the Little Vehicle. If any foreign ecclesiastic (Bikshu[1]) arrive amongst them, they are all ready to entertain him for three days,[2] after which they bid him seek for himself a resting place. Tradition says, "When Buddha visited North India, he at once came to this country. When he left he bequeathed to them an impression of his foot." The appearance of the impression is large or small, according to the intensity of the religious feeling of the person who beholds it. It exists to the present day. The stone on which Buddha dried his clothes, and the place where he converted the malevolent dragon (Apalâla), still remain. The stone is about 12ft. high and 24ft. square, and smooth on one side. From this place the three pilgrims, Hwui King, To Ching, and Hwui Ta, went on in advance towards the kingdom of Na-kie (Nagrâk[3]), where the shadow of

[1] A Bikshu is a mendicant priest (using the word priest in an accommodated sense). It is a term peculiarly applied to Buddhist disciples when living in community. The title of Shaman is older, but less applicable to Buddhists as a community.

[2] This was a custom of the country so early as the time of Alexander the Great. (Q. Curtius.) Appollonius also said that, after three days, he would leave the King of Taxila, who had entertained him for that time. (Cunningham.)

[3] This province is mentioned by Hiouen Thsang as Na-kie-lo-ho-lo, that is, Nagarahâra. It is the province included by the basin of the Cophes or Cabul river. It is mentioned by Ptolemy. The town or village of Nagrâk is close to Jellâlabad. (Viv. St. M.)

Buddha is to be seen. Fah Hian[1] and the others remained in this country during the season of the Rains. After this they descended towards the south, and arrived at the kingdom of Su-ho-to.[2]

[1] A detailed account of the several circumstances mentioned in this chapter may be found in Hiouen Thsang. (Jul. ii., 131–149.)

[2] This kingdom may be identified with the country of the Svât or Swât. It probably includes the district to the west of that river and bordering on the Cabul river. It is included by later Buddhist writers in the country of Udyana, before named.

CHAPTER IX.

In this country also the law of Buddha is in a flourishing condition. This is the place where, in ancient times, the divine ruler Sekra,[1] with a view to tempt Bodhisatwa, caused the appearance of a hawk, pursuing a small bird (like a dove); (on which, Bodhisatwa), tearing his own flesh, gave it in substitution for that of the bird. When Buddha had arrived at complete wisdom,[2] he passed by this place with his disciples, on which he spake to them thus: "It was here that, in one of my former births, I tore my flesh in substitution for that of a bird." The people of the country having thus gained knowledge of this event, erected a tower[3] upon the spot, and enriched it with gold and silver ornaments.

[1] Sekra or Indra, the ruler of Devas of the thirty-three heavens (Triyastriñshas), situated on the summit of Sumeru; in early times the most venerated of all the Hindu Deities. He is supposed to have an especial care over the affairs of the world, and in this and other respects corresponds with the Olympian Jupiter.

[2] The expression, "arriving at complete wisdom," alludes to the attainment of Bôdhi, complete knowledge, which marks the epoch of Sakya's emancipation. (For further account of this event see the subsequent chapters.)

[3] The word here rendered tower, signifies, ideally, "accumulated earth," *i.e.*, a mound, for mounds of earth were the first erected memorials of important events. Afterwards heaps of stones, and then towers, were raised for the same purpose. When any relics are enshrined in these towers they are called "Po tah," *i.e.*, precious towers. Throughout the present work allusions are made to memorial towers, erected on spots rendered famous in Buddhist history by various circumstances. The Chinese Pagoda is the latest developement of this kind of building, and is intended to represent the mystic universe of the northern Buddhists; each stage reprcsenting a world, or platform of worlds, surrounded by bells, flags, and railings, descriptive of their being "perfectly adorned."

CHAPTER X.

From this point, still descending[1] in an eastward direction, after five days' journey, we arrive at the country of Kin-to-wai[2] (Gandhâra). This is the kingdom formerly governed by Fah Yih,[3] the son of Askôa.[4]

[1] The expression, "descending," throughout this translation is rendered from the Chinese word "hea," but, in most cases, this is a misprint in the original for "hing," going.

[2] Gandhâra, a famous kingdom in the history of Buddhism. It is situated between the river Indus and the Kouner river. Ptolemy speaks of the Gandari, "Inter Suastum (Swât) et Indum sunt Gandhari." At the time of Hiouen Thsang (630 A.D.), the royal family had become extinct, and the kingdom of Gandhâra was a dependency of Kabul or Kapisa. With respect to the termination, "wai," in the Chinese equivalent Kin-to-wai, as a rule I am of opinion that this termination corresponds to the Sanscrit "Vastu," a town or city (ἄστυ), which is also the meaning of the Chinese "wai." In the case of She-wai (Sravasti) this is probably the case, and certainly so in Ka-po-lo-wai (Kapilavastu). In the present instance, however, I cannot ascertain that Gandhâra was ever known as Gandhâvasti or Gandhâra vastu, "the city of perfumes."

[3] Fah-yah corresponds to Dharmavivardhana, *i.e.*, increase of the law. This was the son of Asoka. He was otherwise called Kunâla, from the beauty of his eyes, which resembled those of the Kunâla bird. The touching history of this prince may be read in Burnouf (I. B.), p. 404, and Jul. ii., 154.

[4] Asôka (the sorrowless), called in the text A-yu (which is a fault for A-chu-ka), the Piyadasi of the Edicts. The date of this monarch, called in the Pali records Dharmasôka, is a subject of contention between the southern (Ceylonese) school of Buddhism, and that of the north (Nipal, China, Thibet). The former place him 218 years after the death of Buddha, *i.e.*, 325 B.C., the latter 100 years after the death of Buddha.

At the time when Buddha was Bôdhisatwa, he also, in this country, performed an act of sublime charity by sacrificing his eyes. Men have erected on this spot likewise a tower, enriched with gold and silver.

In the former case the date of Buddha's death is assumed to be 543 B.C. This date is founded on a pretended prophecy of Buddha, that, on the day of his Nirvâṇa, Vijaya should land on the island of Lankâ (Ceylon). The traditional date given to Vijaya (the conqueror) is 543 B.C., therefore, they argue, this is the date of the Nirvâṇa. The Ceylonese place another Asôka (Kalasôka) between Buddha and Dharmasôka, 100 years after Buddha, and assert that the second great council was held under his auspices. It is, however, allowed that the Great Asôka was grandson of Chandragupta, who has been identified as the Sandrocottus of Megasthenes, with whom Seleucus concluded a treaty about 315 B.C. From this date it has been gathered that Asôka began to reign about 263 B.C. If, then, we accept the northern legend, the death of Buddha would have occurred about B.C. 363, and, therefore, his birth, B.C. 443; if, on the other hand, we assume that 218 years had elapsed since the Nirvâṇa and Asôka, then Buddha would have died about 477 B.C. (*Vide* Max Müller, Hist. Sansc. Lit., p. 298.)

CHAPTER XI.

From this spot, going eastward seven days, there is a country called Tchu-sha-si-lo[1] (Takshasilâ). This word, being interpreted, signifies, "the severed head." Buddha, when he was Bôdhisatwa, in this place gave his head in charity; men, therefore, have given this name to the country. Still going to the eastward two days' journey, you come to the place where he gave his body to feed a starving tiger.[3] In these two places they have raised great towers, adorned with all the

[1] Takshasilâ is the Taxila of the Greeks (*ἐις Τα'ξιλα ἀφίκετο πόλιν μεγαλην και εὐδαίμονα.*) (Arrian, Lib. V.) This town stood near the site of the present Hassan-Abdal. Cunningham places it near Shah-deri, twelve miles south-east of Hassan-Abdal, one mile north-east of Kalâ-ka-Sarâ, seventy-four miles east of Hashtnagar. Pliny, however, says that Taxila was only sixty miles east of Peukelaotis (Hashtnagar), which would place the site near Hassan-Abdal.

[2] This is an error of Fah-Hian, as the name seems to be derived from the root Taksa, to build, (or, figuratively, to cut to pieces), and Sila, a rock (instead of Sira, a head). Our author's mistake, however, is easily accounted for, by considering the legend which follows in the text, and which is also related by Hiouen Thsang.

[3] The tower erected on this spot has been identified as the Great Tope at Mânikyâla, explored by General Court, close to the Huta-Murta Vihara, or the body-oblation Vihara, referring to Buddha's sacrifice of his body to feed some starving tiger cubs. (C. p. 65.) It was, probably, erected by Kanishka. (For the legend of Buddha feeding the tigress and her cubs, *vide* M.B. 92.

precious substances. The kings, ministers, and people of all the surrounding countries vie with each other in making religious offerings at these places, in scattering flowers, and burning incense continually. Including the two towers mentioned in the previous section, men of that district call these four the four great Stûpas.

CHAPTER XII.

From Gandhâra, going south four days' journey, we arrive at the country of Fo-lau-sha (Purushapura[1] or Peshâwar). In old times Buddha, in company with all his disciples, travelled through this country, on which occasion he addressed Ânanda[2] thus, "After my Nirvâna there will be a king of this country called Ka-ni-ka[3] (Kanishka), who on this spot will raise a Pagoda."

[1] Hiouen Thsang (who describes the antiquities of the place in great detail) speaks of Purushapura as the capital of Gandhâra. It is the present Peshâwar (the frontier town, so named by Akbar).

[2] Ânanda, the nephew of Buddha (being the son of Dotódano, younger brother of Sâkya's father), and his personal attendant. He obtained the condition of an Arhân, after Buddha's death, in time to take part in the first great convocation, where he propounded the Sûtra Pitaka. He is represented in Chinese works as young and smooth faced; whilst Kâsyapa is old and wrinkled. Hence Kâsyapa's saying, "this child has yet to learn his destiny." (Turnour, Essay I., July, 1837.)

[3] Kanishka, a name as celebrated in the history of Buddhism as that of Asôka. He was a chief of the people known as the Great Yuchi or Tochari. According to Chinese accounts these people belonged to the race of the eastern Tartars (Tungnu), who, several centuries B.C., had founded an empire in western Tartary, extending from the Muz-tagh mountains on the north 100 leagues, to the Kuenlun mountains on the south, and from the upper Hoang Ho, in Shensi, on the east, to Kotan on the west. About 180 B.C. they were driven by the Hiungnu westward, to the borders of the Ili river. Again, B.C. 163, they pressed southwards, and occupied the provinces now called Yarkand, Kashgar, and Khotan, driving out the original inhabitants, called Su or Sus by the Chinese. Again, 126 B.C.,

In after times King Kanishka was born, and, on one occasion, as he was going on a tour of inspection, the divine ruler Sekra, wishing to originate the first thoughts of such a purpose, caused to appear before him a little shepherd boy making a Pagoda on the road. The King then stopped and asked him what he was doing, to which he replied, "I am making a tower in honour of Buddha." The King said, "you are a very good boy," and immediately set about building a great tower over that of the little shepherd boy. The height of it was 470ft. and more, and it was decorated with every sort of precious substance, so that all who passed by and saw the exquisite beauty and graceful

the Yuchi advanced still southwards, and occupied Sogdiana and Tahia (or, the country of the Dahæ. [Dahæ qui inter Oxum et Jaxartem non procul a Maris Caspii littore habitabant, Justin, xii. 6, not.] The Hiungnu having become tributary to China, B.C. 60, the Yuchi consolidated their power, and about 39–26 B.C. the King of the most powerful of their tribes (the Kwai-tchang or Gouchang tribe), uniting the other four tribes with his own, advanced still south and conquered Ariana, Caubul, and Gandhâra. The name of this chief was Khiu-tsiu-hi (supposed to be the same as Hyrkodes of the coins). His son, Yen-kao-Ching (Hima Kadphises), continued his father's conquests, and subdued all India to the west of the Jamna. He ruled from about 35 B.C., to 15 B.C. His son was the celebrated Kanishka, who, with his brothers Hushka and Jushka, ruled over Cashmir for 60 years. He was converted to Buddhism, which gave a sudden impulse to that religion, and caused it to spread rapidly throughout the Tocharian dominion. The third great synod (that is according to Northern accounts,—the Southern school do not recognise this Council) was held in Cashmir during his reign. The finest Stûpas in the Cabul Valley and Panjab were built under his auspices. His reign extended, probably, from B.C. 15 to A.D. 45. (C.) Lassen places the reign of Kanishka between 10 A.D. and 40 A.D. (*Viv.* St. M. 300.)

proportions of the tower and the temple attached to it, exclaimed in delight, "these are incomparable for beauty." Tradition says that this was the highest tower in Jambudwipa.[1] When the King had finished his tower, the little one, built by the shepherd boy,[2] immediately came out of it, and removed itself to the south of the great tower, its height was about 3ft. 6in.

Buddha's alms bowl[3] is also preserved in this

[1] Jambudwipa, the continent to the south of Mount Sumeru, which according to Chinese Buddhists includes both India and China. The following is an extract relating to this continent: "The great Âgama Sûtra (Dirghâgama) says, "To the south of mount Sumeru is a country called Chim-fau-tai (Jambudvipa). [The meaning of this word is 'excelling in gold.' The Vibâsha Shaster calls it Chim-po, *i.e.*, Jambu. (Ch. Ed.).] This country in shape is narrow towards the south, and wide towards the north. It is 7,000 yojanas long. The people's faces are the same shape as the country. This continent has a great tree called Chim-fau (Jambu). It is seven yojanas in girth, and 100 yojanas high. The spread of its branches 50 yojanas. The men live 100 years. Beneath this tree is found abundance of the gold called Chim-fau-na-tan (Jambunada), and hence the name." (Fah-kai-lih-to.)

[2] This legeud is somewhat differently narrated by Hiouen Thsang. (Jul. II., 107.) According to that account the shepherd boy related the prophecy found in the text to Kanishka, and this was the cause of his conversion. It also states that the small tower increased continually in size, remaining three feet higher than the one Kanishka built. The circumference of the tower was $1\frac{1}{2}$ li (about 580 yards).

[3] The alms bowl or Pâtra, is the distinctive mark of the Buddhist mendicant. Numerous directions are given how to carry it, how to eat from it, how to cleanse it, etc. [*Vide* Pratimôksha (Sekkhiya Damma).] It must either be earthenware or iron, not gold, silver, copper, or pewter, of uniform size, either black or red. The Shaman may have a bag for it, and in walking carry it over the shoulder. (Rules for the Shamans.) It must be held breast-high, evenly, and not at arms' length. It must not be filled higher than the rim. (Respecting the Pâtra spoken of in the text, *vide* cap. 39.)

country. In former times a King of the Yu-tchi,[1] having raised a great army of soldiers, came with them all to invade this country, desiring to carry off the alms bowl. When he had subdued the country, the King of the Yu-tchi, being a firm believer in the law of Buddha, wished to take the bowl and to go. He, therefore, prepared to make religious offerings, and, having performed his vows to the three Sacred objects of worship, he caparisoned a great elephant, and placed the alms bowl upon its back. No sooner had he done so, than the elephant fell to the ground, and was unable to advance a step. He then caused a four-wheeled car to be constructed to convey the alms bowl, and eight elephants to be harnessed to it; but once more they were unable to advance. The King was then convinced that the destiny of the alms bowl (in that kingdom) was not yet completed, and, being deeply ashamed of himself, he forthwith raised a tower upon the spot, and also a Sañghârâma; moreover he delayed his own departure, and remained to guard the relic, and performed every kind of religious service in its honor. There are about 700 priests at present (in this temple). When mid-day approaches, the members of the community bring forth the alms bowl, and, in company with the laity,[2] who are in attendance, pay it every kind of

[1] The Yu-tchi, or Tochari, a tribe of Tartars who broke up the Greek Bactrian Kingdom, 126 B.C., and afterwards possessed themselves of India.

[2] Rémusat's translation "clad in white garments," referring to the priests,

religious honour. So, again, after the mid-day meal, as evening approaches, at the time of burning incense (*i.e.*, evening service), they do likewise. The bowl contains about two Tau (a dry measure, equal to $1\frac{1}{8}$ galls.).[1] It is of a mixed color, but mostly black. The seams where the four parts join together[2] are bright. It is about two inches thick, and it is kept well polished and bright. Poor people, with the few flowers which they cast into it, are able to fill it; whilst there are very rich men who, being wishful to pay their devotions with very many flowers, are unable to fill it up, though they offer a hundred, or a thousand, or ten thousand bushels. The two pilgrims, Po Wan and Tsang King, having merely paid their reverence to the alms bowl of Buddha, forthwith returned (homewards). The three pilgrims Hwui King, Hwui Ta, and To Ching (as we have before stated), had gone on in advance to the country of Na-kie, to pay their devotions to the shadow of Buddha, as well as his tooth and skull-bone. Hwui

is erroneous. The expression "white clothed" relates to the laity. Mrs. Spiers has been led into error by this translation (Ancient India, p. 335). The whole of the following translation differs widely from Rémusat's.

[1] Either its size is exaggerated or the relic a fictitious one.

[2] This refers to the following legend:—After Buddha had arrived at complete wisdom the four guardian deities brought each an alms bowl of emerald to present to him, but he would not accept them. They then bought four bowls made of stone and of the colour of the mung fruit; and when each entreated that his own bowl might be accepted, Buddha caused them to appear as if turned into a single bowl, the upper rim showing one within the other as it were (M.B. 183). This also explains the allusion in cap. 39 to the bowl dividing itself again into four parts.

King, however, having fallen sick, To Ching remained with him (at Na-kie), to take care of him, so that Hwui Ta alone returned to Peshâwar, and, after a conference with the two former pilgrims, Po Wan and Tsang King (who had not yet set out), they all three resolved to return to China. (Meanwhile) Hwui King having set out for the temple of Buddha's alms bowl, after his arrival, died there.[1] On this Fah Hian went on by himself, towards the place of Buddha's skull bone.

[1] The whole of this passage is obscure, and if it were not for some addenda to the work, would be untranslatable. I have regarded the expression "wou sheung" as equivalent to "died," for it is used in this sense in the 20th chapter; and for the word "shan" "a mountain," which has no sense or meaning at all in the connection of the text, I have substituted "ju," "thus," forming the well-known phrase "ju shi" "accordingly." The addenda by the Chinese editor confirm these renderings.

CHAPTER XIII.

Going westwards sixteen yôjanas,[1] we arrive at the borders of the country of Na-kie[2] (Nagrâk). In the city of Hi-lo[3] (Hiḍḍa), is the Vihâra, containing the

[1] The distance now begins to be measured by yôjanas. This measurement differs in different districts. It is equal to 4 kôs. But the value of the kôs again varies. In the N.W. provinces we may take 40 kôs = 1 deg., which would make the yojana equal to 7 miles. In Maghada and the neighbourhood, on the other hand, we find the yôjana to be about 4½ miles.

[2] Two miles to the west of Jellâlabad, or less, is a site where once stood a town called Adjôuna or Oudyâna; this was the capital of the district called Naghenhar, and a village close to it is still called Nagarak (V. St.M).

[3] This is the present town of Hidda, about five miles south of Jellâlabad, and about seven miles from Nagrâk. (V. St. M. says Nagrâk is N.E. of Hidda, but Hiouen Thsang says that Hidda is S.E. of the capital of Nagarahâra. Nagrâk, therefore, ought to be N.W. of Hidda.) Hiouen Thsang's account of the skull-bone is this:—"About 30 li to the S.E. of the capital (Nagrâk) is a town called Hī-lo, the circuit of which is four of five li (one mile). It is situated on a height, and defended by nature. In the neighbourhood are flowery groves, and pools of water bright as a mirror. The inhabitants of the town are upright, honest, and truthful. There is here a chapel (pavilion) of two stories, the joists ornamented with paintings, and the pilasters coloured red. In the upper stage is a small Stûpa, constructed of the seven precious substances, where Buddha's skull-bone is deposited. The circumference of the bone is 1 foot 2 inches; the marks of the hair are distinctly visible,—its colour whitish yellow. It is enclosed in a casket, which is placed in the centre of the Stûpa. Those persons who wish to know the measure of their virtues or faults, make a soft cake of scented powder and take a cast of the bone, and on this appear certain marks and lines, according to the character of the person using it."

relic of the skull-bone of Buddha.[1] This Vihâra is entirely covered with plates of gold, and decorated with the seven precious substances.[2] The King of the country reverences, in a high degree, this sacred relic. For fear lest any man should carry off the true bone and substitute another in its place, therefore he appoints eight persons belonging to the principal families of the country to seal up (every night) the door of the shrine, each one with his own seal, so as to guard and protect it. At early dawn these eight men all go to the temple, and each one observes if his seal is as he left it. They then open the door, and having washed their hands with perfumed water, they take out the bone of Buddha, and place it upon a lofty throne which is erected outside the shrine. On this throne is a circular table composed of the seven precious substances, with a crystal bell-shaped cupola on the top. Both the table and the cover are highly decorated and enriched with gems. The bone is of a yellowish-white

[1] The high part of the skull-bone (ouchnîcha) has a sacred character among Buddhist relics. These relics, called in China Shé-li (Sarira), are supposed to be imperishable and indestructible. They are found among the refuse of ashes after the cremation of any great saint. The elevated skull-bone is one of the marks of Buddha's person, and is yet regarded by phrenologists as the index of great religiousness of character.

[2] The seven precious substances are gold, silver, lapis lazuli, crystal, cornelian, coral, ruby. (Jul. ii. 482, translates musâragalva [tche-kià] by "amber." E. Burnouf renders it "coral," Sansc. Dict.) Fragments of these precious substances are frequently found in small relic-boxes in Buddhist Stoûpas, as *e.gr.* at Sanchi. (Cunningham, Bhilsa Topes.)

colour, about four inches square,[1] and somewhat elevated in the middle. Each day[2] after it is thus removed, certain men appointed for the purpose ascend a lofty belfry and beat a great drum, blow the conch, and clash the cymbals. When the King hears it he immediately repairs to the Vihâra and offers flowers and incense; having done this, he repeatedly bends his head to the ground in adoration and departs.[3] He enters by the eastern gate and departs by the western one. Thus does the King discharge his religious duties every morning, and after worship he proceeds to attend to governmental affairs. The chief men[4] and nobles also attend to these acts of worship first, and then to their household duties, this, in fact, is the first and unfailing duty of every day. After the acts of worship are over, they then return the relic to its shrine. In this Vihâra is a Dagoba[5] ornamented with the seven precious sub-

[1] The expression "fang ün" may either mean a circle or square; but the meaning here is evidently 4 inches each side, making it about 14 inches round, supposing it to be of a roundish shape. This agrees with Hiouen Thsang's account.

[2] Rémusat translates this "every day at sunrise."

[3] This passage is rendered by Rémusat, "he places the relic on his head and goes away." The expression "teng tai" cannot possibly have this meaning. It is unnatural also. I have no doubt the phrase should be "teng lai," "to bow the head." But even if "tai" be retained, we may translate it as in the text.

[4] The phrase "ku sse," a householder, corresponds to guha pati.

[5] This passage is ambiguous, it may be translated either "in this Vihara are seven Dagobas, some of which are solid, and some hollow;" or "in this Vihara is a Dagoba partly hollow, and partly solid, ornamented with the seven precious substances." I prefer the latter translation, because

stances, partly solid and partly hollow, and about five feet in height. In order to enable worshippers to present their offerings at this Dagoba there are men appointed to sell flowers and incense at the gate of the Vihâra every morning, so that all those who desire to make religious offerings may purchase every thing necessary for the purpose. All the neighbouring princes depute commissioners to present religious offerings in this chapel. The site of the chapel is a square of forty paces a side. Though the heavens should quake, and the earth open, this place would remain unmoved. Going north from this place one yôjana, we arrive at the chief city of the country of Na-kie (Nagrâk). This is the place where Bôdhisatwa, in one of his former births, gave money in exchange for some five-stalked[1] flowers with which he might pay religious reverence to Dipañkara Buddha.[2]

it agrees so closely with Hiouen Thsang's remark. The phrase "kiai thou tah," "tower of emancipation," is the same as a Dagoba, a small relic tower (Dhâtu + garba, a relic shrine).

[1] This is the force of the original; but I have not been able to find the name of any such flower.

[2] Dipañkara Buddha (Ting Kwang Fuh, but commonly written "In Kwang") was the twenty-fourth predecessor of the present Buddha, and from whom Sakya (or, as he was then called, Sumédha Bráhmana) received a definite assurance of his becoming Buddha. He is not an historical character, as the following particulars will shew. "Dipañkara was born in the city of Rammawatí, his father was the King Sudéwa, his mother, Sumédha; he reigned 10,000 years before he became an ascetic. His queen was called Paduma, his son Usabhakkhanda. He exercised asceticism, previous to the reception of the Buddhaship, ten months. He lived 100,000 years; he was 80 cubits high; he had a retinue of 100,000

In this town also is a tower of Buddha's tooth-relic,[1] which is worshipped in the same way as the skull-bone. One yojana to the N.E. of this city we reach the entrance of a defile where is preserved Buddha's religious staff.[2] A Vihâra is erected in which religious offerings are made to it. The staff is made of sandal-wood, of the kind called Gôsîrchañdana,[3] and is about one chang and six or seven-tenths[4] long (between 19 and 20 feet).

Rahats; and the name of Gotama (Sâkya) was Sumédha Bráhmana" (M.B. 94). Hiouen Thsang mentions this offering of flowers to Dipañkara Buddha, but he describes the scene of it as some two miles to the S.W. of the town (Jul. II. 97).

[1] The Stûpa in which this relic was enshrined is spoken of by Hiouen Thsang. He describes it as a great Stoûpa, the foundations of which only remained. The tooth, too, had disappeared.

[2] The religious staff is one of the articles of personal property allowed to the Buddhist monk. The Chinese is "Sih-chang," *i.e.* tin staff, and the Sanscrit Khakkharam. Take the following account of it: "Sih-chang, in Sanscrit kih-hi-lo, *i.e.* a metal staff. When it is shaken, it makes a ringing noise like metal striking against metal. Hence its common name is the 'sounding staff.' It may be made of copper, iron, or tin. The staff generally used in India has only one round ring on the top, two or three inches perhaps in size. This hangs on a hollow metal tube about four or five fingers long. The staff itself is wood, heavy or light according to circumstances, in height up to the breast, with an iron ferrule on the foot about two inches long. . . . . The staff is used at the time of begging food . . . . it must not be used to strike dogs with; but when begging in front of a house it must be shook two or three times, and if no one come to give charity, then immediately pass on to the next house without ringing the staff again. The staff may be used to remove or frighten noxious insects or wild animals." (Sha-men-jih-yung).

[3] The most valuable kind of sandal-wood is that called "Gôsîra" (bull's head—Bucephalus). Rémusat's translation is erroneous.

[4] Rémusat translates this "six or seven fathoms (toises) long." But M. Julien has already pointed out the error of this and similar computations (Jul. I. xi. n). In explanation of the extraordinary length of this

It is contained in a wooden tube case, from which no human power can remove it. Entering the defile and travelling westward for four days there is a Vihâra erected for the purpose of paying religious reverence to Buddha's robe (Sanghâti).[1] When there is a drought in that country the chief personages of the kingdom assemble together, and taking out the robe of Buddha, they worship it and pay to it religious devotions. The heavens then yield abundance of rain. To the south of Nagrâk, half a yôjana, is a cave on the S.W. face of a large mountain. In this cave Buddha left his shadow.[2]

staff (about 19ft.), we must recollect the account given of Buddha's stature—"Buddha is sometimes said to be 12 cubits in height, and sometimes 18 cubits" (M.B. 364).

[1] The Sanghâti, or great garment of the Buddhist monk, is that worn over all, and composed of many pieces from nine up to twenty-five. Originally the dress of the monks was made from scraps of cloth picked up in grave-yards, or that which had been used for a signal flag, or that which had been discarded, or that which had been polluted. These scraps were sewn together, hence the custom in more wealthy times of sewing pieces together in imitation of their former poverty.

[2] Hiouen Thsang places the cave of the Shadow of Buddha twenty li to the S.W. of Hiḍḍa. This agrees nearly enough with that of the text. The account given by Hiouen Thsang of his visit to this cave is too curious to be omitted. Having set out alone from Hidda and arrived at the town of Teng-kouang-tching (Pradîparasmi poura (Jul.) [but is not Teng-kouang equivalent to Dipâñkara ?], he entered a Sañghârâma and enquired his way. He found no one to accompany him, except a boy who said, "the farm of the convent is not at a great distance from here, I will accompany you so far." When they arrived at the farm they passed the night there, and having found an old man who knew the spot, the two set out together. Five brigands attacked them before long, but Hiouen Thsang by his courage and address converted them. They arrived at the cave which is situated to the east of a stream running between two mountains. The entrance was scooped out in a sort of rocky wall, and admitted one in a

At about ten paces off you may see it, like the true resemblance of Buddha, of a golden color, with all its characteristic signs[1] perfectly bright and shining. On turning away or going nearer, the resemblance to the reality becomes less and less distinct. The kings of all the surrounding countries have deputed skilful artists to take a copy of this figure, but they have been unable to accomplish it. A tradition common amongst the

stooping posture only. All within was dark. Hiouen Thsang, having entered and advanced to the eastern side of the cave, then stepped back fifty paces and halted, keeping his eyes fixed on the east wall. "Then animated with a profound faith, he made one hundred prostrations, but saw nothing. He bitterly reproached himself for his faults, wept and cried aloud, and gave himself up to grief." He then recited some sacred texts and prostrated himself anew after each verse. Suddenly there appeared on the east wall a halo of light, large as an alms bowl, but it vanished instantly. Again it appeared and vanished. The pilgrim in a transport of enthusiasm and love, swore never to quit the place till he had looked on the shadow. He continued his worship, and after two hundred prostrations, suddenly the whole cave was inundated with light, and the shadow of Tathâgata (Buddha), of a brilliant whiteness, projected itself on the wall; a dazzling brightness lit up the lineaments of its sacred face. Hiouen Thsang gazed on it for some time, ravished with an ecstacy of delight. The body of Buddha and its robes (Kachâya) [so called from their color (kaça, green)] were of a yellowish red color. Above his knees all the characteristic beauties exhibited themselves in a brilliant manner, but below the lotus throne on which he sat, there was a sort of glimmering appearance. On the right and left were the shadows of Bôdhisatwas and Sramanas, who formed the suite of Buddha. When a light was brought the shadow vanished. Hiouen Thsang then paid his religious offerings and departed" (Jul. i. 81). This cave was originally the abode of the dragon Gôpala. Buddha having converted him bequeathed him his shadow as a safeguard and token of affection.

[1] The characteristic signs, are certain marks of Buddha's person, by which he was distinguished, 108 on each foot, 32 superior signs on his person, 80 inferior signs (M.B. 368).

men of that country says that all the thousand Buddhas of the present Kalpa will leave their shadows in this place. About a hundred paces west of this is a place where Buddha during his lifetime shaved his head and pared his nails. Here Buddha, assisted by his disciples, raised a tower from seventy to eighty feet high, as a model for all future buildings of the sort, and this still exists. By the side of this tower is a temple in which about 700 priests reside. In this place also is a tower erected in honor of all the Rahats and Pratyêka Buddhas,[1] of whom as many as a thousand in number have dwelt in this place.

[1] A Pratyêka Buddha is one who attains the condition of Buddha for himself alone (sc. pratyêkam [êka] individually.) "Pratyêka Buddha, un Buddha personnel, qui n'a pas la charité universelle et n'opére que son propre salut." (E. Burnouf, Sansc. Dict. *sub voc.*) In the early history of Buddhism these beings (or, this condition of mind) were unknown. The three grades recognised were "Sravakas (hearers, ἀκουσται), Arhats, Buddhas. But when the system developed itself the grave question arose, is it possible for a man by the unaided power of his own religious exertions to become perfectly enlightened (Buddha)? This was necessarily answered in the affirmative, but with certain restrictions. Such persons may become Buddhas, but for themselves only, they can benefit no one else; they cannot release any other being from the miseries of successive existence; they cannot preach the law, just as a dumb man, though he may have seen a remarkable dream cannot explain it to others, or as a savage who enters a city and is sumptuously fed by a citizen, is unable, on his return to the forest to give his fellow savages an idea of the taste of the food he has eaten (M.B. 38). This distinction sprang up under the influence of the doctrine of the successive causes of existence (Nidanas), and was no part of the early Hinayana system (Wasseljew, § 65). In the Sutra of the forty-two Sections, however, this condition of being is recognized, 'To feed a hundred learned men is not so meritorious as to feed one virtuous man. To feed a thousand virtuous men is not so

meritorious as to feed one man who keeps the five precepts (a religious man). (The five precepts are: 1. Not to kill; 2. Not to commit adultery; 3. Not to steal; 4. Not to lie; 5. Not to drink intoxicating liquors). To feed ten thousand such is not as meritorious as to feed one Sakradagamin (*vide* Chap. vi. *n.*). To feed ten million such is not as meritorious as to feed one Anagamin. To feed ten one hundred million such is not so meritorious as to feed one Arhat. To feed a thousand million such is not so meritorious as to feed one Pratyêka Buddha. And to feed one hundred thousand million such, is not so meritorious as to feed one Buddha, and learn to pray to him, to deliver all mankind" (§ 10).

CHAPTER XIV.

In the second month of winter, Fah Hian and his two companions[1] going to the South, crossed the Little Snowy Mountains.[2] The snow continually accumulates on these mountains, both in winter and summer. The exceeding cold which came on suddenly in crossing the Northern slope of the mountain, which lies in the shade, caused the men generally to remain perfectly silent (to shut their mouths) through fear. The pilgrim Hwui Ying[3] was unable, after repeated efforts, to proceed any further. His mouth was covered with a white foam; at last he addressed Fah Hian and said, "It is impossible for me to recover; whilst there is time do you press forward, lest we all perish," and upon this he presently died. Fah Hian cherished him (to supply warmth) and piteously invoked him by his familiar name, but it was all ineffectual to restore life. Submitting therefore to his destiny, he once more gathered up his strength and pressed forward. Having (at length) surmounted

[1] That is To Tchang and Hwui Ying.

[2] The pilgrims probably crossed the highest part of the Khyber range near the Saféd Koh (W.).

[3] Hwui King in the original, but he was dead (chap. xii.). There is a dissertation on this passage in the Appendix to the Chinese work, in which this error is clearly pointed out, and Hwui Ying substituted for the name in the Text.

the ridge of the mountains and passed to the southward of them, they arrived at the country of Lo-I (Roh or Rohi, another name for Afghanistan).[1] In this neighbourhood there are 3000 priests belonging both to the Small and Great Vehicle. The two pilgrims remained here during the season of Rest[2]; after this they proceeded to the south ten days' journey, and arrived at the country of Po-Na.[3] Here also there are about 3000 priests, all belonging to the system called the Little Vehicle. From this, going eastwards three days' journey, they again crossed the river Indus. Both sides of the river are now level and plain country.

[1] The principal tribes of the Afghans between the Solimâni hills and the Indus are known collectively by the term Lohanis, and in them we may perhaps have the Lohâs of the Hindoo geographers, and the Lo-I of the Chinese (W.).

[2] The season of Rest, *i.e.*, the summer season of Rain. From this it may be gathered that Fah Hian and his companions set out to cross the Khyber range in the second month of the Indian winter season, *i.e.* in the month Mâgha, which might be as late as the 16th of January. But in any case, unless they travelled some distance to the south before halting, they must have remained stationary in Lo-i some time previous to the rainy season, which would commence about the end of June.

[3] This has been identified with Bannu, a name still found on our maps, and exactly three marches west of the Indus (C.).

CHAPTER XV.

On the other side of the river is a country[1] called Pi-cha.[2] The Law of Buddha is prosperous and flourishing[3] here, and is known both in connection with the Small and Great Vehicle. On seeing disciples from China coming among them they were much affected and spoke thus, "How wonderful to

[1] The expression used in the original denotes merely the fact of there being such a country. It has not the force of "tao" (the expression usually employed "to arrive at,") denoting personal knowledge.

[2] This may be a corruption for Panchanada (Panjab), but more probably it indicates Bhiḍa or Bhiṛa on the Jhelam, which was for a short time the capital of the Brahman Kings of the Panjab. It lies on the direct route between Bannu and Mathura. The narrative of this part of the pilgrim's route is much confused. Probably, however, he followed the usual route towards Lahore, and from thence to the Jumna. This route is still marked upon our maps (Elphinstone's India), and agrees with the few particulars recorded by Fah Hian.

[3] It is difficult to understand why no particulars are given in connection with the flourishing state of Buddhism in this country. The expression used in the original, may indeed only signify "beginning to flourish," although on the other hand, it is used as an idiom denoting fulness, complete prosperity (*vide* Medhurst's Dict. *sub* Hing). At first, from the few notices recorded by the Pilgrim, taken in connection with the use of the word "yu" instead of "tao," I thought it very likely that he followed the course of the Indus until near its junction with the Chenab, and then continued in a S.E. direction across the desert by Bhatnir and Hissar to the Jamna. This distance would very well agree with the eighty yojanas (about 560') of the next chapter. In this case he would have had few opportunities for observing or recording particulars respecting the Panjábi Buddhists. But here another difficulty presents itself. Why, if this was his route, has he given us no particulars respecting the difficulties and privations of the inhospitable deserts through which he must have passed?

think that men from the ends of the earth, should know the character of this religion (lit., that there is a system of religion requiring one to leave one's family), and should come thus far to seek the laws of Buddha." We received from them all that we required and were treated according to the provisions of the law.

He does indeed barely allude to them in the following chapter, but in the most general manner. Perhaps, however, his own remark made in the concluding sentences of the last chapter of this work may account for his silence.

CHAPTER XVI.

From this, proceeding in a south-easterly direction somewhat less than eighty yojanas, we pass in succession various Temples,[1] containing very many priests, in all amounting to 10,000 and more. Having passed by all these places, we arrived at a certain kingdom called Ma-teou-lo.[2] Here, again, we followed the course of the river Po-Na (Jumna). [The force of "again" seems to be that they had followed previously the course of the Indus.] On the banks of this river there are twenty Sañghârâmas, containing perhaps 3000 priests. The Law of Buddha is in a reviving condition.[3] All the kingdoms beyond the sandy deserts are spoken of as belonging to western India.[4] The kings

[1] These temples as Rémusat remarks were probably Brahmanical Devâlayas. Hiouen Thsang records concerning the district of Tehaka (in the centre of the Panjâb), that "there are few who believe in the law of Buddha, the greatest number adore the spirits of heaven (Devas).' (Jul. ii. 189.)

[2] This must be Mathôura (Mattra) below Delhi.

[3] This denotes that the religion of Buddha had been in a depressed state,

[4] This passage may also be translated thus, "The continuation of sandy deserts being passed (we arrive at) the various kingdoms of western India." If this be the true rendering of the passage it may either denote that Fah Hian himself had passed through these deserts (which appears most probable) or it may simply be an observation made by the way.

of all these countries firmly believe in the Law of Buddha. When they pay their religious offerings to the priesthood, they uncover their heads. Both they and the members of their households and the ministers of state (frequently) conduct the priests to their several palaces, for the purpose of providing them with food. Having placed their entertainment before them, they spread a carpet on the ground opposite the lofty daïs on which the priests sit, and there take their places in front of them, for in the presence of the priesthood it is not allowed (to laymen) to sit on a loftier seat.[1] These rules for the conduct of princes when offering their religious devotions, have been handed down by tradition from the time when Buddha was in the world to the present day. To the south of this, the country is called Madya Dêsa (*i.e.* the middle country). The climate of this region is exceedingly equable, there is neither frost nor snow. The inhabitants are prosperous and happy. There are no Boards of Population and Revenue. Those only who farm the Royal demêsnes, pay a portion of the produce as rent. Nor are they bound to remain in possession longer than they like. The King in the administration of justice, inflicts no corporal punishment,

[1] According to the Sekhiyâ damma section of the Pratimôksha (§§ 68 and 69 according to the Pali, 88 and 89 Chinese version) it is not allowed to priests to sit on the ground or in a lower position, when a person for whose benefit he is present, is sitting in a chair (the word employed in the text) or seated on a loftier platform (*vide* Pratamôksha, translation of, R.A.S. Jour.).

but each culprit is fined in money according to the gravity of his offence; and even in cases where the culprit has been guilty of repeated attempts to excite rebellion, they restrict themselves to cutting off his right hand. The chief officers of the king have all allotted revenues. The people of this country kill no living creature nor do they drink intoxicating liquors. And, with the exception of the Chandâlas,[1] they eat neither garlic or onions. The word "chandâla" signifies a wicked man, who lives apart from others. If such a man enters a town or a market place, he strikes a piece of wood, in order to keep himself separate; people, hearing this sound, know what it means and avoid touching him or brushing against him. In this country they do not keep swine or fowls, they do not deal in living animals, nor are there shambles or wine shops round their markets. They use shells for money in their traffic. The Chandâlas alone go hunting and deal in flesh. From the time of Buddha's Nirvâṇa, the kings and nobles of all these countries began to erect Vihâras for the priesthood, and to endow them with lands, gardens, houses, and also men and oxen to cultivate them. The Records of these endowments, being engraved on sheets of copper, have been handed down from one king to another, so that no one has dared to deprive them of possession, and they continue to this day to enjoy their proper Revenues.

[1] The Chandâlas (Tsandâlas) were outcasts of Indian society, those who had no caste, the lowest of mortals (Menu).

All the resident priests have chambers, beds, coverlets, food, drink and clothes provided for them without stint or reserve. Thus it is in all places. The priests, on the other hand, continually employ themselves in works of benevolence, in reciting their Scriptures, or in profound meditation. When a strange priest arrives amongst them, the senior brethren go out to meet him, and conduct him on his way, carrying for him his clothes and alms dish. They then present him with water to wash his feet and cleanse them from mire,[1] and they prepare an extraordinary repast.[2] After a little pause, when the stranger has rested, they ask him his age,[3] according to which they allot him a chamber with proper materials, in every respect as the Law directs. In every place where the priests take up their fixed abode,[4] they erect towers in honour of Sâriputra,[5]

[1] I do not think there is any allusion to "oil" here, as R. supposes. I take "tsuh yu" to signify any pollution of the feet, whether dirt, or the heat of travel.

[2] That is, a repast at an unusual hour. The Buddhists are bound by their rule not to eat after mid-day except when sick or travelling.

[3] Julien has well pointed out (ii. 65 *n.*) that the expression "la," "a sacrifice," signifies also a year of one's life. Hence the translation in the text, which differs from R.

[4] This refers to the priests' residence during the rainy seasons. Fah Hian is still speaking generally of the customs in Mid-India, and not of himself or his companions, as R. supposes.

[5] Sâriputra, one of the great disciples of Buddha, the representative of complete (esoteric) wisdom. Take the following account: "Sâriputra is equivalent to son of the Tsau bird (S'ari, a kind of hawk with remarkable eyes), this was a name derived from his mother. At first he was a disciple of the heretic Sañgha (M.B. 195), he was versed in all the eighteen

Mogalan,[1] Ânanda,[2] and also towers in honour of the Abhidharma,[3] Vinaya, and Sûtra Pitakas. · After

S'astras, unrivalled in discussion, and ever open to instruction; nevertheless, he was unable to obtain knowledge of the true Doctrine. He was moreover disgusted with the rude manners and mode of living common amongst unbelievers. One day as he was going along the road he met by chance Assaji the Bikshu, carrying his staff and his alms bowl, his garments clean and properly arranged, his gait slow and dignified. Pleased at these circumstances, he asked him, 'Who is your master?' Assaji (Ma-shing, *i.e.* Asvajit), replied, 'The great Shaman Buddha, he is my teacher.' Again he asked, 'And what law does he teach?' To which he replied, 'I am but the disciple of a day, and know but little, but in brief, one gáthá (verse) may exhibit his doctrine, and it is this: All things (all conditions of Being, or conditional Being, or the Conditioned, (tehu fah [yé dhamma]) proceed from connection of cause and effect. The destruction of things results from the same. I, Buddha, the Great Shaman, always make this the principle of my teaching.' Sâriputra, on hearing these words, understood the mode of deliverance, and became a believer" (Life of Buddha, from the Chinese, § 77).

[1] Mogalan (Ch. Mou-lien, Sansc. Maudgalyâyana), formerly a fellow-disciple of Sâriputra. As a condition of obtaining saving knowledge (Amrita, sweet dew) he said, "Should I obtain it, I vow to dispense it freely to all." That day, on seeing Sâriputra coming back with a happy and lightened mien, he said, "Has my brother obtained knowledge of the excellent Doctrine?" Sâriputra then told him whom he had met, and repeated the verse (gáthá) to him. On this Mogalan at once gained perfect enlightenment, and both agreed to reject the teaching of all heretical schools. These two men each brought 250 of their disciples to follow Buddha, who shaved their heads and assumed the religious garments (chívara). Buddha then addressing the assembly, said, "With respect to these two disciples (Sâriputra and Mogalan), the first shall become pre-eminent for wisdom, the other for force of divine faculties;" (*i.e.* extension of natural faculties for divine purposes). (Life of Buddha, § 78.)

[2] Ânanda, nephew of Buddha, the great composer of Sutras, and the second Buddhist patriarch.

[3] The Abhidharma, the third of the three Pitakas or treasures of Buddhist doctrine, containing the metaphysical portion of the creed, or the explanation of the doctrine laid down in the Sûtras.

the first month of residence the principal religious families in the neighbourhood, exhort them to commence their Religious Services. On this, the priests partake of an extraordinary collation, and being assembled in a great congregation they repeat the Law; this being over, they present religious offerings to the tower of Sâriputra, every kind of incense and flowers, and throughout the whole night they burn lamps provided by those men for the purpose. Sâriputra was originally a Bráhman. On one occasion having met Buddha, he sought to become a disciple. So also did the great Kâsyapa[1] and the great Mogalan. The Bikshunîs principally affect the worship of the tower of Ânanda, because it was Ânanda who requested Buddha to permit females to become disciples. The Samaneras[2] principally affect the worship of

[1] Maha Kâsyapa, or the Great Kâsyapa, was one of three brothers, all of whom were fire worshippers. Maha Kâsyapa was converted by Buddha, and became instrumental in the conversion of his brothers. They each brought with them 250 disciples. These, with the 500 of Sâriputra and Mogalan, make up the 1250 followers of Buddha, of whom frequent mention is made in the Sutras. Maha Kâsyapa was the first Buddhist patriarch.

[2] Samaneras (Ch. Sha-mi) are novices or candidates for the priesthood. A Novice must be at least eight years of age, and must have received permission of his parents to abandon the world. He cannot receive ordination till he is twenty years old. He is not regarded as a member of the Chapter or Sañgha; he can perform any religious rite, but he is not allowed to interfere in matters of government or discipline. The place of residence having been chosen, the novice must declare his intention to a superior priest, or he must take his robe, and after having shaved his head and bathed, he must give it to a priest and then receive it

Râhula.[1] The professors of the Abhidharma pay their religious offerings to that work, and so also with the masters of the Vinaya. Every year there is one such religious service, each individual having his own day. Men who belong to the Great Vehicle worship the Prâjna Pâramita,[2] Man-

of him again. He must then request the priest to impart to him the threefold protective formulary (Sansc. tri sarana, Ch. san kwei), viz.: I take refuge in Buddha, in the Law, in the Associated Priesthood. And he then repeats the ten obligations, which are, (1.) Not to kill; (2.) Not to steal, (3.) Not to marry; (4.) Not to lie; (5.) Not to drink intoxicating liquors; (6.) Not to eat after mid-day; (7.) Not to attend dancing, singing, music parties or theatres; (8.) Not to use perfumes, unguents, or ornamental flowers; (9.) Not to seek high or honourable seats or couches in company; (10.) Not to covet or receive gold, silver or precious articles" (The duties of the Shami may be learned from the Catechism of the Shamans, or from M. B. pp. 24, 25).

[1] Râhula, the son of Buddha by his wife Yasodâri. R. translates this very differently.

[2] This expression refers to a class of works in Buddhist literature so called. Prâjna is knowledge, sanctified knowledge. Pâramita [pâra + mita, pp. from, mâ (E. Burnouf), but rather from pâra (sc. pâram) and ita, pp. from i (êmi) to go], is, literally, "transported across," therefore the whole phrase is equivalent to this, "the knowledge (of one who has been) transported across," or as we might say "Divine wisdom." The idea is fully explained and tediously dwelt upon, by commentators of the Chinese Pâramita works. Let us content ourselves with the following, which occurs in the commentary of Tai Teen, on the Hṛidaya Prâjna Pâramita Sûtra. "Prâjna (wisdom) is like the pole that propels the boat, so it advances the human soul. The heart putting forth its power (*i.e.* of this wisdom), emerges from the surging sea of life. The body advances straight to the shore of Bòdhi (perfect enlightenment) with free and elastic gait; the man assumes his original nature, like the moon emerging from the clouds. Pâramita (that shore). After emerging from the sea of life and death the shore on which we land is called 'that shore,' whilst the shore on which men are subject to the necessity of life and death is called 'this shore.' Those who corrupt

jusri,[1] and Avalôkitêśwara.[2] The Priests' harvest being finished (or it may be, the season when the priests receive presents being over), then the nobles, and householders, and Bráhmans, all provide themselves with different sorts of material for making garments such as priests require and present them to the clergy. The priests likewise make presents one to another. These rules of courtesy for the direction of the holy Congregation, have been handed down without

themselves remain on this shore, whilst the enlightened arrive at that shore." The Prâjna Pâramita works occupy a most important place in the development of Buddhist doctrine. They occupy a middle place between the Elementary school (which insists principally on the practice of morality for emancipation) and the advanced Mystical school (which regards Salvation as consisting in a union of soul with the Universal mind, brought about by intense self-reflection). Two of these works have been translated and appear in the Trans. of the R.A.S.

1 Mañjusri, a semi-historical character deified by the Nepalese and Thibetans. He is said to have drained the valley of Nipal, and civilised the inhabitants, just what Kâsyapa is said to have done for Kashmir (Burnouf, Lotus, 505). By the Chinese on the other hand he is spoken of "as a teacher of the highest flight of doctrine found in the Great Vehicle, and the founder of a school called 'that of the One Nature,' which affirmed that all creatures possess the one nature of Buddha." It is in this latter sense, no doubt, he is referred to in the text (*vide* Lotus of Good Law, 498, sqq., and Life of Buddha from Chinese, § 182).

2 Avalôkitêśwara, an imaginary being. Literally, "the manifested God" (avalôkita + îswara). Called by the Chinese "kwan shai yin," where "shai yin," "voice of men," has been supposed to indicate "swara," a voice, and that this has been mistaken by the Chinese priests for "îswara," a "god," but I think erroneously. Kwan-shai-yin is equivalent to the "manifested voice," where "voice" stands for "vach," and "vach" is a well-known object of Hindoo and Vedic worship. The characteristic of Avalôkitêśwara is intense love of man, hence he is the "Saviour of men." (For further particulars see Translation of the Ritual of Kwan-yin, R.A S. Transact.)

interruption from the time of Buddha's Nirvana till now. From the river Sin-to (Indus) to south India, where it borders on the southern sea, a distance of forty or fifty thousand li, the land is all plain and level. There are no great mountains or valleys,[1] but still there are rivers.

[1] For the use of the word "ch'uen" in this sense, *vide* Jul. iii. 207.

CHAPTER XVII.

GOING S.E. from this place (i.e. Mathoura) eighteen yôjanas, there is a kingdom called Sang-ka-shi (Sãnkasya M.B. 300, *n.*).[1] When Buddha went up to the Triyastriñshas heaven,[2] to say Bana[3] for the sake of his mother,[4] after three months he descended at this place. On this occasion he exerted his spiritual power so that his disciples did not know where he had gone. Seven days before the completion of the three months, he again scattered his spiritual influence, so that Aniruddha,[5] by his divine sight was able to behold the World-Honored one afar off. Immediately he addressed

[1] Sangkâsya is the present Sankisa, on the banks of the Kali Nada, about twenty-five miles from Farakhabad. It is called Kapitha by Hiouen Thsang. "It is now a village consisting only of from fifty to sixty houses; all around it for a circuit of six miles are ruins of brick and earth, said to be the walls of an old city" (J.W.L.). General Cunningham visited this place in 1862, and has given a full account of its Buddhist remains (Report of the Archæolog. Surveyor of India, 1862-63).

[2] The thirty-three heavens on the top of mount Sumeru.

[3] To say Bana is the common expression used in Ceylon for preaching (S.H.). The Chinese expression is "shwoh fah," "to say the Law."

[4] The mother of Buddha was called Mâya (illusion) she died seven days after Buddha's birth, and was transported to the heaven of Indra (Triyastriñshas). As she had not had the opportunity of hearing the doctrine of Buddha preached, he is represented as ascending to that heaven to declare it for her sake.

[5] Anuruddha, the son of Amitôdana, the brother of Sudhôdana (the father of Buddha). He was cousin to Buddha. He became a disciple and an Arhat. He was chief of those who have supernatural vision and

the venerable Maha Mogalan, "You now can go and pay reverence to the World-Honored one."[1] Mogalan forthwith proceeded and prostrated himself in adoration of the marks on the foot of Buddha.[2] This act of adoration being over, Buddha addressed him and said, "After seven days more I shall descend to Jambudvîpa." Then Mogalan returned. At the appointed time the Maharâjas of the eight kingdoms and all the ministers and people, not having seen Buddha for so long, greatly desired to meet him. They flocked therefore in great crowds to this country to await the return of the World-Honoured one. Then the Bikshuni Utpala[3] began to think thus with herself, "To day the king, ministers, and people are all going to meet Buddha and render homage to him, but I—a woman—how can I contrive to get the first sight of him." Buddha immediately, by his divine power, changed her into a holy Chakravarttî[4] Râja, and in that capacity she was the

received divine eyes by which he could see all things in a 100,000 systems of worlds, as easily as he could perceive a mustard seed in his hands" (M.B. 227).

[1] The expression in the original "man sun" means "to pay reverence" and not "to enquire" as R. translates it.

[2] The Mangalya Lakshana, 216 in number, 108 on each foot.

[3] In the travels of Hiouen Thsang she is called Pouṇḍarîkavarṇâ (Jul. ii. 240).

[4] A Chakravartti, is an universal monarch, one in whom the chakra (discus) of Vishnu abides (varttate). The grammatical etymology is, "He who abides in, or rules over, an extensive territory, called a Chakra" (Wilson. M.B. 126). So called probably because the "chakra" or discus precedes him in his tour through the territory he governs (M.B. 127).

very first to reverence Buddha on his return. Buddha was now about to descend from the Triyastriñshas heavens. At this time there appeared a threefold precious ladder. Buddha standing above the middle ladder which was made of the seven precious substances began to descend. Then the king of the Brahmakâyikas[1] caused a silver ladder to appear, and took his place on the right hand, holding a white chowry in his hand. Whilst the divine Sekra caused a bright golden ladder to appear, and took his place on the left hand holding a precious parasol in his hand.[2] Innumerable Dêvas were in attendance whilst Buddha descended. After he had accomplished his return the three ladders all disappeared in the earth except seven steps, which still continued visible. In after times king Asôka, wishing to find out the utmost depth to which these ladders went, employed men to dig and examine the matter. They went down till they came to a spring of yellow water, but yet had not arrived at the bottom. The king deriving from

[1] The Brahmakâyika heaven, the lowest of the heavens in the world of forms (Rupa loka). The Brahmakâyikas are the followers of Brahmâ. They inhabit three heavens on the same platform." In the middle come the Mahâ Brahmânas, on the right the Brahma purôhitas (ministers of Brahma), on the left Brahmaparishadyas (those who compose the assembly of Brahma)." (Fah kai li to). The Thibetan account is different, admitting four heavens belonging to Brahma. The work from which the above extract is taken is in agreement with the ordinary account (*vide* Burnouf, Introd. p. 608.)

[2] The legend connected with Buddha's descent from the Tryastriñshas heaven, is known to the southern Buddhists (M.B. 300). It is probable of an early date therefore.

this an increase of faith and reverence, forthwith built over the ladders a Vihâra, and in the middle of it placed a standing figure (of Buddha) sixteen feet high. Behind the Vihâra he erected a stone pillar thirty cubits high, and on the top placed the figure of a Lion.[1] Within the pillar on the four sides are placed figures of Buddha; both within and without it is shining and bright as glass (lapis lazuli). It happened once that some heretical Doctors had a contention with the Shamans respecting this, as a place of residence. Then the Shamans agreed to any condition for settling the question that might be considered reasonable. On which they all bound themselves to this compact, "If this place properly belongs to the Shamans, then there will be some supernatural proof given of it." Immediately on this, the lion on the top of the pillar uttered a great roar. Witnessing this testimony, the unbelievers abashed withdrew from the dispute and submitted.

The body of Buddha, in consequence of his having partaken of Divine food during the three months (he was in the Triyastriñshas heavens), emitted a divine fragrance,[2] unlike that of men. Immediately after his

[1] General Cunningham, who visited the spot (1862), found a pillar, evidently of the age of Asôka, with a well carved elephant on the top. The elephant, however, was minus trunk and tail. He supposes this to be the pillar seen by Fah Hian, who mistook the animal on the top of it for a lion. It is possible such a mistake may have been made, as in the account of one of the pillars at Srâvasti, Fah Hian says an ox formed the capital, whilst Hiouen Thsang calls it an elephant (C. p. 19, Arch. Surv.).

[2] R. has taken the connection differently, the translation in the Text, however, is the most natural.

descent, he bathed himself. Men of after ages erected in this place a bath house, which yet remains. There is also a tower erected on the spot where the Bikshuni Utpala was the first to adore Buddha (on his return). There is also a tower on the spot where Buddha when in the world cut his hair and his nails, and also on the following spots, viz., where the three former Buddhas,[1]

[1] According to Buddhist doctrine there are to be five supreme Buddhas in the present (Bhadra) Kalpa (age, or cycle of years of fanciful duration). Four of these have already appeared. The last is yet to come. The four are (1) Kakusunda Tathâgata (Tathâgata is a term applied to all the Supreme Buddhas). (2) Kónâgamana Tathâgata. (3) Kâśyapa Tathâgata. (4) Gotama (Sakya Muni) Tathâgata. And the one yet to come is (5) Mâitrêya Buddha. It is impossible to know whether there may not be a fragment of History connected with these Buddhas; at any rate the Chinese copy of the Pratimôksha supplies a distinct dogma for each of them, as follows:—

Kakusanda (Kin-Lim-sin) taught:

"The heart, carefully avoiding idle dissipation,
Diligently applying itself to religion,
Forsaking all lust, and (consequent) disappointment,
Fixed and immovable, attains Nirvana (rest).

Konagamana (Ku-na-tum-mu-ni) taught:

"Practising no vice,
Advancing in the exercise of virtue,
Purifying mind and will,
This is the doctrine of all the Buddhas."

Kâsyapa (Ka-ih) taught:

"To keep one's tongue,
To cleanse one's mind,
To do no ill,
This is the way to purify oneself throughout,
And to attain this state of discipline
Is the doctrine of all the great Sages."

Shi-kia (Sâkya) taught: (The doctrine of the present Buddha).

—(*vide* Translation of the Pratimôksha from the Chinese R.A.S. Transact.)

as well as Sâkya Muni, sat down, and also where they walked for exercise, and also where there are certain marks and impressions left on the stones by the feet of the different Buddhas (Jul. ii. 239); these towers still remain. There is also one erected where Brahma, Sekra and the Dêvas attended Buddha when he came down from heaven. In these different places there are perhaps 1000 male and female disciples who (in their several establishments) have their meals in common. They belong promiscuously to the systems of the Great and Little Vehicle, and agree to occupy the same place. A white-eared dragon (or, the dragon yih-pih-i, *i.e.* one white ear) is the patron of this body of priests.[1] It is he who causes fertilizing and seasonable showers of rain to fall within their country, and preserves it from plagues and calamities, and so causes the priesthood to dwell in security. The priests, in gratitude for these favours, have erected a Dragon-chapel, and within it placed a resting place (seat) for his accommodation, and moreover they make special contributions,[2] in the shape of religious offerings, to provide the dragon with food. The body of priests every day select from

[1] This dragon (Nâga) is still made an object of religious veneration by the people of Sankisa. He is called Kârewar, and the tank which he is supposed to occupy is termed "Kandaiya Tal." Milk is offered to him every day during the month Vâisâkh (August, the beginning of the rainy season) C.

[2] R. terms this "happy food," but the expression "fuh" (happy), is a common one in Buddhist works, denoting "meritorious," or that which causes "merit" (and therefore happiness).

their midst three men to go and take their meal in this Chapel. Towards the end of each season of Rest (Varchâs), the dragon incontinently assumes the form of a little serpent, both of whose ears are edged with white. The body of priests, recognizing him, place in the midst for his use a copper vessel full of cream. The serpent then proceeds to come down from the highest part of the alcove, constructed for his accommodation, to the lowest part, all the while moving as though he would pay his respects[1] to all those around him. He then suddenly disappears. He makes his appearance once every year. This country is abundantly productive: the people in consequence are very prosperous, and rich beyond comparison. Men of all countries coming here, may without any trouble obtain all they require. Fifty yojanas to the north of this temple[2] there is another temple called "Fire Limit," which is the name of an evil spirit. Buddha in one of his incarnations converted this evil spirit, whereupon men in after ages raised a Vihâra on the spot. At the time of the dedication of the Vihâra, an Arhat spilt some of the water, with which he was cleansing his hands, on the earth, and the place where it fell is still visible; though they have often swept and cleansed the

[1] The phrase "man sun," as we have already stated, signifies "to pay respect to," and not "to enquire." We cannot mistake the peculiar motion of the snake's neck in moving, here regarded as a token of salutation or respect.

[2] This carries us into Nipal, or even further north.

place, yet the mark still remains and cannot be destroyed. There is, besides, in this place, a tower of Buddha which a benevolent Spirit ever keeps clean and waters, and which at first (was built) without a human architect. There was once an heretical King who said, "Since you are able to do this, I will bring a great army and quarter it here, which shall accumulate much filth and refuse. Will you be able to clear all this away, I wonder?" The Spirit immediately caused a great tempest to rise and blow over the place, as a proof that he could do it. In this district there are a hundred or so small towers; a man might pass the day in trying to count them without succeeding. If any one is very anxious to discover the right number, then it is customary to place a man by the side of each tower and afterwards to number the men. But even in this case, it can never be known how many or how few men will be required. There is also a Sañghârâma here, containing about six or seven hundred priests. In this is a place where a Pratyêka Buddha ate (the fruit of Nirvâṇa);[1] the spot of ground where this took place is just in size like a chariot wheel, all the ground around it is covered with grass, but this spot produces none. The earth also where he dried his clothes, is bare of vegetation; the traces of the impress of the clothes remain to this day.

[1] So I have ventured to translate this passage. It may, however, simply imply that he ate his usual food here, but this appears too trivial an occurrence to record in connection with his Nirvâṇa, for the subsequent passage, is, when literally rendered, "the spot of ground where he entered Nirvâṇa is," etc.

CHAPTER XVIII.

Fah Hian resided in the Dragon Vihara during the summer Rest. After this was over, going south-east seven yôjanas, he arrived at the city of Ki-jou-i (Kanouj).[1] This city borders on the Ganges. There are two Sañghârâmas here, both belonging to the system of the Little Vehicle. Going from the city six or seven li in a westerly direction, on the north bank of the river Ganges,[2] is the place where Buddha delivered the Law

[1] This city was for many hundred years the capital of North India. In 1016 A.D. when Mahmud Ghâzni approached the town of Kanouj, the historian relates that "he there saw a city which raised its head to the skies, and which in strength and structure might justly boast to have no equal." All the Buddhist monuments, however (of which Hiouen Thsang speaks), were ruthlessly destroyed by the fanatical Mahomedans. (C.) Kanouj is mentioned by Ptolemy, A.D. 140, as Κανόγιζα. The name itself is stated to be a corruption of Kanya Kubja, "the humped-backed maiden." According to the Puranas, this relates to the curse of the sage Vahu on the hundred daughters of Kusanabu, in consequence of which they became hump-backed. Hiouen Thsang, however, relates that when this town was called Kusumapura, under the king Brahmadatta, that a Rishi called Mahâvriksha pronounced a similar curse on his ninety-nine daughters, because they had refused to accept him in marriage, and hence the name was changed. Hiouen Thsang describes the town as flourishing under a powerful monarch, Harsha Vardhana, and as being three and a half miles long, and three-quarters of a mile wide.

[2] There is a difficulty in this account, for if Kanouj be on the west bank of the Ganges, how, by going west six or seven li, can we suppose a tower on the north bank of the river? It has been supposed (C.) that Fah Hian's account is wrong, especially as Hiouen Thsang (Jul. II. 265) speaks

for the good of his disciples. Tradition says that he preached concerning impermanency and sorrow,[1] and also on the body being like a bubble and so on. On this spot they have raised a tower, which still remains. Crossing the Ganges, and going south three yojanas, we arrive at a forest called Ho-li.[2] Here also Buddha preached the Law. They have erected towers on this spot and also where he sat down and walked for exercise.

of a similar tower on the S.E. of the capital, and to the S. of the river. I am unwilling, however to believe him capable of so great an inaccuracy as this would imply. I rather think that he here alludes to the tower mentioned by Hiouen Thsang (Jul. II. 262), on the N.W. of the city "erected by Asoka, and where Buddha explained the most excellent laws," and it seems very likely that the dry Nala to which Cunningham refers as existing on the N.W. of the city, was in Fah Hian's time a tributary of the Ganges, as the Chota Ganga was on the S.W. side. It is to be remarked also that in the text Fah Hian does not speak of the *river* Ganges (Heng Ho) but the waters or affluents of the Ganges (Heng Shwui).

[1] The three subjects on which he preached were, no doubt, anitya (impermanence), dukha (sorrow), anâtmâ (unreality), these are called the Trividyâ, or three subjects of knowledge. There is an allusion also in the text to the concluding passage of the Diamond Sutra (Vajra-chhedikâ Sutra), "Wherefore the conclusion is this, that all things which admit of definition (the conditional) are as a dream, a phantom, a bubble, a shadow, as the dew and lightning flash" (Vajra-chhedikâ, R.A.S. Journal).

[2] This is supposed to be the same as the Nava-deva-Kula of Hiouen Thsang, at present swept away by the Ganges (C.)

CHAPTER XIX.

GOING S.E.[1] from this place ten yôjanas, you arrive at the great country of Sha-chi.[2] Leaving the southern gate of the capital city, on the east side of the road is the place where Buddha once located himself. Whilst here, he bit off a piece from the Dântakachta (Jul. II. 291) stick with which he cleansed his teeth, and fixing it in the earth it immediately grew up seven feet high, neither more or less. All the unbelievers and Brahmans, filled with jealousy, cut it down, and tore away and scattered the leaves far and wide, but yet it always sprung up again in the same place as before. Here also they raised towers on the place where the four Buddhas walked for exercise and sat down. The ruins of these still exist.

[1] Rémusat has written S.W., but my copy says S.E., which is no doubt correct.

[2] We must observe that Fah Hian speaks of a great country and not of a great city in this passage. The capital of the country is probably the same as that referred to by Hiouen Thsang (Jul. II. 290), which he calls the capital of Vaisâkha. Vaisâkha was probably a later name for Sha-chi (Kasi). There can be but little doubt that Fah Hian travelled in a south-easterly direction until he entered the borders of this great country, and then proceeded to the capital by a route not mentioned. If we regard the country Sha-chi, as Kasi, which we know bordered on Kôsala (M.B. 218), then we may be sure that the capital was Ayôdyâ or Oude on the river Gogra and close to Fyzabad. By this supposition we shall find Fah Hian's account a consistent one, and in agreement with Hiouen Thsang.

CHAPTER XX.

Going eight yôjanas southwards[1] from this place, we arrive at the country of Kiu-sa-lo (Kôsala)[2] and its chief town She-wei (Srâvastî).[3] There are very few inhabitants in this city, altogether perhaps about two hundred families. This is the city which king Prasê-

[1] We are here compelled to acknowledge an error in the text. It should be undoubtedly north instead of south.

[2] We observe here again that Fah Hian speaks first of the country, and then (without further detail) of the capital. The country Kusala or Kôsala, is famous in Buddhist history. "It is the country along the bank of the Sarayu, forming a part of the modern province of Oude. It was the pristine kingdom of the solar race. In the time of Buddha, the principal city was Sewet (Srâvastî)" (Wilson. M.B. 188 *n.*). This country must not be confused with the Kôsala of Hiouen Thsang, which is in the Deccan (Dakshina Kôsala).

[3] She-wei (Srâvastî). I have before observed that Fah Hian uses the expression "wei," as synonymous with "vastu," and although in the present case that word may not be a component part of the name of the town, it is so similar as easily to mislead our author. Srâvastî (Sewet) is said to have been built by Raja Sravasta, of the solar race, and tenth in descent from Sûrya himself (the Sun) (C.) This town is placed by C. on the south bank of the river Rapti, about fifty-eight miles north of Ayôdyâ (Oude). There are still ruins of a great town existing on this site, the name given to the place being Sâhet Mâhet (Arch. Rep. 39.). It was in this town Buddha passed twenty-five years of his life, after arriving at enlightenment. The memorials of his teaching and history here are very numerous. From Râjagriha to Srâvastî was forty-five yôjanas (M.B. 218) which at seven miles per yôjana, agrees exactly with this site.

najit[1] governed. Towers have been erected in after times on the site of the ruined Vihâra of Mahâ Prajâpatî,[2] also on the foundations (of the house) of Sudatta[3] the Nobleman, also on the spot where the Añgoulimâlya[4]

1 In the Chinese Po-sse-no, but according to Hiouen Thsang, Po-lo-sse-na-chi-to, *i.e.* Prasênajit (victorious army), the Pasé-nadi of Ceylon. He was contemporary with Sakya Buddha (*vide* his history M.B. 285 and elsewhere).

2 This passage R. translates, "They are there extremely attached to the Law," but the phrase Ta-'ai-Tao, is the Chinese form of Mahâprajâpatî, the aunt of Buddha (sister of Mahâ Mâyâ, Buddha's mother. She was his foster mother also, as she nursed him after Mâya's death). It was for her sake that Ânanda besought Buddha to admit females into the priesthood (community). She possessed a Vihâra in Srâvastî, which Prasênajît had built for her (Jul. ii. 294).

3 Sudatta (Shen-chi) was the minister of Prasênadjît. He was surnamed Anâthapiṇḍika (he who gives to orphans: the Beneficent). Having been informed of the merits and virtue of Buddha, he desired to build for him a Vihâra. He begged Buddha to condescend to come and see the site of it. There was a famous plot of ground called the Che-to-yuen (Jêtavana, the garden of the Prince Jêta). But when he asked the Prince to dispose of it, he replied that he would not let him have it unless he covered the ground with golden coins called masurans. This condition was complied with. After this, Anâthapiṇḍaka began to erect the Vihâra, around it were houses for the priests, suitable for day and for night; there was an ambulatory, tanks also, and gardens of fruit and flower trees, and around the whole a wall eighteen cubits high, and extending 4000 cubits. This is the famous Jêtavana Vihâra, where Buddha delivered so many of his discourses, and dwelt for many years (M.B. 219).

4 The Añgulimâlyas were fanatics who killed all the persons they could, to cut off their fingers (añgoula) to make necklaces with. One of these was about to kill his mother, when he saw Buddha, and left his mother to attack him. Buddha slowly stepped back and the man followed him, but could not touch him. Buddha then said, "Why do you persevere in your wicked design, why leave the possibility of being good, for the certainty of misery?" On this the Añgulimâlya was converted and afterwards entered Nirvâṇa (Jul. ii. 295).

was burnt who was converted and entered Nirvâṇa; all these Towers are erected in the midst of the city. The unbelieving Brahmans, entertaining a jealous feeling, desired to destroy these various edifices, but on their attempting to do so the heavens thundered and the lightnings flashed, so that they were unable to carry their design into execution. Leaving the city by the south gate, and proceeding twelve hundred paces on the road, on the west side of it is the place where the nobleman Sudatta built a Vihâra.[1] This chapel opens towards the East. The principal door is flanked by two side chambers, in front of which stand two stone pillars, on the top of the left hand one is the figure of a wheel, and on the right hand one, the image of an ox.[2] The clear water of the tanks, the luxuriant groves, and numberless flowers of variegated hues, combine to produce the picture of what is called the Vihâra of Chi-ûn (Jêta).[3] When Buddha ascended into the Triyastriñshas heavens, to repeat the Law for the sake of his mother, after ninety days absence, king Prasênajit desiring to see him again, carved out of the sandal wood called Gôsîrcha-

[1] This is the Jêtavana Vihâra previously described. Hiouen Thsang places it four or five li in the same direction, which is near enough for identification.

[2] Hiouen Thsang states that these pillars were seventy feet high, and had been erected by Asôka. On the top of one he places a cupola or dome, and on the other an Elephant. (C.) supposes that the trunk of the elephant might have been broken off and so Fah Hian have mistaken it for an ox.

[3] Chi-ün, probably a contraction of Chi-to-yuen, the garden of Jêta, *i.e.* Jêtavana.

chandana (ox-head) an image[1] of the saint and placed it on the seat that he usually occupied. When Buddha returned and entered the Vihâra, the image immediately quitting its place, went forward to meet him. On this Buddha addressed these words to it, "Return I pray you to your seat. After my Nirvâṇa you will be the model from which all my followers (lit. the members of the four schools or classes) shall carve their images of me." On this the Figure immediately returned to its seat. This image, as it was the very first made of all the figures of Buddha, is the one which all subsequent ages have followed as a model. Buddha subsequently removed and dwelt in a small Vihâra on the south side of the greater one, in a place quite separate from that occupied by the image, and about twenty paces from it. The Chi-ûn Vihâra originally had seven stories. The monarchs of all the surrounding countries and their inhabitants, vied with each other in presenting religious offerings at this spot. They decked the place with flags and silken canopies, they offered flowers and burnt incense, whilst the lamps shone out day after day with unfading splendor. Unfortunately, a rat gnawing at the wick of one of the lamps caused it to set fire to one of the hanging canopies, and this resulted in a general conflagration, and the entire destruction of the seven stories of the Vihâra. The kings and people of the surround-

[1] The account of this statue resembles that given by Hiouen Thsang (Jul. ii. 284), relating to Oudâyana, king of Kòsâmbî.

ing countries were all deeply grieved, supposing that the sandal wood figure had also been consumed. Four or five days afterwards, on opening the door of the eastern little chapel, they were surprised to behold the original figure there. All the people were filled with joy, and they agreed to re-build the chapel. Having completed two stories they removed the image from its new situation back to where it was before. When Fah Hian and To Ching arrived at this chapel of Chi-ûn, they were much affected to think that this was the spot in which Buddha had passed twenty-five years of his life. Around them stood many strangers, all occupied in similar reflections. They had traversed a succession of strange countries. Perhaps they might be spared to return home, perhaps they would die.[1] Gazing thus upon the place where Buddha once dwelt, but was no longer to be seen, their hearts were affected with very lively regret. Whereupon the priests, belonging to that community, came forward and addressed Fah Hian and his companion thus, "From what country have you come?" To which they replied, "We come from the land of Han." Then those priests, in astonishment, exclaimed, "Wonderful! to think that men from the remotest corner[2] of the earth should come so far as this, from a desire to search for the Law;" and then talking between themselves they said, "Our various Superiors

1 The phrase "wou shang" is used also (Chap. xii.) in this sense.

2 China is commonly spoken of as the "Middle country;" but in this work it is characterised as a Frontier country—in deference to the superior claims of India.

and Brethren who have succeeded one another in this place, from the earliest time till now, have none of them seen men of Han come so far as this before." Four li to the N.W. of the Vihâra is a copse called "Recovered sight" (Âptanêtravana, Jul. ii. 308), Originally there were five hundred blind men dwelling on this spot, who were in the habit of attending the Chapel. On one occasion Buddha declared the Law on their account, after listening to his sermon, they immediately recovered their sight. The blind men, overcome with joy, drove their staves into the earth and fell down on their faces in adoration. The staves forthwith took root and grew up to be great trees. The people, from a feeling of reverence, did not presume to cut them down, and so they grew and formed a grove, to which this name of "Recovered sight" was given. The priests of the chapel of Chi-ûn resort in great numbers to this shady copse to meditate after their midday meal. Six or seven li to the N.E. of the Vihâra of Chi-ûn is the site of the chapel which Visâka-mátawi[1] built (Jul. II. 305), and invited Buddha and the priests to occupy. The ruins of this chapel still exist.[2] The great Garden enclosure of

[1] Visâkha-matawi, *i.e.* mother Visâkha, because she became Mother or Superior of all the Upásikáwas or female disciples of Buddha. She was the daughter of a rich merchant (Dhananja); she distributed much alms among the followers of Buddha and built a Vihâra for him called the Pûrvârâma (M.B. 220) *i.e.* eastern monastery. The direction given by Fah Hian, N.E., is probably correct, as this would indicate E. from the city. (Cunningham prefers S.E)

[2] It will be observed that most of this translation differs from R. The word "ku" used in the original, although generally used adverbially,

the Vihara of Chi-ûn has two gates,[1] one opening towards the East the other towards the North. This garden is the plot of ground which the nobleman Sudatta bought, after covering it with gold coins. The chapel is placed in the exact centre of it; it was here Buddha resided for a very long time and expounded the Law for the Salvation of men. Towers have been erected on the various spots where he walked for exercise or sat down. These towers have all distinctive titles given them, as for example, the place where Buddha was accused of murdering the Chaṇḍâla woman.[2] Leaving (the garden of) Chi-ün by the eastern gate, and going north seventy paces, on the west side of the road is the place where Buddha formerly held a discussion with the followers of the ninety-six heretical schools. The king of the country, the chief ministers, the landowners and people all came in great numbers to hear him. At this time a woman, who was an unbeliever, called Chiñchimana,[3]

denoting "a consequence of an action," has also the sense of "ku," ancient or old.

[1] R. translates this "the town has two gates," which has misled Cunningham in § 333 of his cap. on Srâvastî (Arch. Surv. Rep. 1862-63, p. 41).

[2] "Behind the convent is a narrow passage where some heretical Brahmachâris killed an abandoned woman and buried her at the foot of a tree, and then denounced Buddha as a murderer and adulterer. But above all their accusations a voice from heaven declared, 'The Brahmans are the criminals, their charge is an infamous calumny'" (Jul. ii. 300).

[3] The history of this woman's plan to defame Buddha may be read in Spence Hardy (M.B. 275). She is there called Chinchi, and by Jul. (ii. 302) Tchñatcha.

being filled with jealousy, gathered up her clothes in a heap round her person so as to appear big with child, and then accused Buddha, in the midst of the great assembly, of having acted towards her contrary to the Law. On this, Sekra, the heavenly king, taking the appearance of a white mouse, came and gnawed through the sash which bound the woman's clothes up in the heap; on this the whole fell down, and then the earth opened and she herself went down alive into Hell.[1] Here also is the place where Dêvadatta,[2] having poisoned his nails for the purpose of destroying Buddha, went down alive into Hell. Men in after times signalised these various places so that they might be known. Where the discussion took place they raised a Chapel, which was more than six cheung (seventy feet) high, and within it placed a sitting figure of Buddha. To the east of the road is a Temple (Dêvâlaya) belonging to the heretics, which is named "Shadow covered." It is

[1] There were five persons living in the time of Buddha of whom it is recorded they went down alive into hell. 1. The noble Dhagineyya, who attempted the virtue of the priestess Upulwan; 2. The Brahman Mágandi, who reviled Buddha for seven days; 3. Chinchi, who brought a false accusation against Buddha; 4. Supra Buddha, the father-in-law of Buddha. 5. Dêvadatta, who attempted to take the life of Buddha (M.B. 61).

[2] Dêvadatta was the son of Supra Buddha, the father-in-law of Sakya Buddha (M.B. 61). But another account states that his father was Dronodana Raja, the brother of Sudhôdana Raja, Buddha's Father (Jul. ii. 301). I would here remark, that General Cunningham has identified the spots mentioned in the text, but I am not prepared to accept his correction of Fah Hian's statement that these spots are "north of the east gate," because he supposes the pilgrim to be speaking of the gate of the Vihâra, whereas he alludes to the east gate of the Garden.

just opposite the Vihâra erected on the place of the discussion, and of the same height. It has received the name of "Shadow-covered," from the fact that when the sun is in the west, the shadow of the Vihâra of Buddha (the honourable of the age)[1] covers the temple of the heretics, but when the sun is in the east the shadow of the latter is bent to the north, and does not at all overshadow the chapel of Buddha. The heretics being in the habit of appointing persons to take care of their temple, to sweep and water it, to burn incense and light lamps for religious worship, (it was found) that towards the approach of morning their lamps disappeared and were discovered in the middle of the Buddhist chapel. On this the Brahmans, being angry, said, "These Shamans take our lamps for the purpose of their own religious worship, why do we not put a stop to it?" Whereupon, the Brahmans, placing themselves in watch at night, saw how the thing was done, for lo! their own gods came and taking the lamps proceeded with them to the chapel of Buddha, and having three times moved round the building in solemn procession, and thus paid their homage to Buddha, they suddenly disappeared. On this the Brahmans, recognising the greatness of Buddha's spiritual power, forsook their families and became his disciples. Tradition says that about the time when these things happened, there

[1] This is one of thecommon epithets of Buddha, "world-honoured," or "honoured by men" (Lôkajyêsta).

where ninety Saṅghârâmas surrounding this chapel of Chi-ün, all of which, with one exception, were occupied by priests. In this country of mid-India there are ninety-six heretical sects,[1] all of whom allow the reality of worldly phenomena. Each sect has its disciples who beg their food, but do not carry alms-dishes. They build hospices[2] by the side of solitary roads (lit. "houses of merit," *i.e.* for obtaining merit) for the shelter of travellers, where they may rest, sleep, eat and drink, and are supplied with all necessaries. The followers of Buddha also, as they pass to and fro, are entertained by them, only different arrangements are made for their convenience. Dêvadatta also has a body of disciples still existing; they pay religious reverence to the three past Buddhas,[3] but not to Sâkya Muni.

Four li to the S.E. of Srâvastî[4] is the place where the World-Honored one, stood by the side of the road when king Viroûdhaka (Leou-li)[5] wished to destroy the

[1] These sectaries originated in times subsequent to Buddha; they were offshoots from the six principal heretical schools named by Spence Hardy (M.B. 290). They are called in general Tîrthakas, although this term ought properly to be confined to Brahmans (Pure-livers).

[2] Puṇyasâlâs, *i.e.* hospices.

[3] This is to Krakusanda Buddha, Kunaka Muni, and Kâsyapa Buddha.

[4] Mr. Laidlay's translation gives S.W. by mistake, the French is correct. Cunningham has followed Laidlay. (Archæolog. Survey Report, p. 45, § 351.)

[5] This King, who reigned at Koli, near Kapilavastu, and was the son of Prasênajit, exterminated the family of the Sâkyas, of which Buddha was a member. It is to this circumstance that Wassiljew (Der Buddhismus, § 11) attributes the conversion of Buddha to a religious life.

country of the Sâkya family;[1] on this spot there is a tower built. Fifty li to the west of the city we arrive at a town called To-wai,[2] this was the original birthplace of Kâsyapa Buddha. Towers are erected on the spot where he had an interview with his father and also where he entered Nirvâṇa. A great tower has also been erected over the relics of the entire body of Kâsyapa Tathâgata.[3]

[1] In the text "the country of She-i." I have translated it the "country of the Sakya family," although the equivalent of Sakya is not that used in the text, but it is phonetically of the same value, and therefore may represent it. The expression "i" I take to be equivalent to family or race. It is possible, however, the country may be called "She-i," though I know not how to restore it. The capital of the Sâkyas was Kapilanagara (now called Nagar, near Basti) (C).

[2] Cunningham (Rep. § 353) identifies this place with Tadwa, a village nine miles to the west of Sâhet-Mâhet. The Singhalese accounts state that Kâsyapa Buddha was born at Benares (M.B. 97).

[3] The title Tathâgata, corresponds to the Chinese "ju-lai," *i.e.* "thus-come," "he who has come according to expectation."

CHAPTER XXI.

LEAVING the city of Srâvastî, and going twelve yôjanas to the south east, we arrive at a town called Na-pi-ka.[1] This is the birthplace of Krakuchanda Buddha. There are towers erected on the spots where the interview between the father and son took place, and also where he entered Nirvâṇa. Going north from this place less than one yôjana, we arrive at a town[2] where Kanakamuni Buddha was born; there are towers also erected here over similar places as the last.

[1] The Singhalese accounts states that Krakusanda was born at Mékhalâ, but where that was, or the Napika of the text, I am unable to find.

[2] The birthplace of this Buddha (called by the Singhalese Konâgamana) was Sódhawati.

CHAPTER XXII.

FROM this spot going eastward less than a yôjana we arrive at the city of Ka-wei-lo-wei (Kapilavastu).[1] In this city there is no government or people, it is just like a great desert. There is simply a congregation of priests and about ten families of lay people. In the place where stand the ruins of the palace of Sudhôdana,[2] there is a picture of the Prince-apparent and his mother, (supposed to be) taken at the time of his miraculous conception.[3] The Prince is represented as descending towards his mother, riding on a white elephant. Towers have been erected on the following spots—where the royal Prince left the city by the Eastern gate,[4] where he saw the sick man, and where

[1] Ka-wai-lo-wei, evidently a mistake for Ka-pi-lo-wei, *i.e.* the city of Kapila (Kapilavastou), corresponding to the Mongolian Kabalik, and the Nepalese Kapilapúra. This city, which is the birthplace of Buddha, was situated about sixty miles adove Gorackpur on the river Rapti.

[2] Buddha's father.

[3] The fable relates that Bodhisatwa descended from the Tusita heaven, in the shape of a white elephant, surrounded by light like the sun, and entered the left side of his mother. But in the text he is described as descending *seated* on an elephant, which account seems far more natural. (*Vide* Lalita Vistara, p. 61, and also Life of Sakya Tathâgata, R.A.S. Journal, § 10.)

[4] This refers to the universally received account of Sakya's conversion. It may be read in extenso, in the Lalita Vistara, and Spence Hardy. In brief, the account states that Sakya had been carefully guarded by his father, and kept in a secluded palace, surrounded by every luxury. On

he caused his chariot to turn and take him back to his Palace. There are also towers erected on the following spots—at the place where the (Rishi) Asita[1] calculated the horoscope of the royal Prince; where Nanda[2] and the others struck the elephant and seized it; where the arrow[3] going south-east thirty li, entered the earth, from which bubbled up a fountain of water, which, in after

one occasion having gone out for a ride, he passed in succession an old man, a sick man, a dead man, and a Shaman. Being impressed by the sights, and convinced of the vanity of all earthly sources of happiness, he entered on a religious life (*vide* Life of Buddha, from the Chinese, § 31). This account of Sakya's conversion was so generally known and accepted in Europe in the Middle Ages, that in a work of Metaphrastus (technically known as "the Paradise"), a Christian writer of about the tenth century, this part of Sakya's history is referred to a Christian monarch of India known as Joasaph (*vide* The Paradise. Venice, 1856).

[1] In the original the name of this Rishi is A-i. He is probably the same as Asita mentioned in the Lalita Vistara (and Life of Buddha, from the Chinese, § 23). Having been summoned to predict the child's fortune, he declared from the marks on his person that he would become a supreme Buddha.

[2] The story referred to here, is this, "The royal Prince, with his cousin Nanda and his uncle Dêvadatta, leaving the grounds where some athletic sports had been held, Dêvadatta saw a great elephant standing in the gateway; hitting it with his fist he killed it. Then Nanda seeing the carcase lying in the road, seized it with his hand and dragged it on one side. Afterwards the royal Prince, passing by the carcase, raised it with one hand and hurled it outside the city walls, and where it fell it indented the earth so that the place was called the elephant dyke (Hastigarta) (Jul. ii. 313).

[3] "The royal Prince when he was fifteen years old contended with all the Sâkyas in athletic sports. He drew a bow and with one arrow perforated seven golden drums, and with another seven iron blocks. These arrows passing through the targets went in a south-east direction and stuck in the earth, from these spots two fountains of water gushed." Shing To, § 27.

generations, was used as a well for travellers to drink at; also on the spot where Buddha, after arriving at Supreme Wisdom, met his father;[1] where the five hundred Sâkyas,[2] having embraced the faith, paid reverence to Upâli; at the place where the earth shook six times in succession; at the place where Buddha expounded the Law on behalf of all the Dêvas, whilst the four Heavenly Kings guarded the four gates of the hall, so that his father could not enter; at the place where Mahâ Prajâpatî[3] presented Buddha with a Sañghâti[4] whilst he was sitting under a Nyagrôdha[5] tree, with his face to the East, which tree still exists; at the place where Viroûdhaka Râja killed the offspring of the Sâkyas,[6] who had previously entered on the path Srôtapânna. All these towers are still in existence. A few li to the north-east of the city is the royal field, where the Prince, sitting underneath a tree, watched a ploughing match. Fifty li to the east of the city is the royal garden, called Lumbinî;[7] it was here the Queen en-

[1] The account of this interview may be read (M. B. 200).

[2] *Vide* M. B. 309. The events named in the text may all be found in the Life of Buddha in Spence Hardy.

[3] Mahâ Prajâpatî, the aunt of Buddha, also called Gâutamî (Lal. Vistara).

[4] The Sañghâṭi, the cloak or mantle of the Buddhist priests.

[5] The trees in the Nyagrodha garden, near Kapilavastu (M.B. 200).

[6] Viroûdhakha carried away five hundred of the female Sâkyas, in order to introduce them into his harem. On their refusal to submit to such disgrace, they were cruelly mutilated and left to die. Whilst in this state they were able to believe in Buddha and attained the condition of Dêvas (Jul. ii. 307).

[7] The Lumbinî garden, situated between Kapila-vastu and Koli, to

tered the bath to wash herself, and having come out on the northern side, advanced twenty paces, and then holding a branch of the (Sala)[1] tree in her hand, brought forth the Prince. When born he walked seven[2] steps; two dragon Kings washed the Prince's body,—the place where this occurred was afterwards converted into a well, from which the priests draw their drinking water. All the Buddhas have four places universally determined for them: 1. The place for arriving at Supreme Wisdom; 2. The place[3] for turning the wheel of the Law; 3. The place for expounding the true principles of the Law, and refuting the heretics; 4. The place for descending to earth after going into the Triyastriñshas heaven to explain the Law to their mothers. With respect to other places, they are chosen according to the time when the several Buddhas come into the world. The country of Kapila-vastou is now a great desert, you seldom meet any people on the roads, for they are much in dread of the white elephants and the lions (which frequent the neighbourhood), and render it impossible to travel negligently. Going east five yôjanas from

which the inhabitants of both cities were accustomed to resort for recreation (M.B. 144).

[1] The Sâla tree, the *Shorea robusta.*

[2] All these particulars may be read in the several lives of Buddha already alluded to.

[3] To turn the wheel of the Law is a Buddhist expression, denoting the continuity and identity of all Buddhist doctrine.

the place where Buddha was born, there is a country called Lan-mo (Râmagrâma).[1]

[1] The distance here given between Kapilavastu and Râmagrâma, corresponds to the 200 li of Hiouen Thsang. This place is identical with Râmagamo of the Mahâwanso. In that work the relic tower of Râmagamo is spoken of as being on the banks of the Ganges, *i.e.* one of the affluents of the Ganges, most probably the small affluent above the Little Gandak River (*vide* Laidlay's Notes). I do not see, however, how Mr. Laidlay can refer this tower to the Gogra River.

CHAPTER XXIII.

THE King of this country obtained one share of the Relics of Buddha's body.[1] On his return home he built a tower (over these relics), which is the same as the Tower of Râmagrâma. By the side of it is a tank, in the middle of which resides a Dragon,[2] who constantly guards and protects the tower, and performs religious service in it, morning and night. When King Asôka was born (and came to the throne), he wished to destroy the eight towers (which had been erected over the different portions of the relics), and to build eighty-four thousand others (throughout the land). Having destroyed seven of them, he next proceeded to treat this one in the same way The Dragon therefore assumed a body,[3] and conducted the King within his abode, and having exhibited to him all the vessels and appliances he used in his religious services, he addressed the King, and said: "If you can excel me in these particulars, then you may destroy the tower, go and do so at once, I will have no quarrel with you." King Asôka, knowing that these vessels were of no

[1] The relics of Buddha after his cremation were divided into eight parts, and one part given to each of the eight claimants (*vide* M. B. 351).

[2] For another account of this fable, *vide* Jul. ii. 327.

[3] Namely that of a Brâhman (*vide* Jul. *ut supra*).

human workmanship, immediately returned to his home (without carrying his purpose into execution). In the midst of this (sacred spot) grass and weeds were allowed to grow. There was no one either to water it or sweep it; but ever and anon a herd of elephants, carrying water in their trunks, piously watered the ground, and also brought all sorts of flowers and perfumes to pay religious worship at the Tower. Buddhist pilgrims from all countries came here to pay their vows and worship at the shrine. On one occasion some of these (or, one of these) met the elephants, and being very much frightened, concealed themselves amongst the trees. They then saw the elephants perform their Service according to the Law. The disciples of Buddha on this were greatly affected. They grieved to think that in this sacred spot there was neither temple nor priests to perform religious service, so that the very elephants had to water and sweep it. On this they immediately gave up the great Precepts[1] of the lay disciple, and took upon them the vows[2] of a Sama-

[1] That is, the five great precepts which bind the lay disciples (*i.e.* the Upâsaka and Upâsikâwa). 1. Not to kill; 2. Not to commit adultery; 3. Not to steal; 4. Not to lie or slander; 5. Not to drink intoxicating drinks.

[2] The ten rules of the Novice (Shami or Shamini, *i.e.* Samaneras) require not only abstinence from adulterous intercourse, but strict celibacy. And besides the five mentioned above, 6. Not to use perfumery or flowers for ornament; 7. Not to witness theatrical performances; 8. Not to occupy a luxurious couch; 9. Not to eat at forbidden hours; 10. Not to possess money or precious goods. I need scarcely point to the confusion which M. Klaproth has introduced into this chapter, by supposing the text to refer to Tauist priests.

nera. They then began to pluck up the brushwood, and level the ground, and arrange the place so that it became neat and clean. They further stimulated the King of the country to help make residences for the priests. Moreover, they built a temple, in which priests still reside. From about the time when these things occurred there has been a regular succession of priests till now, only the Superior of the temple has always been a Samanera. Three yôjanas[1] east of this place is the spot where the royal Prince dismissed his charioteer Tchandaka[2] and the royal horse, previous to their return. Here also is erected a tower.

[1] Hiouen Thsang makes the distance one hundred li in the same direction. The two accounts therefore correspond. This distance and direction will place us immediately between the small affluent on which Ramagrâma stood and the Little Gandak River.

[2] The charioteer was called Chandaka and the horse Kanika. The common account states that the royal Prince travelled eight hundred li through the air on the night when he left his home, and on arriving at the Snowy Mountains he dismissed his charioteer saying, "Go now, return with the horse Kanika, difficult as the task has been you have accomplished it. Return home!" On this Chandaka filled with grief replied, "Who shall be my master now, returning alone to the Palace?" (Shing To, § 36.) (*Vide* also Jul. ii. 330.)

CHAPTER XXIV.

PROCEEDING eastward from this place four yôjanas[1] we arrive at the tower raised over the ashes selected after the burning of Buddha's body. Here also is a Saṅghârâma. Again advancing twelve yôjanas[2] to

[1] Hiouen Thsang makes the distance to this spot 180 li, which would nearly correspond with four yôjanas. According to him, however, the direction is S.E. instead of E.; and considering the situation of Kusinagara (Kasia) in the following section, this must have been the direction. His account is as follows: — "To the S.E. of the tower constructed on the spot where the royal Prince cut off his locks, after travelling over a wild country for 180 or 190 li, we arrive at a wood of Nyagrôdha trees. Here there is a tower of about thirty feet in height. After the Nirvâṇa of Buddha, when his relics were divided, the Brâhmans having received none, went to the place of the cremation and collected the ashes and cinders, and having brought them to their place, they built this tower over them. Wonderful miracles of healing are wrought by their efficacy" (Jul. ii. 332). This fable is also found in the Lalita Vistara, p. 425.

[2] This distance is a misprint in the original, derived either from the previous twelve yôjanas recorded from Kapilavastu, or else from the same distance mentioned subsequently. Hiouen Thsang places Kusinagara to the N.E. of the "Tower of the Ashes," but records no distance. He merely mentions a dangerous and difficult forest through which he travelled (Jul. ii. 333). But in the Life of Hiouen Thsang it is said that the kingdom of Kusinagara borders on the forest, which extends for one hundred li to the east of Ramâgrama (Jul. i. 130). I have failed, however, to verify the statement of M. V. St. Martin, that Hiouen Thsang repeats his account of the "Tower of the Ashes" in his list of buildings near Kusinagara (*vide* Jul. iii. 357 *n*). The site of the city of Kusinagara has been identified by Cunningham and others, with that of a village called Kasia, thirty-five miles to the east of Goruekpúr, on the borders of the Little Gandak River. V. St. Martin places it fifty miles S.E. of Goruckpúr (Jul. iii. 358), and only two or three li from the Tower of Ashes.

the eastward we arrive at the town of Kusinagara. To the north of this town, on the place where the world-honoured Buddha, lying by the side of the Hiraṇyavatî River,[1] with his head to the North, and a Sal tree on either side of him, entered Nirvâṇa. Also in the place where Subhadra[2] was converted, the very last of all his disciples. Also where, for seven days, they paid reverence to the world-honoured Buddha, lying in his golden coffin.[3] Also where Vajrapâṇi threw down his golden mace, and where the eight kings divided the relics; in each of the above places towers have been raised and Sanghârâmas built, which still exist. In this city also there are but few inhabitants; such families as there are are connected with the resident congregation of priests. Going south-east[4] twelve yôjanas from this place we arrive at the spot where all the Litchavas,[5] desiring to follow Buddha to

[1] Otherwise called the Adjitavatî, identical with the Little Gandak River.

[2] Subhadra was an old Brahman, aged eighty-one, and was the last convert of Buddha previous to his Nirvâṇa (Jul. ii. 339).

[3] For an account of Buddha's death, see Spence Hardy (M.B. 352) and (Jul. ii. 340).

[4] Laidlay has by mistake translated the French S.W. instead of S.E. But the French editors have also mistranslated the distance, which is twelve yôjanas and not twenty. We have thus nineteen yôjanas between Kusinagara (Kasia) and Vâisâlî (Besarh), which is as nearly correct as possible.

[5] The Litchavas or Lichawi princes, were residents of Vâisâlî, who founded that city and shared its government (M. B. 235 *n.*). The city of Vâisâlî is mentioned in the following section. In the time of Buddha

the scene of his Nirvâṇa, were forbidden to do so. On account of their great affection to Buddha they were unwilling to go back, on which Buddha caused to appear between them and him a great and deeply-scarped river, which they could not cross. He then left with them his alms-bowl as a memorial, and exhorted them to return to their houses. On this they went back and erected a stone pillar, on which they engraved an inscription (to the above effect).

there were 7707 of these Litchavas, resident in Vâisâlî, and each in his separate palace. The translation I here give differs widely from the French.

CHAPTER XXV.

GOING eastward from this spot five yôjanas we arrive at the country of Vâisâlî.[1] To the north of the city of this name (or, to the North of the capital city of Vâisâlî) there is the Vihâra of the great forest[2] (Mahâvana Vihâra) which has a double tower[3] (or a tower of two stories). This chapel was once occupied by Buddha.[4] Here also is the tower which was built over half the body of Ânanda.[5] Within this city dwelt Âmradârikâ,[6] who built a tower in honour of Buddha, the ruins of which still exist. Three li to the south of the city, on the west side of the road, is the garden which Âmradârikâ presented to Buddha as a

[1] Vâisâlî, a very famous city in the Buddhist Records. Cunningham identifies it with the present Besarh, twenty miles north of Hajipûr.

[2] This chapel was situated in the neighbourhood of the present village of Bakhra, about two miles N.N.W. of Besarh. It is alluded to in the Singhalese Records as the Mahâvano Vihâro. From Burnouf we find it was built by the side of a Tank known as the Markaṭa-hrada, or Monkey Tank (Introd. to Indian Bud., p. 74) (M. B. 356).

[3] This tower is called by Burnouf the Kutâgâra Hall, *i.e.* Upper Storied Hall.

[4] Namely, during the fifth year of his teaching.

[5] *Vide* Chap. 26.

[6] That is the daughter of the âmra or mango tree. There are two fables connected with the miraculous birth of this female from the tree (*vide* Jul. ii. 388 *n.*). The garden which she presented to Buddha is called the Âmravana. She is also called Ambapâli (M.B. 456).

place for him to rest in. When Buddha was about to enter Nirvâṇa, accompanied by his disciples, he left Vâisâlî by the western gate, and turning his body to the right as a token of respect[1] (Pradakshaṇa) he beheld the city and thus addressed his followers:—"In this place I have performed the last religious act of my earthly career." Men afterwards raised a Tower on this spot. Three li to the north-west of the city is a tower called "the tower of the deposited bows and clubs." The origin of this name was as follows:—On one of the superior affluents of the river Ganges there was a certain country ruled by a king. One of the concubines of this monarch gave birth to an unformed fœtus, whereupon the wife of the king, being filled with jealousy, said, "Your conception is one of very bad omen."[2] So they immediately closed it up in a box of wood and cast it into the middle of the Ganges. Lower down the stream there was a certain Râjah, who, as he was taking a tour of observation, caught sight of the wooden box as it floated on the surface of the stream. On bringing it to the shore and opening it, to see what was inside, he beheld a thousand little children very fair and just of a size. The king hereupon took them and brought them up.

[1] So I would translate the passage, although Mr. Laidlay has an ingenious note on the subject. Turning to the right in token of respect is a well-known Buddhist custom (Jul. iii. 554).

[2] This absurd legend is otherwise given by S. Hardy, but the account is equally monstrous (M.B. 235 *n.*).

Afterwards, when they grew up, they turned out to be very brave and warlike, and were victorious over all whom they went to attack. In process of time they marched against the kingdom of the monarch, their father. The king was filled with great consternation in anticipation of their approach. On this his concubine asked the Râjah why he was so terrified, to whom he replied, "The king of that country has a thousand sons, brave and warlike beyond compare, and these are coming to waste my territories, this is why I am alarmed." To this the concubine replied, "Fear not! but erect on the east of the city a high tower, and when the robbers come, place me on the top of it, and I will restrain them." The king did as she requested, and when the invaders arrived the concubine, from the top of the tower, addressed them, saying, "Are you my children all? Then why are you engaged in such rebellious acts as these?" They replied, "Who are you, that say you are our mother?" The concubine replied, "If ye will not believe me, all of you look up towards me, and open your mouths." On this the concubine, with both her hands, compressed her breasts, and from each breast forthwith proceeded five hundred jets of milk, which fell into the mouths of her thousand sons. On this the robbers, perceiving that she was indeed their mother, immediately laid down their bows and clubs. The two royal fathers, by a consideration of these circumstances, were able to arrive at the condition of Pratyêka Buddhas, and two Towers, erected in their honour, remain to the present day. In after times, when the world-honoured Buddha arrived at Supreme Reason, he addressed all his disciples in these words, and said, "This is the place where I formerly laid aside my bow and my club." Men in after times, coming to know this, founded a Tower in this place, and hence the name given to it. The thousand young children are in truth the thousand Buddhas of this Bhâdra Kalpa. Buddha, when standing beside this tower, addressed Ânanda in these words, "After three months I must enter Nirvâṇa," on which occasion Mâra Râja so fascinated the mind of Ânâṇda that he did not request Buddha to remain in the world.[1] Going east from this point three or four li there is a tower. One hundred years[2] after the Nirvâṇa of Buddha there were at Vâisâlî certain Bikshus who violated the rules of the Vinaya by their conduct, in ten particulars, justifying themselves by saying

[1] Had he done so we are required to believe that Buddha would not have died.

[2] This refers to the second great Council of the Buddhist church. According to Singhalese authorities (Mahawanso) there were three great convocations or councils: 1. At Râjagriha, immediately after Buddha's death, to compile the authorised Scriptures; 2. At Vâisâlî, under Kalâsoka, to refute certain errors that had crept into the church; 3. Under the Great Asôka (Dharmâsoka), at Pataliputra. But the northern accounts know nothing of the first Asôka, but place the second council at Vâisâlî, under Asôka (Dharmâsokha), and the third they refer to the time of Kanishka, 400 years after the Nirvâṇa.

that Buddha had said "thus it was,"[1] at which time all the Rahats and the orthodox Bikshus, making an assembly of seven hundred ecclesiastics and more, compared and collated the Vinaya Pitaka afresh. Afterwards men erected a tower on this spot, which still exists.

[1] This alludes to the well-known phrase, used to indicate the true words of Buddha, "Thus (ju shi) have I heard" (evam mayá śrutam).

CHAPTER XXVI.

GOING four yôjanas east[1] of this, we arrive at the confluence of the five rivers. When Ânanda was going from the country of Magadha towards Vâisâlî, desiring to enter Nirvâṇa, all the Dêvas acquainted king Ajâsat[2] of it. The king immediately placed himself at the head of his troops, set out after him and arrived at (or, towards) the banks of the river. All the Litchhavas of Vâisâlî, hearing that Ânanda was coming, likewise set out to meet him and arrived at the side of the river. Ânanda then reflected that if he were to advance, king Ajâsat would be much grieved, and if he should go back, then the Litchhavas would be indignant. Being perplexed he forthwith entered the Samâdhi,[3] called the "brilliancy of flame," consuming his body, and entered

[1] My copy of the original says "going east," yet as this is omitted in the French version, it is possible mine is wrong. Certainly the direction from Vâisâlî to the confluence of the rivers near Patna, would rather be south than east.

[2] That is Ajâtasatru, the son of Bimbasâra, king of Magadha, the country south of the river Ganges, now called Behar. According to Hindoo records he flourished about 250 years before Chandragupta, *i.e.* B.C. 560.

[3] Samâdhi is a state of complete ecstasy, in which the soul, or spiritual portion of the agent, is wrapt away from the body, and assumes a condition corresponding to the character of the ecstacy enjoyed. Here the Samâdhi is called that of "Fire" (Agnidhâtou).

Nirvâṇa in the very midst of the river. His body was divided into two parts, one part was found on either side of the river, so the two kings, each taking the relics of half his body, returned and erected towers over them.

CHAPTER XXVII.

CROSSING the river, and proceeding towards the south one yôjana, we arrive at Magadha, and the town of Pa-lin-fou (Patna).[1] This is the town in which king Asôka reigned. In the middle of the city is the royal palace, the different parts of which he commissioned the genii (demons) to construct. The massive stones of which the walls are made, the doorways and the sculptured towers, are no human work. The ruins of this palace still exist. The younger brother[2] of king Asôka having arrived at the dignity of a Rahat, was in the habit of residing in the hill Khi-chi-kiu[3] (Gridhrakûta), finding his chief delight in silent contemplation.

[1] This is the Παλιμβοθρα of Arrian (Indica), which he places in the territories of the Prasii (Vrijjis ?), and just at the junction of the Erranoboas with the Ganges. Taking the former river to represent the Sône, and bearing in mind that the mouth of the Sône is now some twenty miles to the west of its former course (V. St. Martin, Jul. iii. 372, *n.*), the position of the modern Patna will correspond with the ancient town. This city, which is otherwise called Kusumapûra (the city of flowers), was not in existence in Buddha's time: there was, however, a small fort erected on the site, to check the encroachments of the Litchhavas of Vâisâlî; and in the interval between Buddha's death and the arrival of the Greek embassy to Chandragupta under Megasthenes, this fort had increased into a vast and important city (μεγιστη δε πολις Ινδοισιν εστι Παλιμβοθρα).

[2] Referring probably to Mahêndra, who became the celebrated apostle of Buddhism to Ceylon. In the Singhalese records he is indeed spoken of as the son of Asôka; but as Hiouen Thsang expressly designates him Mo-hi-in-to-lo, there can be no doubt of the allusion.

[3] The Vulture's Peak,—will be mentioned again in Chap. 29.

The king, having a great regard and reverence for his brother, requested him to come to his house to receive (or present) his religious offerings. His brother, pleased with his tranquility in the mountain, declined the invitation. The king then addressed his brother, saying, "If you will only accept my invitation, I will make for you a hill within the city." The king then, providing all sorts of meat and drink, invited the Genii to come, addressing them thus, "I beg you all to accept my invitation for to-morrow, but as there are no seats (fit for you), I must request you each to bring his own." On the morrow all the great Genii came, each one bringing with him a great stone, four or five paces square. Immediately after the feast (the session), he deputed the Genii to pile up the great stones and make a mountain of them, and at the base of the mountain with five great square stones to make a Rock chamber, in length about thirty-five feet and in breadth twenty-two feet, and in height eleven feet or so.

In this city (*i.e.* of Pâṭalipoutra or Patna) once lived a certain Brâhman,[1] called Lo-tai-sz-pi-mi,[2] of large mind and extensive knowledge, and attached

[1] This passage is obscure in consequence of the uncertainty of the time when this celebrated Brâhman (*i.e.* a disciple, who had been a Brâhman) lived. Most probably Fah Hian alludes to him, as then existing, and in more than one respect his description agrees with the account we have of Buddha Ghôsa, the celebrated translator of the Singhalese Buddhist Scriptures into Pali, who certainly must have been living, probably at Patna, at the time when Fah Hian visited the place.

[2] I can offer no very satisfactory opinion as to the correct restoration of this name. It may be, perhaps, Artâ Svâmin, that is, as we should now say, Chief Pandit.

to the Great Vehicle. There was nothing with which he was unacquainted, and he lived apart occupied in silent meditation. The King of the country honoured and respected him, as his religious superior (Guru). If he went to salute him he did not dare to sit down in his presence. If the King, from a feeling of affectionate esteem, took him by the hand, the Brahman immediately washed himself from head to foot. For something like fifty years the whole country looked up to this man and placed its confidence on him alone. He mightily extended the influence of the Law of Buddha, so that the heretics were unable to obtain any advantage at all over the priesthood.

By the side of the tower of king Asôka is built a Sañghârâma belonging to the Greater Vehicle, very imposing and elegant. There is also a Temple belonging to the Little Vehicle. Together they contain about six or seven hundred priests, all of them exceedingly well conducted. In the College attached to the temple one may see eminent Shamans from every quarter of the world, and whatever scholars there are who seek for instruction, they all flock to this temple. The Brahman teacher[1] (of whom we have just spoken) is also called Mañjusrî.[2] The great Shamans of the

[1] The French version renders this passage "The masters of the sons of Brahmans are called also Manjusri;" but I conceive the translation I have adopted is borne out by the text, and is certainly more natural.

[2] Mañjusrî, as before explained, is a semi-historical character. If in the text the reference is to some great Teacher who lived in former times,

country, and all the Bikshus attached to the Great Vehicle, universally esteem and reverence him; moreover he resides in this Sañghârâma. Of all the kingdoms of mid-India, the towns of this country are especially large. The people are rich and prosperous and virtuous. Every year on the eighth day of the second month there is a procession of Images. On this occasion, they construct a four-wheeled car, and erect upon it a tower of five stages, composed of bamboos lashed together, the whole being supported by a centre post resembling a large spear with three points, in height twenty-two feet and more. So it resembles a Pagoda. They then cover it over with fine white linen, on which they afterwards paint all sorts of gaily-coloured pictures. Having made figures of all the Dêvas, and decorated them with gold, silver, and coloured glass (lapis lazuli), they place them under canopies of embroidered silk. Then at the four corners (of the car) they construct niches (shrines) in which they place figures of Buddha, in a sitting posture, with a Bôdhisatwa standing in attendance. There are perhaps twenty cars thus prepared, and decorated each one differently from the rest. During the day of the procession, both priests and laymen assemble in great numbers. There are all sorts of games and amusements (for the latter), whilst the former offer flowers and

i.e. before Fah Hian, then, it may be, this person was the original bearer of the name, and the source of many stories related of Mañjusrî, the Apostle of Nipal and Thibet.

incense in religious worship. The Bramachârîs (sons or disciples of Brâhmans) come forth to salute Buddha, and one after the other the cars enter the city. After coming into the town they take up their several positions. Then all night long the people burn lamps,[1] indulge in games, and make religious offerings. Such is the custom of all those who assemble on this occasion from the different countries round about. The respective nobles and landowners of this country have founded hospitals within the city,[2] to which the poor of all countries, the destitute, cripples, and the diseased, may repair (for shelter). They receive every kind of requisite help gratuitously. Physicians inspect their diseases, and according to their cases order them food and drink, medicine or decoctions, every thing in fact that may contribute to their ease. When cured they depart at their own convenience. King Asôka having destroyed seven (of the original) pagodas, constructed 84,000 others.[3] The very first which he built is the great tower which stands about three li to the south

[1] From the whole of this account, it would seem that the Buddhist worship had already begun to degenerate from its primitive simplicity and severity. Plays, and music and concerts are strictly forbidden by the rules of the Order. We can begin to see how Buddhism lapsed into Sivite worship, and finally into the horrors of Jaganâth.

[2] They were probably first instituted by Asôka, as we read in the Edicts, and their existence in this city of Asôka is therefore only natural. These hospitals are distinctively Buddhist. The hospices founded by Brahmans were houses of shelter and entertainment for travellers, rather than places for the restoration of the sick.

[3] The number here spoken of is of course conventional. Buddhists say

of this city. In front of this pagoda is an impression of Buddha's foot, (over which) they have raised a chapel, the gate of which faces the north. To the south of the tower is a stone pillar, about a chang and a half in girth (eighteen feet),[1] and three chang or so in height (thirty-five feet). On the surface of this pillar is an inscription to the following effect,[2] "King Asôka presented the whole of Jambudwîpa to the priests of the Four Quarters, and redeemed it again with money, and this he did four times." Three or four hundred paces

there are 84,000 sources of sin or trouble in the world, and 84,000 methods of salvation. With respect to the erection of these pagodas the Chinese account is this, "One hundred years after the division of the relics, there arose an iron-wheel king called Asoka (a-yu). He was the grandson of A-che-si (Ajâtasatru) (sic). He erected all the stûpas of the five Indies. He moreover took the relics from the Dragon Palaces. He then commissioned the king of the demons to take small fragments of the seven precious substances and in one night to perfect 84,000 stûpas. This was done. There was a Rahat called Yasna, who, spreading out his five fingers like the spokes of a wheel, scattered rays of light from their points in 84,000 directions, and who ordered the flying demons (Yakshas) each one to follow a ray, and erect a stupa wherever it alighted, and so throughout Jambudwîpa were they constructed" (Life of Buddha, § 170). It has been conjectured that the allusion in the latter portion of this account is to the discovery of the art of writing, and the consequent edicts which were issued. The rays of light from the fingers of Yasna, might easily be supposed to refer to the vowels used in the Edict character.

[1] The French version gives "four or five chang in circumference," mistaking the mode of Chinese notation.

[2] Hiouen Thsang speaks of this inscription (Jul. ii. 423). He states that in his time it was incomplete and mutilated. The purport of it was this, "King Asôka, gifted with invincible faith, has given thrice the whole of Jambudwîpa to Buddha, the Law and the Assembly, and three times has redeemed it with all the valuable property in his possession."

to the north of the pagoda is the spot where Asôka was born (or resided). On this spot he raised the city of Ni-lâi,[1] and in the midst of it erected a stone pillar also about thirty-five feet in height, on the top of which he placed the figure of a lion, and also engraved an historical record on the front of the pillar, giving an account of the successive events connected with the city of Ni-lâi, with the corresponding year, day, and month.

[1] The town of Nâla (mentioned in the Singhalese Annals) is situated to the S.E. of the gates of Pâṭaliputra (V. St. Martin, 383 *n.*).

CHAPTER XXVIII.

From this city, proceeding in a south-easterly[1] direction nine yôjanas, we arrive at a small rocky hill[2] standing by itself, on the top of which is a stone cell facing the south. On one occasion, when Buddha was sitting in the middle of this cell, the Divine Sekra took with him his attendant musicians, each one provided with a five stringed lute, and caused them to

[1] Mr. Laidley has south-west, by mistake.

[2] This isolated rock is mentioned by Hiouen Thsang, and called In-to-lo-chi-lo-kiu-ho, *i.e.* Indrasilâguhâ, "the cave of the stone of Indra." It has been identified with a peak now called Giryek (giri + eka, one rock) (Cunningham). There are numerous remains of Buddhist temples in the neighbourhood. In order to understand the general appearance of this celebrated neighbourhood, I here quote from the Report of the Archæological Surveyor to the Government of India (1861-62, p. 6), "From the neighbourhood of Gaya two parallel ranges of hills stretch towards the N.E. for about thirty-six miles to the bank of the Panchâna river, just opposite the village of Giryek. The eastern end of the southern range is much depressed, but the northern range maintains its height, and ends abruptly in two lofty peaks, overhanging the Panchâna river. The lower peak on the east is crowned with a solid tower of brick work, well known as Jara-sandha-ka-baithak, *i.e.* "Jarasandha's throne," while the higher peak on the west, to which the name of Giryek peculiarly belongs, bears an oblong terrace covered with the ruins of several buildings. The principal building would appear to have been a Vihâra, or temple, on the highest point of the terrace, which was approached by a steep flight of steps leading through pillared rooms." This latter peak is the one named in the text, the former is spoken of by Hiouen Thsang, as the site of a Stûpa built in honor of a Wild Goose (Jul. iii. 61).

sound a strain in the place where Buddha was seated. Then the divine Sekra proposed forty-two questions to Buddha, writing each one of them singly with his finger upon a stone. The traces of these questions yet exist. There is also a Sanghârâma[1] built upon this spot. Going south-west from this one yôjana we arrive at the village of Na-lo.[2] This was the place of Sâriputra's birth. Sâriputra returned here to enter Nirvâṇa. A tower therefore was erected on this spot, which is still in existence. Going west from this one yojâna we arrive at the New Râjgariha.[3] This was

[1] This allusion is probably to the Sanghârâma built on the neighbouring peak, and afterwards called the Hansa Sanghârâma, *i.e.* the Wild Goose convent.

[2] Otherwise called Nâlandagrâma. It was near this village, which has been identified with the present Baragaon (Baragong sc. Vihâragrâma), that the celebrated convent of Nâlanda was constructed. Hiouen Thsang dwelt five years in this magnificent establishment, where every day a hnndred professors elucidated the principles of Buddhist philosophy to thousands of hearers. Hiouen Thsang (i. 143) makes Nâlandagrâma the birth place of Mâudgalyâyana (Mogalan), and he speaks of a country or town called Kâlapinâka as the birth place of Sâriputra (Jul. iii. 54.). In a subsequent account Hiouen Thsang speaks of a village called Kulika as the birth place of Mogalan (Jul. iii. 51). We may therefore assume that Kulika and Nâlandagrâma are different names of the same place. It is probable that Fah Hian confused the birth place of Sâriputra with that of Mâudgalyâyana.

[3] This town is called New Râjagriha to distinguish it from the old town of the same name. It is said to have been built by king Srenika, or Bimbasara, the father of Ajâsat. The Archæological Surveyor of India, in his account of this place, makes its circuit somewhat less than three miles; it was built in the form of an irregular pentagon, with one long side and four shorter ones (Report, 1861, p. 9). It is a town celebrated in Buddhist history, and close to the scene of Buddha's complete inspiration. At present there is on the site a village retaining the name of Radjgir, about fifteen miles S.W. of the town of Behar.

the town which king Ajâsat built. There are two Sanghârâmas in it. Leaving this town by the West gate, and proceeding 300 paces, (we arrive at) the tower which King Ajâsat raised over the share of Buddha's relics which he obtained. Its height is very imposing. Leaving the south side of the city, and proceeding southwards four li, we enter a valley situated between five hills[1] (or, we enter a valley that leads to (a space) between five hills). These hills encircle it completely like the walls of a town. This is the site of the old town[2] of King Bimbasara. From east to west[3] it is about five or six li, from north to south seven or eight li. Here Sâriputra[4] and Mogalan first met Asvajit. Here also the Nirgrantha[5] made a pit with fire in it, and poisoned the food, of which he invited Buddha

[1] These five hills, which surrounded the old city of Râdjagriha (or, as it was also called Kusâgârapura, *i.e.* the city of the Kusa grass) are very celebrated ones; in the Mahâbhârata they are called Vaihâra, Varâha, Vrishabha, Rishigiri, and Ghaityaka. They are at present named Baibhrâ-giri, Vipula-giri, Ratna-giri, Udaya-giri, and Sona-giri.

[2] That is, the old Râjagriha, or Kusâgârapura. Hiọuen Thsang speaks of this city as encompassed by hills, which form as it were an outer wall to it. These hills represent a circuit of about ten miles (Arch. Surv.). The site of the old town is now called Hansu Tanr (Kitto).

[3] These figures would make the circuit of the city about four and one-third miles.

[4] For an account of this interview see chapter xvi.

[5] The Nirgranthas were ascetics who went naked. The one alluded to here was called Srîgupta (Jul. iii. 18). His object was to cause Buddha to fall into the pit, which was lightly covered over; but instead of that, when Buddha approached, the fire was extinguished, and the pit filled with water.

to partake. Here also is the spot where King Ajâsat, intoxicating a black elephant,[1] desired to destroy Buddha. To the north-east of the city, in the middle of a crooked defile, (the physician) Djîvaka[2] (Ki Kau) erected a Vihâra in the garden of Ambapâlî,[3] and invited Buddha and his 1250 disciples to receive her religious offerings. The ruins[4] still exist. Within the city all is desolate, and without inhabitants.

[1] This crime is generally ascribed to Dêvadatta and not to Ajâsat.

[2] Called by Hiouen Thsang Chi-po-kia. He is referred to (Lotus, 450) and (E.M. 116).

[3] Also called Âmradârikâ. She was a very beautiful female, but a courtezan (M.B. 457). Buddha, however, honored her with his presence at a feast she prepared for him, and also accepted the Amravana garden from her (Chapter 25).

[4] The whole of the context differs from the French version.

CHAPTER XXIX.

Entering the valley, and skirting the mountains along their south-eastern slope for a distance of fifteen li, we arrive at the hill called Gridhrakôuṭa[1] (Ki-che-kiu). Three li from the top is a stone cavern facing the south. Buddha used in this place to sit in profound meditation (dhyâna). Thirty paces to the north-west is another stone cell, in which Ânanda practiced meditation (dhyâna). The Dêva Mâra Pâpîyan[2] having assumed the form of a vulture, took his station before the cavern, and terrified Ânanda. Buddha, by his spiritual power (of Irrdhi), penetrated the rock, and with his outspread hand touched[3] the head of Ânanda. On this he bore up against his fear, and found peace. The traces of the bird and of the hand-hole still plainly exist, and from this circumstance the hill is called

[1] That is the Vulture-peak, or, the peak of the vultures, called in the Pali books Ghedjhakato. The translation I have given of the Text may be questionable. It is, however, in agreement with Hiouen Thsang, who places the Vulture-peak N.E. of the city (Jul. i. 154).

[2] Pâpîyan, another name for Mâra, the supreme ruler of the world of desires (Kamâdhâtu). Mâra means "death," and Pâpîyan, "the very wicked one."

[3] I here translate "ma," by "touched the head," and "kin" (the shoulder) by "able to bear." It may, however, be rendered, "touched the shoulder of Ânanda, on which his fear was immediately allayed."

"the hill of the vulture cave" (Gridhrakôuṭa). In front of the cave are spots where each of the four Buddhas sat down. Each of the Arhats likewise has a cave (in this neighbourhood) celebrated as the place where he practiced meditation (sat in meditation (dhyâna)). Altogether there are several hundreds of these. Here is the place where, during the lifetime of Buddha, when he was walking to and fro, from east to west, in front of his cell, Dêvadatta, standing on the mountain between the northern eminences, rolled down athwart his path a stone which wounded a toe of Buddha's foot. The stone[1] is still there. The hall[2] in which Buddha delivered the law has been overturned and destroyed; the foundations of the brick walls still exist however. The peaks of this mountain are picturesque and imposing; it is the loftiest one of the five mountains that surround the town. Fah Hian having bought flowers, incense, and oil and lamps, in the New Town, procured the assistance of two aged Bikshus to accompany him to the top of the peak. Having arrived there, he offered his flowers and incense, and lit his lamps, so that their combined lustre illuminated the gloom of the cave. Fah Hian was deeply moved, even till the tears coursed down his cheeks, and he said, "Here

[1] Hiouen Thsang gives the height of this rock fourteen or fifteen feet, and the girth thirty paces.

[2] In this Hall, which was built on the western slope of the mountain, Buddha is represented as having delivered some of his most important discourses.

it was in bygone days Buddha dwelt, and delivered the Surañgama Sutra.[1] Fah Hian, not privileged to be born at a time when Buddha lived, can but gaze on the traces of his presence, and the place which he occupied." Then taking his position in front of the cave, he recited the Surañgama (Sutra), and remained there the entire night.

[1] The Surañgama Sutra, called in Chinese the Shau-Leng-yen Sutra, is one most highly esteemed amongst them. Its doctrines and arguments were highly commended by the celebrated Choo-foo-tsze. It is a voluminous work, in ten volumes, containing an elaborate argument to prove the existence of an inward faculty (alâya) corresponding somewhat to our idea of the "soul." It also contains the celebrated Dhâranîs used by the priests in their worship. A translation of this Sutra is much to be desired.

CHAPTER XXX.

Returning towards the New city, after passing through the Old town, and going more than 300 paces[1] to the north, on the west side of the road, we arrive at the Kalandavênouvána Vihâra[2] (the chapel in the Bamboo garden of Kalanda). This chapel still exists, and a congregation of priests sweep and water it. Two or three li to the north of the chapel is the Shi-mo-she-na[3] (Samasana) which signifies "the field of tombs for laying the dead." Skirting the southern hill,[4] and proceeding westward 300 paces, there is a stone cell called the Pipal cave,[5] where Buddha was accustomed

1 About 250 yards, or the seventh of a mile. Hiouen Thsang gives the distance one li.

2 Called by the Singhalese writers Wéluwana (venouvana, *i.e.* bamboo garden). According to the legend, a squirrel (Kalanda) having saved the life of a king of Vâisâlî, who was asleep in this wood, by chirping, in his ear when a snake was approaching, the king made a decree that no one in his dominions should kill a squirrel on pain of death, and also that the squirrels in this garden should be regularly supplied with food (M.B. 194). There was a rich householder living in this neighbourhood, to whom the name of Kalanda was given, and he built the Vihâra and presented it to Buddha (Jul. iii. 30). Some of Buddha's most celebrated discourses were delivered here. It is also stated that king Bimbasara gave it to Buddha (M.B. 194).

3 The word S'amas'ana (श्मशान) signifies "cemetery."

4 I have translated it thus, contrary to the French version, which would take us across the mountain.

5 In the original Pin-po-lo, rendered "Pipal cave" by Jul. iii. 24.

to sit in deep meditation (dhyâna) after his mid-day meal. Going still in a westerly direction five or six li, there is a stone cave situated in the northern shade of the mountain, and called Che-ti.[1] This is the place where 500 Rahats assembled after the Nirvâṇa of Buddha to arrange the collection of sacred books. At the time when the books were recited, three vacant seats were specially prepared and adorned. The one on the left was for Sâriputra, the one on the right for Maudgalyâyana. The assembly was yet short of 500 by one Rahat; and already the great Kâsyapa was ascending the throne, when Ânanda stood without the gate unable to find admission;[2] on this spot they have raised a tower, which still exists. Still skirting the mountain we find very many other stone cells used by all the Rahats for the purpose of meditation. Leaving the old city and going N.E. three li we arrive at the stone cell of Dêvadatta,[3] fifty paces from which there is a great square black stone. Some time ago, there was a Bikshu who spent his time in walking forward and backward on this stone meditating on the imperma-

[1] This is plainly the Sattapanni cave of the Mahawanso, where the first great Convocation was held. I do not know on what authority it is stated (Archæolog. Survey, 1861-62, p. 8) that this cave was situated on the southern face of Mount Bhaibâra. It is plain both from this account and also from Hiouen Thsang's description, that the cave was on the northern face, in the shade.

[2] Having succeeded in attaining the condition of a Rahat (for a full account of this incident, *vide* Jul. iii. 33).

[3] That is, where Dêvadatta practised meditation (Jul. iii. 27).

nency, the sorrow, and vanity of his present life. Arriving thus at an unsound state of mind, disgusted at the sorrows of life, he drew his knife, and would have killed himself. But then he reflected that the world-honoured Buddha had forbidden[1] self-murder in the precepts left for his followers. But then again he thought "although that is so, yet I am simply anxious to destroy the three miseries that rob (me of my rightful enjoyment) (*i.e.* raga, dwesa, moha—evil desire, hatred, ignorance). Then again he drew his knife and inflicted a wound upon himself (cut his throat). On the first gash he obtained the degree of Su-to-un (Sowan); when he had half done the work he arrived at the condition of A-na-hom (Anagami); and after completing the deed he obtained the position of a Rahat, and entered Nirvâṇa.

[1] Namely, in the Pratimoksha. The third rule of the Parajika section (*vide* Translation from Chinese R.A.S. Journal). With reference to the remark of Mr. Laidlay, "that the practice of self-immolation ascribed by the Greek historians to the Buddhists, was, like that of going naked, a departure from orthodox principles." I doubt very much whether there is any reference to Buddhists in the Greek accounts.

CHAPTER XXXI.

Going west from this four yôjanas we arrive at the town of Gayâ.[1] All within this city likewise is desolate and desert. Going south twenty li, we arrive at the place where Bôdhisatwa, when alive, passed six years[2] in self-inflicted austerities. This place is well wooded. From this spot, proceeding westward[3] three

[1] The town of Gayâ, near which Buddha arrived at complete enlightenment, is situated on the west or left side of the river Phalgou. "It is commonly known now as 'the old town,' to distinguish it from a modern suburb, called Sahebgandj, or Sahîbgrâma, that is, the Sahib's village, because it was constructed by an English resident" (V. St. M.) It is ordinarily stated, however, that there are two Gayâs, viz., Buddha Gayâ, and the present town of Gayâ, the latter being six miles north of the former (C.) But we may take for granted that what is called Buddha Gayâ is but the scene of ruin of the numerous sacred buildings which at one time flourished here, and that the town of Gayâ is in fact the very town which Fah Hian visited. It is built on the N.E. extremity of a mountain known in the legends as Gayâsiras, the present Gayâsir, or as Hiouen Thsang calls it the mountain of Gayâ, or the divine mountain. On the summit of this hill Asôka erected a tower, one hundred feet in height. At the base of this mountain, and between it and the river is built the village of the Sahîb.

[2] This is the valley to the east of the village of Ourouvilva (urú, great, and welyáyâ, sands (Turnour, Mahav. lxvi.), where Bôdhisatwa practised the most severe austerities for six years. It borders on the river Nairañjânâ (the upper portion of the Phalgou) and is described as a delightful retreat (Lalita Vistara). It is called the forest of Uruwela in the Pali accounts (M.B. 164).

[3] If Buddha bathed in the Nairañjânâ, one would think that it should be eastward from Ourouvilva.

li, we arrive at the spot[1] where Buddha, entering the water to bathe himself, the Dêva held out the branch of a tree to him to assist him in coming out of the water.[2] Again, going north two li, we arrive at the place where the village girls[3] gave the milk and rice to Buddha. From this, going north two li, is the spot where Buddha, seated on a stone under a great tree, and looking towards the east,[4] eat the rice and milk. Both the tree and the stone remain to the present day. The stone is about six feet square, and two in height. In mid-India the heat and cold are so equalized that trees will live for thousands of years, and even so many as ten thousand. Going north-east from this half a yôjana, we arrive at a stone cell,[5] into which Bôdhi-

[1] This spot is called Supratishtita (M.B. 168).

[2] The ordinary account is "bathing himself in the Nairañjânâ river all the Dêvas waited on him with flowers and perfumes, and threw them into the midst of the river. After he had bathed, a tree-deva, holding down a branch as with a hand, assisted Bôdhisatwa to come out of the water" (Shing To, § 45).

[3] The legend states that Bôdhisatwa having failed to arrive at complete wisdom by the practice of six years mortifications, resolved to relax his austerities. He therefore received the rice and milk which the two daughters of Sújâta, the lord of the village (of Ourouvilva), offered him. These damsels are named in Burnouf's account, Nandâ and Nandabalâ, but elsewhere Trapusha and Bhallikâ. But in the Singhalese account only one damsel is mentioned, and she is called Sujâtá (M.B. 168).

[4] The river therefore was to the east of him, as we read that having finished the meal he cast the rice bowl into the river at his feet, and Sekra taking it up returned with it to his heavenly abode, and erected over it a pagoda (*vide* also M.B. 168).

[5] This was situated half way down the mountain Prâgbôdhi, on the east side of the river (compare Jul. ii. 458). It is to be observed that these incidents are not mentioned in the Singhalese Records.

satwa entering sat down with his legs crossed, and his face toward the west.[1] Whilst thus seated, he reflected with himself: "If I am to arrive at the condition of perfect wisdom, then let there be some spiritual manifestation." Immediately on the stone wall there appeared the shadow of Buddha, in length somewhat about three feet. This shadow is still distinctly visible. Then the heavens and the earth were greatly shaken, so much so that all the Dêvas resident in space cried out and said, "This is not the place appointed for the Buddhas (past or those to come) to arrive at Perfect Wisdom; at a distance less[2] than half a yôjana south-west from this, beneath the Pei-to[3] tree, is the spot where all the Buddhas (past or yet to come) should arrive at that condition." The Dêvas[4] having thus spoken immediately went before him, singing and leading the way with a view to induce him to follow. Then Bôdhisatwa, rising up,

[1] And therefore with his back to the entrance of the cave, and looking, towards the river. (Compare Jul. ii. 458.)

[2] Hiouen Thsang states the distance to be fourteen or fifteen li S.W., which agrees with the text.

[3] Respecting this tree we read "that it is indigenous in Maghada, of about sixty feet or seventy feet high, and never casts its leaves." Pei-to, is an Indian word (Patra) which signifies a "leaf;" it is on the leaves of this tree books are written" (Jul. ii. lxv. *n.*). In all other accounts the sacred tree here named is called the Pi-pal or "ficus religiosa."

[4] "From the Sal tree (probably near the cave alluded to in the text) to the Bo tree (*i.e.* the Pei-to), the Déwas made an ornamental path 3000 cubits broad, and at night the prince proceeded along its course attended by a vast concourse of Déwas, Nágas and other beings" (M.B. 170).

advanced after them. When distant thirty paces from the tree, the Dêvas presented to him the grass mat of Ki-tseung (Santi).[1] Bôdhisatwa, having accepted it, again advanced fifteen paces. Then 500 blue birds came flying towards him,[2] and having encircled Bôdhisatwa three times in their flight, departed. Bôdhisatwa, then going forward, arrived under the Pei-to tree, and spreading out the mat of Santi, sat down upon it, with his face towards the east.[3] Then it was that Mâra[4] Râja dispatched three pleasure girls[5] from the northern quarter to come and tempt him, whilst Mâra himself coming from the south,[6] assailed him

[1] "On his way he was met by the Brahman Santi, who gave him eight bundles of Kusa grass, as he knew they would be required and prove a great benefit" (M.B. 170).

[2] The fourth dream of Buddha (Bôdhisatwa) on the night previous to his complete inspiration was "that numbers of the birds called Lohini flew to him from the four quarters; when they were at a distance they were all of different colours, but as they approached they all became of a golden hue" (M.B. 167).

[3] The Singhalese accounts say that he sat down facing the west (M.B. 170).

[4] Mâra is represented as having for six years striven with Bôdhisatwa with a view to prevent his final enlightenment. "No reason is assigned for his opposition to Buddha, but the fear that by his discourses many beings would attain the blessedness of the Brâhma Lôkas, and the privilege of Nirvâṇa, which would prevent the re-peopling of the lower worlds over which he ruled. There can be no doubt that the whole history of this battle was at first an allegorical description of an enlightened mind struggling with the power of evil" (M. B.).

[5] These three women are spoken of as the daughters of Mâra, and named Tanhâ, Rati, Ranga.

[6] The account of Bôdhisatwa's temptation on this occasion is given in the Southern records with that amplification and luxuriance of description

likewise. Then Bôdhisatwa striking the toe of his foot against the earth, the whole army of Mâra was scattered, and the three women were changed into hags. On the place above-mentioned,[1] where he inflicted on himself mortification for six years, and on each spot subsequently mentioned, men in after times erected towers and placed figures (of Buddha), which still remain. Buddha having arrived at Supreme Wisdom[2] for seven days,[3] sat contemplating the Tree,

which is usual amongst those imaginative people (M. B. 172, etc.). It is said that Mâra approached from the western quarter, and that his army extended 164 miles.

[1] The French translation is incorrect here, as it would make Bôdhisatwa undergo a second term of mortification for six years.

[2] The condition of complete enlightenment to which a Buddha arrives, consists in the entire destruction of every evil desire, and the acquisition of that Supreme Wisdom by which he knows the exact circumstances of all the beings who have ever existed in the endless and infinite worlds, and all the causes, from their beginning to their end, that lead to repetition of existence. In other words, the condition of a Buddha is supposed to be one of complete Holiness, infinite Wisdom, and its consequent, perfect Joy. At the moment of Buddha's arrival at this condition he uttered the following gâthas: "Performing my pilgrimage through an eternity of countless existences, in sorrow have I unremittingly yet vainly sought the artificer of the abode (*i.e.* of my body). Now, O! artificer, thou art found! Henceforth no receptacle of sin shalt thou form! Thy frames (ribs) broken, thy ridge pole shattered, my mind detached from all existing objects,—I have attained the extinction of Desire." From this moment Buddha became the Teacher of men, and the Lord of the three worlds.

[3] After repeating the stanzas just mentioned, Buddha thought thus: "I have attained the Buddhaship; I have overcome Mâra; all evil desire is destroyed; I am lord of the three worlds; I will therefore remain longer in this place." Thus reflecting, he remained in a sitting posture on the throne (Bôdhimaṇḍa) for the space of seven days; afterwards he arose from the throne and ascended into the air, where he remained for a moment, and then descended to the N.E. side of the tree, where he sat for seven days with his eyes immoveably fixed on it (M. B. 181).

experiencing the joys of emancipation. On this spot they have raised a tower, as well as on the following, viz. where he walked[1] for seven days under the Pei-to tree, from east to west; where all the Dêvas, having caused the appearance of a hall[2] composed of the seven precious substances, for seven days paid religious worship to Buddha; where the blind dragon Manlun[3] (Mouchalinda, Lalita Vistara 355), for seven days encircled Buddha in token of respect; also where Buddha seated on a square stone beneath a Nyagrôdha tree, and with his face to the east, received the respectful salutation of Brahmá; also where the four Heavenly Kings[4] respectfully offered him his alms bowl; also where the 500 merchants[5] presented him with wheat and honey; also where he converted the Kâsyapas,[6] elder and younger brothers, each of whom was at the head of 1,000 disciples. In the place where Buddha arrived at perfect[7]

[1] The Déwas made a golden path, on which Buddha continued for seven days to walk from end to end (M. B.).

[2] The Déwas then made a golden palace on the N.W. side of the tree, where he resided seven other days (M. B.).

[3] In the sixth week after his enlightenment he went to the lake Muchalinda, where he remained at the foot of a Midella tree. At that time a rain began to fall, which continued during seven days. The Nâga Muchalinda having ascended to the surface of the lake, sheltered Buddha with his extended hood, as with a canopy (M. B.).

[4] That is, the four kings who reign over the four quarters, and whose palaces are at the foot of Mount Sumeru. They each brought an alms bowl for Buddha, and he caused the four to be joined together in one.

[5] For this event, see (M. B. 182).

[6] We have before alluded to this event.

[7] This place is called the Bôdhi-maṇḍala, *i.e.* the precinct of Bôdhi. It is supposed to be in the exact centre of Jambudwipa. The tree itself is

reason, there are three Saṅghârâmas, in all of which priests are located. All the ecclesiastics are supplied with necessaries by the people, so that they have sufficient and lack nothing. They scrupulously observe the rules of the Vinaya with respect to decorum. They exactly conform to the regulations established by Buddha when he was in the world, which relate to sitting down, rising up, or entering the assembly; and they have ever done so from the first till now. The sites of the four great Pagodas have always been associated together from the time of the Nirvâṇa. The four great Pagodas are those erected on the place where he was born, where he obtained emancipation, where he began to preach, and where he entered Nirvâṇa.

called the Bodhi-drûm, *i.e.* the tree of knowledge. It still (1861) exists, but very much decayed; one large stem with three branches to the westward is still green, but the other branches are barkless and rotten. The tree must have been renewed frequently, as the present Pipal is standing on a terrace at least 30 feet above the level of the surrounding country. It was in full vigour in 1811 A.D., when seen by Dr. Buchanan, who describes it as probably not exceeding 100 years in age (Arch. Surv. 2).

CHAPTER XXXII.

Formerly, when King Asôka was a lad, when he was playing on the road, he encountered[1] Sâkya Buddha going begging. The little boy, rejoiced to have the opportunity, immediately presented him with a handful of earth, as an offering. Buddha received it, and on his return sprinkled it on the ground on which he took his exercise. In return for this act of charity the lad became an iron-wheel king, and ruled over Jambudwîpa. On assuming the iron wheel[2] (*i.e.* when he became a universal monarch) he was on a certain occasion going through Jambudwîpa in the administration of justice, at which time he saw one of the places of torment[3] for the punishment of wicked men, situated between two mountains, and surrounded by an iron wall. He immediately asked his attendant

[1] This is evidently an anachronism here, as Asôka could not have been born till many years after Buddha's Nirvâṇa. The second council (100 years after Buddha) was held under his auspices. Yet the Northern accounts relate that Upagupta, who had seen Buddha, was alive at this time.

[2] Refer to Spence Hardy's account of a Chakravarti (M.B. pp. 127, 7).

[3] The Buddhists are believers in future punishment, and have framed many accounts of the different hells in which sinners will be for a time subject to torment. Some of the little hells they believe to be situated between high mountains in particular parts of the earth, and no doubt this was one which Asòka saw.

ministers, "What is this place?" To this they replied and said, "This is the place where Jemma,[1] the infernal king, inflicts punishment on wicked men for their crimes." The king then began to reflect and said, "The Demon King, in the exercise of his function, requires to have a place of punishment for wicked men. Why should not I, who rule these men (on earth), have a place of punishment likewise for the guilty?" On this he asked his ministers, "Who is there that I can appoint to make for me a Hell, and to exercise authority therein for the punishment of wicked men?" In reply they said, "None but a very wicked man can fulfil such an office." The king forthwith dispatched his ministers to go in every direction to seek for such a man. In the course of their search they saw, by the side of a running stream, a lusty great fellow of a black colour, with red hair and light eyes, with feet like talons, and a mouth like that of a fish. When he whistled to the birds and beasts they came to him, and when they approached he mercilessly shot them through, so that none escaped. Having caught this man, he was brought before the king. The king then gave him these secret orders, "You must enclose a square space with high walls, and with this enclosure plant every kind of flower and fruit (tree), and make beautiful lakes and alcoves, and arrange everything with such

[1] Jemma is the god of the infernal regions, the judge of the dead—he allots them their various punishments.

taste as to cause men to be anxious to look within the enclosure. Then, having made a wide gate, the moment a man enters within the precincts, seize him at once, and subject him to every kind of infernal torture. And whatever you do, let no one (who has once entered) ever go out again. And I strictly enjoin you, that if I even should enter the enclosure, that you torture me also and spare not. Now then, I appoint and constitute you Lord of this place of Torment!" It happened that a certain Bikshu, as he was going his rounds begging for food, entered the gate. The Infernal Keeper seeing him, (seized his person) and made preparations to put him to torture. The Bikshu, being very much frightened, suppliantly begged for a moment's respite, that he might, at least, partake of his mid-day meal. It so happened that just at this moment another man entered the place, on which the keeper directly seized him, and, putting him in a stone mortar, began to pound his body to atoms, till a red froth formed on the surface of the mass. The Bikshu having witnessed this spectacle, began to reflect on the impermanency, the sorrow, the vanity of bodily existence, that it is like a bubble and froth of the sea, and so he arrived at the condition of a Rahat. This having transpired, the Infernal Keeper laid hold of him and thrust him into a caldron of boiling water. The heart of the Bikshu and his countenance were full of joy. The fire was extinguished and the water became cold, whilst in the middle of it there sprung up a Lotus, on the top of which the Bikshu took his seat. The keeper (on witnessing this) forthwith proceeded to the king and said, "A wonderful miracle has occurred in the place of Torture—would that your Majesty would come and see it." The king said, "I dare not come, in consideration of my former agreement with you." The keeper replied, "This matter is one of great moment: it is only right you should come; let us consider your former agreement changed." The king then directly followed him and entered the prison; on which the Bikshu, for his sake, delivered a religious discourse, so that the king believed and was converted[1] (obtained deliverance). Then he ordered the place of Torture to be destroyed, and repented of all the evil he had formerly committed. From the time of his conversion he exceedingly honored the three sacred symbols of his faith (the three precious ones, *i.e.* Buddha, Dharma, Sañgha), and went continually to the spot underneath the Pei-to Tree for the purpose of repentance, self-examination, and fasting. In consequence of this, the queen on one occasion asked, "Where is it the king is perpetually going?" on which the ministers replied, "He continually resides under the Pei-to Tree." The queen hereupon, awaiting an opportunity when the king was not there, sent men to cut the tree down. The king, repairing as

[1] The legend is somewhat differently related by Hiouen Thsang (Jul. ii. 415).

usual to the spot, and seeing what had happened, was so overpowered with grief that he fell down senseless on the ground. The ministers, bathing his face with water, after a long time restored him to consciousness. Then the king piled up the earth on the four sides of the stump of the tree, and commanded the roots to be moistened with a hundred pitchers of milk. Then, prostrating himself at full length on the ground, he made the following vow: "If the tree does not revive, I will never rise up again." No sooner had he done this than the tree immediately began to force up small branches from the root, and so it continued to grow until it arrived at its present height, which is somewhat less than 120 feet.

CHAPTER XXXIII.

From this place, going south three li, we arrive at a mountain called the Cock's-foot (Kukutapâdagiri).[1] The great Kâsyapa is at present within this mountain. (On a certain occasion) he divided the mountain at its base, so as to open a passage (for himself). This entrance is now closed up. At a considerable distance from this spot, there is a deep chasm; it is in this (fastness as in a) receptacle that the entire body of Kâsyapa is

[1] The distance to this mountain is insufficient, as given in the text. I should be inclined to substitute "yôjanas" for "lis." The route, as given by Hiouen Thsang, from Gayâ to Kukutapâdagiri (*i.e.* the Cock's-foot mountain), is "To the east of the Bôdhidrûm we cross the river Nâirânjana; further on to the east we pass the river Mo-ho (the Mahânada, or the Mohana in Klaproth's map); we then enter a great forest, and, after going some hundred li across deserts, we arrive at Kukutapâdagiri, which is also called Gouroupâdagiri, *i.e.* the Mountain of the Master's (*sc.* Kâsyapa's) foot" (V. St. Martin v. 377). There is another difficulty connected with the situation of this mountain. Burnouf (I. B. p. 366, *n.*) states that the celebrated hermitage, known as the Kukuṭa Ârâma, was situated on it. Now, Hiouen Thsang distinctly states that this hermitage was in the neighbourhood of Pâṭalipoutra (Jul. i. 139), some sixty miles (7 yôjanas + 100 li) to the north of Gayâ. To add to the confusion, the Archæological Surveyor's Report (1861, p. 5) identifies Kurkihar, about 16 miles to the east of Gayâ, with the Kukuṭârâma; and then adds, that "this situation agrees exactly with Fah Hian's account, excepting that there is no three peaked-hill in the neighbourhood." I am at a loss to know to what account he refers. On the whole I prefer to consider the hermitage and the hill as distinct localities—the former near Patna, the latter some 15 miles to the E. or S.E. of Gayâ.

now preserved. Outside this chasm is the place where Kâsyapa, when alive, washed his hands. The people of that region, who are afflicted with head-aches, use the earth brought from the place for anointing themselves with, and this immediately cures them. In the midst of this mountain, as soon as the sun[1] begins to decline, all the Rahats[2] come and take their abode. Buddhist pilgrims of that and other countries come year by year (to this mountain) to pay religious worship to Kâsyapa; if any should happen to be distressed with doubts, directly the sun goes down, the Rahats arrive, and begin to discourse with (the pilgrims) and explain their doubts and difficulties; and, having done so, forthwith they disappear. The thickets about this hill are dense and tangled. There are, moreover, many lions, tigers, and wolves prowling about, so that it is not possible to travel without great care.

[1] So I translate the phrase "tsih jih ku"—but it is a most unusual expression.

[2] We must remember the description given of a Rahat in the earliest work translated into Chinese (Forty-two section Sutra), viz., "The Rahat is able to fly, change his appearance, fix the years of his life, shake heaven and earth" (§ 2).

CHAPTER XXXIV.

Fah Hian returning towards Pâtaliputra kept along the course of the Ganges, and after going ten yôjanas in a westerly direction arrived at a Vihâra[1] called "Desert" (Kwang ye) in which Buddha resided. Priests still reside in it. Still keeping along the course of the Ganges, and going west twelve yôjanas, we arrive at the country of Kasi[2] and the city of Benares (Po-lo-nai).[3] About ten li or so to the N.E.[4] of this city is the chapel of the Deer Park of the Rishis. This garden was once

[1] This Vihâra was probably situated in the kingdom of Yuddhapati, mentioned by Hiouen Thsang (Jul. i. 134), somewhere near Ghazipura, but its name is not easily identified with any existing monument.

[2] Kasi, the name of an aboriginal tribe that occupied this district, but afterwards applied generally to the country round Benares (V. St. M. 362).

[3] Benares, a city still celebrated as a seat of learning, was also the scene of Buddha's first appearance as a great Teacher. The statues most commonly found in the neighbourhood therefore represent him in the attitude of teaching, viz. with his left arm pendant, his right fore-arm elevated, the hand level with the shoulder, with the two forefingers raised, and the others closed under the thumb. The city of Benares is situated on the left bank of the Ganges, between the river Barnâ Nadi (or, Varanâ) on the N.E. and the Asi Nâla on the S.W. From the joint names of these two streams the Brahmans derive Varanasi, or Benares. But the most usual derivation is from the Rajah Banâr, who is said to have rebuilt the city about 800 years ago. (C.)

[4] In Laidlay's translation from the French it is N.W. by mistake.

occupied by a Pratyêka Buddha.[1] There are always wild deer reposing in it for shelter. When the world-honoured Buddha was about to arrive at Supreme Wisdom, all the Dêvas who resided in space began to chant a hymn and say: "The son of Sudhôdana Râja, who has left his home that he may acquire supreme wisdom, after seven days will arrive at the condition of Buddha." The Pratyêka Buddha hearing this, immediately entered Nirvâṇa. Therefore, the name of this place is the Deer Park of the Rishi. The world-honoured Buddha having arrived at complete knowledge, men in after-ages erected a Vihâra on this spot. Buddha

[1] The Garden of the Deer Park is one of the most celebrated spots in Buddhist history. The legend relating to it is this: "The Rajah of Benares, who was fond of sport, had slaughtered so many deer that the King of the Deer remonstrated with him and offered to furnish him with one deer daily throughout the year if he would give up slaughtering them. The Rajah eonsented. After some time it came to the turn of a hind, big with young, to be slain for the king. She however objeeted, on the ground that it was not right that two lives should be saerificed. The King of the Deer (who was Bôdhisatwa, the future Buddha Sakhya,) was so affeeted that he went and offered himself in place of the hind. On this the King gave up his elaim and made over the park for the perpetual use of the deer, and henee it was ealled the Deer Park (Mrigadâva) (Jul. ii. 361)." The site of this park has been identified "as a fine wood whieh eovers an area of about half a mile, and extends from the great Tower of Dhamek on the North to the Chaukandi Mount on the South" (Areh. Surv. 40). This garden or park is called the Park of the Rishis (saints or devotees), either beeause the five men or disciples, mentioned hereafter, dwelt there, or, beeause of a Rishi who dwelt at a short distance to the East of it (Jul. ii. 369). It is ealled Isipatanam in the Pali annals for the same reason (Isi, a saint or devotee). It was to this plaee Buddha first proeeeded after his enlightenment. The legend in the text relating to the Pratyêka Buddha, is, so far as I know, not found elsewhere.

being desirous to convert Âdjñâtâ Kâuṇḍinya [1] (Keou lun) and his companions, known as the five men, they communed one with another and said: "This Shaman Gotama,[2] having in his own person for six years practiced the severest mortifications, reducing himself to the daily use of but one grain of millet and one of rice, and in spite of this, having failed to obtain Supreme Wisdom, how much less shall he now obtain that condition, by entering into men's society and removing the checks he placed upon his words and thoughts and actions; to-day when he comes here, let us carefully avoid all conversation with him." On Buddha's arrival the five men [3] rose and saluted him, and here they have erected a tower—also on the following spots, viz. on a

[1] Buddha's first intention was to declare the Law for the conversion of two ascetics, called Alâra and Uddaka (Oudraka Râma pouttra, and Arâḍa Kâlâma) but they had, in the meantime, died. On which he resolved to seek the five ascetics who had for six years practiced austerities with him near Gaya, and who had left him when they saw his efforts were unsuccessful, and that he had begun to relax his mortifications. These five men now dwelt in the Deer Park; they were called Ajñâta Kaûṇḍinya, Asvajit, Vâshpa, Mahânâma, and Bhadrika (or, according to the Pali accounts, Kondanya, Bhaddaji, Wappa, Mahanamá, and Assaji).

[2] Gótama, the common title of Buddha in the Southern schools of Buddhism; it is seldom used in the North. Gotama was the family name of Sakya Muni.

[3] Their conduct is thus explained: "Buddha approached them with slow steps, affecting all beings who saw him, with his Divine appearance. The five men, forgetting their agreement, advanced towards him and saluted him, and then, after having asked his permission, they respectfully followed him. Buddha drew them step by step to his doctrine, and after having dwelt with him during the season of the rains, they obtained enlightenment" (Jul. ii. 369).

site sixty paces to the north of the former place, where Buddha, seated with his face to the east,[1] began to turn the Wheel of the Law (to preach) for the purpose of converting Kâuṇḍinya and his companions, commonly known as "the five men:" also on a spot twenty paces to the north of this, where Buddha delivered his prediction concerning Mâitrêya,[2] also on a spot fifty paces to the south of this, where the Dragon Êlâpatra asked Buddha at what time he should be delivered from his Dragon-form; in all these places towers have been erected which still exist. In the midst[3] (of the Park) there are two Sañghârâmas which still have priests dwelling in them. Proceeding north-west thirteen yôjanas from the Park of the Deer, there is a

[1] So my copy has it. Rémusat translates it "facing the West," and the Archæological Surveyor of India mentions a tablet on the western face of the great Tower of Dhamek (which he identifies with this one) as significant of this position of Buddha. I cannot doubt, however, he was facing the East, according to the orthodox rule. This great Tower of Sârnâth or Dhamek was opened and examined by Cunningham; but, being only a Memorial Tower, nothing was found within it (except one inscribed stone) to reward the labor of fourteen months. The tower was 110 feet high, and of an octagonal shape, 292 feet in circumference at the base.

[2] That is where Buddha declared that Mâitrêya should be his successor. Just as Dipañkara Buddha announced that Sakya would become Buddha.

[3] It is curious that Fah Hian's account of these celebrated monasteries should be so meagre. According to Hiouen Thsang there were in his time no less than 3000 priests in the various Sañghârâmas of the Deer Park. The period between Fah Hian and Hiouen Thsang was evidently one of rapid progress amongst the Buddhists of this neighbourhood. One of these monasteries has been thoroughly examined, and from certain appearances it has been concluded that the whole were suddenly destroyed by fire, probably at the time of the final persecution of the Buddhist religion, in the eighth century.

country called Kau-chang-mi [1] (Kâusâmbî). There is a Vihâra, here called Gochira vana [2] (the Garden of Gochira) in which Buddha formerly dwelt; it is now lying in ruins. There are congregations here, principally belonging to the system known as the Little Vehicle. Eight yôjanas east of this place is a place where Buddha once took up his residence and converted an evil demon. They have also erected towers on various spots where he sat, or walked for exercise, when he was resident in this neighbourhood. There are Sañghârâmas still existing here and perhaps [3] one hundred priests.

[1] So it is in the original, and not Kau-thau-mi, as in the French version. This name represents Kausambi, which has been identified with the village of Kosam on the Jumna, thirty miles above Allahabâd.

[2] The Southern accounts call this the Garden of Ghosika. It has been conjectured that this is the same as Gopsahasa, a village close to Kosam (C).

[3] These notices respecting Kausambi are so poor, that it is plain Fah Hian did not visit the country. This confirms the use of the expression "yau," instead of "to," as indicative of hearsay accounts.

CHAPTER XXXV.

GOING two hundred yôjanas[1] south from this, there is a country called Ta-Thsin (Dakshina. Deccan). Here is a Sanghârâma of the former Buddha Kâsyapa. It is constructed out of a great mountain of rock, hewn to the proper shape. This building has altogether five stories. The lowest is shaped into the form of an elephant, and has five hundred stone cells in it. The second is in the form of a lion and has four hundred chambers. The third is shaped like a horse and has three hundred chambers. The fourth is in the form of an ox and has two hundred chambers. The fifth story is in the shape of a dove and has one hundred chambers

[1] This distance is too great. The conjecture of Colonel Sykes, that the cave here described refers to Ellora, is not improbable. As to the shapes of the various platforms, it is possible that Fah Hian's informant referred in the first instance to the characteristic sculptures found in each set of chambers. For instance, in the great cave of Kailas at Ellora, which has been hewn out of the solid rock to the depth of four hundred feet, we read that "on either side of the base of the portico of the Pagoda are three elephants facing outward, and also at the entrance to the grand area two stone elephants of the size of life; a little further within the area is the chapel of Nandi, with the figure of the bull, and the five chapels beyond are supported on elephants and tigers placed alternately" (Murray). These wonderful sculptures, and those in the adjoining caves, when narrated to Fah Hian, would leave such a general impression on his mind as to lead to the description in the text.

in it. At the very top of all is a spring of water which flowing in a stream before the rooms, encircles each tier, and so, running in a circuitous course, at last arrives at the very lowest story of all, where, flowing past the chambers as before, it finally issues through the door of the building. Throughout the consecutive tiers, in various parts of the building, windows have been pierced through the solid rock for the admission of light, so that every chamber is quite illuminated and there is no darkness (throughout the whole). At the four corners of this edifice they have hewn out the rock into steps, as means for ascending. Men of the present time point out a small ladder which reaches up to the highest point (of the rock) by which men of old ascended it, one foot at a time.[1] They derive the name which they give to this building, viz. Po-lo-yu,[2] from an Indian word signifying "pigeon." There are always Rahats abiding here. This land is hilly and barren and without inhabitants. At a considerable distance from the hill there are villages, but all of them are inhabited by heretics. They know nothing of the law of Buddha, or Shamans, or Brahmans, or of any of the different schools of learning. The men of that country continually see persons come flying to the temple. On a certain oc-

[1] Rémusat seems to have mistaken the wording of this passage, but the translation I have given is not satisfactory to myself.

[2] This may possibly be a corruption of the Sanskrit pârâvata, a pigeon; it signifies "a mountain" also, which may have been the original sense of the word as applied to this particular hill.

casion there were some Budhist pilgrims from different countries who came here with a desire to pay religious worship at this temple. Then the men of the villages, above alluded to, asked them saying, "Why do you not fly to it? We behold the religious men who occupy those chambers constantly on the wing." These men then answered by way of excuse, "Because our wings are not yet perfectly formed." The country of Ta-Thsin (Deccan) is precipitous and the roads dangerous and difficult to find. Those who wish to go there ought to give a present to the king of the country, either money or goods. The king then deputes certain men to accompany them as guides, and so they pass the travellers from one place to another, each party pointing out their own roads and intricate bye paths. Fah Hian, finding himself in the end unable to proceed to that country, reports in the above passages merely what he has heard.

CHAPTER XXXVI.

From Benares going eastward in a retrograde order, we arrive at the town of Pâṭaliputra again. The purpose of Fah Hian was to seek for copies of the Vinaya Pitaka. But throughout the whole of Northern India the various masters trusted to tradition only for their knowledge of the Precepts, and had no written copies[1] of them at all. Wherefore Fah Hian had come even so far as Mid India (without effecting his purpose). But here in the Sañghârâma of the Great Vehicle[2] (at Patna) he obtained one copy of the Precepts, viz. the collection used by the school of the Mahâsañgikas,[3]

[1] This is an important statement; for it shows that even down to the time of Fah Hian, the body of Buddhist doctrine had been preserved in the different central establishments principally by tradition. This, in some degree, accounts for the various schools that sprang up, of which mention will soon be made.

[2] Viz. the Sañghârâma referred to in chap. xxvi.

[3] There is some difficulty in classifying the various schools of Buddhism, owing to the conflicting accounts of the Northern and Southern records. In Nipal, as Mr. Hodgson has explained, there are four principal schools of Buddhist philosophy, viz. the Swabavikas (those who believe in a self-existent Nature), the Aishwarikas (theists), the Kârmikas (those who believe the continuation of existence to be the result of the exercise of conscious moral agency on the part of sentient beings), and the Yatnikas (those who believe the same result to follow from the exercise of conscious intellectual agency). These schools, however (with the exception of the first), do do not represent the most ancient opinions of the followers of Buddha. They belong to a period probably posterior to Nâgârdjuna (who must have lived

which was that used by the first great assembly of priests convened during Buddha's lifetime. In the chapel of Chi-un (Jetavana) there is a tradition that

about the beginning of our era), who was a great opponent of the Swabavikas (the earliest school). In Thibet another division is commonly spoken of, which includes the four following classes: 1. The Vâibâchikas, 2. The Sûtrântikas, 3. The Yogâtcharas, 4. The Madyamikas. The first of these schools, which represents the primitive Buddhist church, is divided into eighteen sects, included under four principal classes with their subdivisions. 1. The followers of Râhula, the son of Sakya (and therefore belonging to the Kshattriya caste). These sectaries repeated the Pratimôksha in the Sanskrit language, and believed in the existence of objects of sense; they were therefore called Sarvâstivâdas, or those who allow the reality of all things. They were divided into seven minor schools, viz. (*a*) Mûlasarvastivadins, (*b*) Kâsyapîyas, (*c*) Mahisasikas, (*d*) Dharmaguptas, (*e*) Bahusrutiyas, (*f*) Tamrasatiyas, (*g*) Vibajyavadinas. 2. The followers of Kâsyapa, who was a Brahman. These repeated the Pratimôksha in the Prakrit language, and were known as Mahâsangikas. They were subdivided into five minor schools: (*a*) Purvasilas, (*b*) Avarasilahs, (*c*) Himavatahs, (*d*) Lokotaravadinas, (*e*) Prajnapativadinas. 3. The followers of Upâli who was a Sudra. They repeated the Pratimôksha in the Paisatyeka dialect, and were generally known as Sammatiyas, *i.e.* the honorable sect; they were subdivided into three classes: (*a*) Kaurukullakas, (*b*) Avantikas, (*c*) Vatsiputriyas. 4. The followers of Kâtyâyana, a Sudra, and were commonly known as the Mahastâvîrâhs; they were subdivided into three classes: viz. (*a*) Mahaviharavasinas, (*b*) Jetavaniyas, (*c*) Abhayagirivasinahs. [These three classes evidently represent the traditions of the three monasteries, Maha Vihâra, Jeta Vihâra (in Kosala), and the Abhayagiri Vihâra (in Ceylon)]. II. The great school of the Sutrântikas consists of those who follow the teaching of the Sutras (in distinction from the teaching of the Vibhâchâ). They are divided into two sects: (*a*) Those who follow the letter of the Sutras, (*b*) those who allow all reasonable deductions from the letter. III. The great school of the Yôgâchâras is divided into nine sects. They all trace their origin to the teaching of Aryasaṁga. The great feature of this school is their belief in the power of profound meditation, accompanied by ritual practices for the emancipation of the soul. IV. The great school of the Madhyamîkas, is divided into two chief sects, viz. the followers of Nâgârjuna, and the

this was originally their copy, (or, that this school originally sprang from them). The eighteen sects in general have each their own Superior, but they are agreed in their dependence on the Great Refuge (found in Buddha, Dharma, Sañgha). In some minor details of faith they differ, as well as in a more or less exact attention to some matters of practice. But this collection (belonging to the school above named) is generally regarded as most correct and complete. Moreover, he obtained one copy of Precepts in manu-

followers of Buddhapalita. These two teachers lived at an interval of four hundred years, and the second revived the declining sect of his predecessor. The Madhyamîka school professed to have discovered a medial course between the two theories of the absolute eternity of matter or its non-existence. But confining ourselves to the school of Kâsyapa, commonly known as the Mahâsañgikas, we find that this school (according to Thibetan accounts, Was. § 224, *n.*) arose at the time of the great council under Asôka. It was at the time of this Convocation that the Sacred Books were first committed to writing. Hitherto the Law had been handed down by word of mouth in the different centres of religious influence. Hence the dialects and many of the customs observed at the recitation of the Law differed in different localities. There arose therefore a considerable difference between the rendering recommended by some of the chief Staviras or heads of convents, and the body of priests, who belonged to the less considerable establishments. They appealed to Asôka, who ordered a general vote to be taken by ballot, each priest voting for the party representing the ancient or traditional rendering, or the modern conventual use. The majority was in favour of the ancient opinions, and this party was called the Mahâsañgika (the great body of priests); the others were called the Staviras or Mahâstaviras, because they followed the opinions of certain great establishments. The Mahâsañgikas were called the followers of Kâsyapa, because they adhered to the rendering of the Law supposed to have been authorized by him, at the first great Convocation at Rajagrîha, over which he presided. The Mahâwanso (Chap. IV.) also dates the origin of the Mahâsañgikas from the time of the second Council.

script,[1] comprising about 7,000 gâthas. This copy was that used by the assembly belonging to the school of the Sarvâstivâdas.[2] The same, in fact, as is generally used in China. The masters of this school also hand down the Precepts by word of mouth, and do not commit them to writing. Moreover, in this assembly he obtained an imperfect copy of the Abhidharma, including altogether about 6,000 gâthas. Moreover, he obtained a collection of Sutras in their abbreviated form, consisting altogether of 2,500 verses. Moreover, he obtained an expanded volume (Vâipoulya)[3] of the Parinirvâṇa[4] Sûtra, containing about 5,000 verses.

[1] In manuscript,—that is, which Fah Hian himself copied, or, perhaps, which one of the priests copied for him.

[2] The Sarvâstavâdas represent the first division of the Vâibhâshikas, who followed Râhula. They believed in the actual existence of all sensible phenomena. The great school of the Vâibhâshikas, represented, in the first instance, the ancient Church of the Buddhists, and were not so called until a comparatively late date, when the various minor divisions compelled them to classify themselves under general denominations. They were so called either because they followed the teaching of a work called the Vibhâshâ (विभाषा *sc.* a work divided into (eight) parts विभाग), composed by Kâtyâyanapoutra and Asvagôsha, or because they employed themselves in discussion on different forms of substance, or that which is substance and non-substance; or more probably still, because they used the popular language (vibasha) in their discussions. The statement that the Vinaya known hitherto in China was that of the Sarvâstavâdas, helps to confirm the opinion that this was the most ancient and orthodox school of Buddhism. We are told also that in Thibet the Vinaya is only known according to the school of the Mûlasarvâstavâdins, the first of the minor divisions of the great school of the Sarvâstavâdas (Was. § 89).

[3] The expanded Sûtras are those of a late date, which contain repetitions of the same idea, in prose and verse, expanded to a tiresome length.

[4] The Parinirvâṇa (Parinibban) Sûtra, a work that professes to have been delivered by Buddha previous to his Nirvâṇa.

Moreover, he procured a copy of the Abhidharma according to the school of the Mahâsañghikas. On this account Fah Hian abode in this place for the space of three years engaged in learning to read the Sanskrit books, and to converse in that language, and in copying the precepts. When To-ching arrived in mid-India and saw the customary behaviour of the Shamans, and the strict decorum observed by the assembly of priests, and their religious deportment, even in the midst of worldly influences,—then, sorrowfully reflecting on the meagre character of the Precepts known to the different assemblies of priests in the border land of China, he bound himself by a vow and said, "From the present time for ever till I obtain the condition of Buddha, may I never again be born in a frontier country." And in accordance with this expression of his wish, he took up his permanent abode in this place, and did not return. And so Fah Hian, desiring with his whole heart to spread the knowledge of the Precepts throughout the land of Han (China), returned alone.

CHAPTER XXXVII.

FOLLOWING down the river Ganges in an easterly direction for eighteen yôjanas distance, we find the great kingdom of Tchen-po[1] (Champa) on its southern shore. In the place where Buddha once dwelt and where he moved to and fro for exercise, also where the four previous Buddhas sat down; in all these places towers have been erected, and there are still priests resident in them. From this, continuing to go eastwards nearly fifty yôjanas, we arrive at the kingdom of Tamralipti.[2] Here it is the river empties itself into the sea. There are twenty-four Sañghârâmas in this country, all of them have resident priests, and the Law of Buddha is generally respected. Fah Hian remained here for two years, writing out copies of the Sacred books (Sûtras), and taking impressions of the figures

[1] Tchampa or Tchampapuri, the name of the ancient capital of a country called Angadesa, governed by Karna, and hence called Karnapura. It corresponds with the present Bhagalpura (Kl.). Hiouen Thsang also visited this country, and he speaks of the number of heretical sects who were mixed together here. Buddhism, in fact, began to assume, in this part of India, a corrupt form at an early period—being mixed up with local superstitions.

[2] Corresponding to Tâmalitta of the Mahawanso (cap. xix.), the present Tamluc, near the mouth of the Hooghly. From this port there was extensive traffic with Ceylon and the southern coasts of India. Buddhism flourished here, but probably under a corrupt form, as the intermixture of races was considerable, and the people superstitiously inclined.

(used in worship). He then shipped himself on board a great merchant vessel. Putting to sea, they proceeded in a south-westerly direction, and, catching the first fair wind of the winter season (*i.e.* of the N.E. monsoon) they sailed for fourteen days and nights and arrived at the country of the Lions[1] (Siñhala, Ceylon). Men of that country (Tamralipti) say that the distance between the two is about 700 yôjanas. This kingdom (of Lions) is situated on a great island. From east to west it is fifty yôjanas, and from north to south thirty yôjanas.[2] On every side of it are small islands,[3] perhaps amounting to 100 in number. They are distant from one another 10 or 20 li, and as much as 200 li. All of them depend on the great island. Most of them produce precious stones and pearls. The Mani gem[4] is also found in one district, embracing a surface perhaps of 10 li. The King sends a guard to protect the place. If any gems are found, the King claims three out of every ten.

[1] So called from "Siñha," a lion, and "lā," to take. A fabulous account states that the first colonization of this island was accomplished by a refugee from India, who had destroyed (taken) his own father, under the shape of a lion. The island is also called Ratnadwipa, "the treasure land," and also Tâmraparna (Taprobane), "the land full of copper," or, "of the colour of copper."

[2] These measurements Remusat remarks are correct, only Fah Hian was deceived—as Eratosthenes was—in giving greater extent to Ceylon in longitude than in latitude.

[3] It has been supposed that Fah Hian here refers to the Maldives.

[4] The Mani gem is a famous one in Buddhist formulæ, e. gr. in the well known Thibetan invocation, "Om mani padme, hum!" Although generally it is rendered by the English "pearl," it probably is the carbuncle.

CHAPTER XXXVIII.

THIS kingdom had originally no human inhabitants, but only demons[1] and dragons dwelt in it. Merchants of different countries (however) resorted here to trade. At the time of traffic, the demons did not appear in person, but only exposed their valuable commodities[2] with the value affixed to them. Then the merchant men, according to the prices marked, purchased the goods and took them away. But in consequence of these visits, and the sojourn of the merchants in the country, men of other countries also hearing of the delightful character of the place, flocked there in great numbers, and so a great populous community was formed. This country enjoys an equable climate, without any extremes of temperature either in winter or summer. The plants and trees are always verdant. The fields

[1] The ordinary account states that Ceylon was inhabited by Rakshasas, female demons, who lived on the flesh of dead men. These were conquered and destroyed by Siñhala, the son of Siñha. The native works state that it was Vijaya (conquest), son of Siñhala, who, at the head of 700 warriors, destroyed these supernatural beings. Vijaya is made to be a contemporary of Sakya Muni. Mr. Turnour has remarked on the singular agreement between Vijaya's adventures on this island, and the account of Ulysses and his followers landing on the island of Circe (Mahawanso, Introd. lxxxvi.).

[2] There is still an account current in the country that this mode of traffie is employed by the natives in their dealings with the Veddah people (the aborigines of the island).

are sown just according to men's inclination; there are no fixed seasons for doing so. Buddha came to this country (in the first instance) from a desire to convert a malevolent dragon.[1] By his spiritual power he planted one foot[2] to the north of the royal city,[3] and one on the top of a mountain, the distance between the two being 15 yôjanas. Over the impression (on the hill), to the north of the royal city, is erected a great tower,[4] in height 470 feet. It is adorned with gold and silver, and every precious substance[5] com-

[1] Fah Hian must here refer to the occasion of Buddha's second visit to the island. His first visit, according to the Mahawanso (cap. i.), was in the ninth month of his Buddhahood, for the purpose of sanctifying the island by the expulsion of the Yakkos, and rendering it habitable for human beings. His second visit was in the fifth year of his Buddhahood, "when, observing that a conflict was at hand between the armies of the Nâgas (dragons) Mahodaro and Chulodaro, out of compassion to the Nâgas, he again visited Nagadipo (an island to the north of Ceylon). At this time, Mahodaro was a Nâga king in a Nâga kingdom 500 yôjanas in extent, bounded by the ocean; his younger sister Kidabbika had been given in marriage to a Nâga king of the Kaunawaddharmano Mountain. Chulodaro was his son. The conflict between the nephew and his uncle was about to begin on account of a gem throne . . . . . To them the Vanquisher (Djina, *i.e.* Buddha) preached a sermon on reconciliation. They were overjoyed at seeing him, and bowed down at his feet. The Divine Teacher procured for 80,000 Kotis of Nâgas, the salvation of the faith and the state of piety."

[2] This occurred on his third visit, when, rising aloft in the air, the Divine Teacher displayed the impression of his foot on the mountain of Sumanekuto (Adam's peak) (Mahawanso, cap. i.; *vide* also M. B. 212.)

[3] That is, Anurádhapura, the ancient capital, said to have been sixteen miles square.

[4] This great Thúpa, or Tower of Ruanwelli, was erected by Dutugaimunoo or Dutthagamini, 157 B.C.; it is described as being 120 cubits high (Mahawanso, Epit. Turnour, 16).

[5] In connection with the erection of this Thûpa we read that two

bines to make it perfect. By the side of this tower, moreover, is erected a Sañghârâma, which is called Abhayagiri[1] (the mountain without fear), containing 5,000 priests. They have also built here a Hall of Buddha, which is covered with gold and silver engraved work, conjoined with all the precious substances. In the midst of this hall is a jasper figure (of Buddha), in height about 22 feet. The entire body glitters and sparkles with the seven precious substances, whilst the various characteristic marks are so gloriously portrayed, that no words can describe the effect. In the right hand it holds a pearl of inestimable value. Fah Hian had now been absent from China (the land of Han) many years; the manners and customs of the people with whom he had intercourse were entirely strange to him. The towns, people, mountains, valleys, and plants and trees which met his eyes, were unlike those of old times. Moreover, his fellow travellers were now separated from him—some had remained behind and some were dead[2]—to think upon the past was all

Samanéra priests repaired to Uturukuru, whence they brought six beautiful cloud-coloured stones, in length and breadth 80 cubits, of the tint of the ganthi flower, without flaw, and resplendent as the sun (M. B. 15, *n.*)

[1] This convent was built by King Welagambahu, 89 B.C.; the dagoba is described as being 180 cubits high (Epit. of Hist. of Ceylon, Turnour, p. 19). It was this prince who brought together 500 priests to a cave in Metale, and, for the first time, had the tenets of Buddhism reduced to writing, 217 years after they had been orally promulgated by Mahindo, Asôka's son (*ib.*).

[2] Of his original companions, two had died, viz. Hwui King (cap. xii.)

that was left him! and so his heart was continully saddened. All at once, as he was standing by the side of this jasper figure, he beheld a merchant present to it, as a religious offering, a white taffeta fan, of Chinese manufacture (made in the land of Tsin). Unperceived (Fah Hian) gave way to his sorrowful feelings, and the tears flowing down filled his eyes. A former King of this country sent an embassy[1] to mid-India, to procure a slip of the Pei-to tree. This they planted by the side of the Hall of Buddha. When it was about 220 feet high, the tree began to lean towards the S.E. The King, fearing it would fall, placed eight or nine props round the tree to support it. Just in the place where the tree was thus supported, it put forth a branch, which pierced through the props, and, descending to the earth, took root. This branch is about 20 inches round. The props, although pierced through the centre, still surround (the tree), which stands now without their support, yet men have not removed them.

and Hwui Ying (cap. xiv.), Three had returned home (cap. xii.); four had separated themselves at an early period (caps. ii. iv.); and his constant companion, To Ching, had remained behind at Pátaliputra, so that Fah Hian was now left alone.

[1] The embassy was sent, according to the native accounts, by Dêvânampiyatissa, shortly after the arrival of Mahindo. "Arittho, the nephew of the king, was deputed to go to Pátaliputra and invite Sanghamittá, sister of Mahindo, to come to Lanká, and, at the same time, he was to request a branch of the Bo Tree, under which Sidhártta (*i.e.* Sakya) had become Buddha" (M. B. 325). The various extravagant details connected with the excision, transportation, and planting of this remarkable branch may be read, as above (*vide* also Mahawanso, cap. xix.).

Under the tree is erected a chapel, in the middle of which is a figure (of Buddha) in a sitting posture. Both the clergy and laity pay reverence to this figure with little intermission, Within the capital, moreover, is erected the chapel of the Tooth of Buddha,[1] in the construction of which all the seven precious substances have been employed. The King purifies himself according to the strictest Brahmanical rules, whilst those

[1] This is the celebrated Deladá or Tooth Relic. It is described as a "piece of discoloured ivory, or bone, slightly curved, nearly two inches in length, and one in diameter at the base, and from thence to the other extremity, which is rounded and blunt, it considerably decreases in size. The sanctuary of this relic is a small chamber in the Vihâra attached to the palace of the former kings of Kandy, where it is enshrined in six cases, the largest of which, upwards of five feet in height, is formed of silver, on the model of a dagoba. The same shape is preserved in the five inner ones, two of them being inlaid with rubies and other precious stones. The outer case is ornamented with many gold ornaments and jewels which have been offered to the Relic; and at night, when the place is lighted by lamps, its appearance is very brilliant, far surpassing that of the British regalia in the Tower of London" (E. M. 224). According to a native work (Daladáwansa), "Khema, one of the disciples of Buddha, procured the left canine tooth of Buddha, which he took to Dantapura, the capital of Kalinga. Here it remained 800 years. Then Paṇdu, the Lord paramount of India, attempted to destroy it, but was unable to do so. Having returned it to Dantapura, it was afterwards transported to Anurádhapura for safety. In the 14th century it was again taken to the continent, but was recovered by Prâkrama Bahu IV. The Portuguese say it was destroyed by Constantine de Braganza in 1560 A.D.; but the natives say it was concealed in a village in Saffragam. In 1815 it came into possession of the British, and although surreptitiously taken away in the rebellion of 1818, it was subsequently found in the possession of a priest and restored to its former sanctuary. It was then placed in charge of the British agent for the Kandian Provinces, and protected by a guard at night, public exhibitions of it being made from time to time. But in 1839 the Relic was finally given up to the native chiefs and priests" (E. M. 226).

men within the city who reverence (this relic) from a principle of belief, also compose their passions according to strict rule. This kingdom, from the time when (this chapel) was erected, has suffered neither from want, famine, calamity, or revolution. The treasury of this congregation of priests contains numerous gems and a Mani jewel of inestimable value. Their King once entered the treasury, and, going round it for the purpose of inspection, he saw there this Mani gem. On beholding it, a covetous feeling sprang up in his heart, and he desired to take it away with him. For three days this thought afflicted him, but then he came to his right mind. He directly repaired to the assembly of the priests, and, bowing down his head, he repented of his former wicked purpose, and, addressing them, said, "Would that you would make a rule from this time forth and for ever, on no account to allow the king to enter your treasury to look (at the jewels), except he is a member of the fraternity and of forty years of age[1] —after that time he may be permitted to enter." There are many noblemen and rich householders within the city. The houses of the Sa-pho[2] (Sabæan) merchants are very beautifully adorned. The streets and passages are all smooth and level. At the head of the

[1] The use of the expression "la" for a year of one's age, has been noticed by Jul. ii. 65, *n.*

[2] I have ventured to translate Sa-pho as Sabæan, merchants of Saba, or Arabia. Saba, according to Marco Polo, a town in Persia (cap. xi. p. 46).

four principal streets there are Preaching Halls;[1] on the 8th, 14th, and 15th day of the month, they prepare a lofty throne within each of these buildings, and the religious members of the community of the four classes[2] all congregate to hear the preaching of the Law. The men of this country say, that there are, in the country, altogether fifty or sixty thousand priests, all of whom live in community (take their meals in common). Besides these, the King supplies five or six thousand persons within the city with food. These persons, when they require, take their alms bowls and go (to the appointed place), and, according to the measure of the bowls, fill them and return. They always bring out the tooth of Buddha in the middle of the third month. Ten days beforehand, the King magnificently caparisons a great elephant, and commissions a man of eloquence and ability to clothe himself in royal apparel

[1] There is an interesting account of the mode of reciting the Law in hese Preaching Halls in E. M. 233. "The readings are most numerously attended on the night of the full moon (14th–15th)." "Whenever the name of Buddha is repeated by the officiating priest, the people call out simultaneously 'sâdhu' ('Good' or 'Blessing'), the noise of which may be heard at a great distance." "The Law is read in a kind of recitative, 'in a manner between singing and reading,' as, it is said, the Psalms were recited in the early Church." "The platform in the centre of the Hall is sometimes occupied by several priests, one of whom reads a portion of the Law at a time." (But for the full account, *vide* as above.) I have also attended such a meeting during the reading of the Law in a preaching hall in Japan. The crowds who filled the hall, and the peculiar mode of recitation adopted by the priests, lent an unusual interest to the performance.

[2] The same expression, no doubt, as that translated by Jul. i. 218: "les quatre multitudes," viz. Bikshus, Bikshunis, Upâsakas, and Upâsikawas.

and, riding on the elephant, to sound a drum and proclaim as follows:—"Bôdhisatwa, during three asankya kalpas,[1] underwent every kind of austerity, he spared himself no personal sufferings, he left his country, wife, and child; moreover, he tore out his eyes to bestow them on another, he mangled his flesh to deliver a dove (from the hawk),[2] he sacrificed his head in alms, he gave his body to a famishing tiger, he grudged not his marrow or brain. Thus he endured every sort of agony for the sake of all flesh. Moreover, when he became perfect Buddha, he lived in the world forty-nine years preaching the Law, and teaching and converting men. He gave rest to the wretched—he saved the lost. Having passed through countless births, he then entered Nirvâṇa. Since that event is 1497 years.[3] The eyes of the world were then put

[1] That is, during an innumerable series of years. According to Buddhist calculation, twenty antah-kalpas make one asankya-kalpa, and an antah-kalpa is the period during which the age of man increases from ten years to an asankya, and decreases from an asankya to ten years. (An asankya is a unit with 140 cyphers after it.) Were the surface of the earth to increase in elevation at the rate of one inch in 1000 years, and the process continue in the same ratio, the elevation would reach 28 miles before the antah-kalpa would be finished (M. B. 7). "According to the Buddhistical creed, all historical data, whether sacred or profane, anterior to the last Buddha's advent, are based on his revelation. They are involved in absurdities as unbounded as the mystification in which Hindu literature is enveloped."

[2] These acts of self-sacrifice indicate the principle necessary to prepare the future recipient of Supreme Wisdom (Bôdhi) for that condition. They are referred to under Chap. XI.

[3] There is a difficulty here in knowing whether this date is the one assigned to the Nirvâṇa by the "eloquent preacher" or by Fah Hian.

out, and all flesh deeply grieved. After ten days the tooth of (this same) Buddha will be brought forth and taken to the Abhayagiri Vihâra. Let all ecclesiastical and lay persons within the kingdom, who wish to lay up a store of merit, prepare and smooth the roads, adorn the streets and highways, let them scatter every kind of flower, and offer incense in religious reverence to the Relic." This proclamation being finished, the King next causes to be placed on both sides of the road representations of the 500 bodily forms which Bôdhisatwa assumed, during his successive births. For instance, his birth as Su-jin-no;[1] his appearance as a bright flash of light;[2] his birth as the king of the elephants,[3] and as an antelope These figures are all beautifully painted in divers colours, and have a very life-like appearance. At length the tooth of Buddha is brought forth and conducted along the principal

The former opinion is less probable, because the period of Buddha's Nirvâṇa (543 B.C.) is now so well established in Ceylon. It is possible, however, that this era may only date from the time of the Mahawanso.

[1] The French edition gives Sou-ta-nou, but mine has Su-jin-nou. The reference is probably to the Jâtaka (previous birth) called Sutana or Sudâna, given by Upham. This Jâtaka is the one related by Spence Hardy (M. B. 116) as the Wessantara Jâtaka, and frequently referred to by Sung Yun (*vide* subsequent Part).

[2] This probably alludes to the fable of the Fraeolin (Jul. ii. 336). A forest having caught fire, and many birds and beasts in risk of perishing miserably, a fracolin with its tail dipped in water tried to extinguish the flames, and on this Sekra accomplished what the bird had failed to do. That bird was Bôdhisatwa.

[3] From Hardy's list we find that Buddha had been born as an elephant six times, and as a stag ten times.

road. As they proceed on the way, religious offerings are made to it. When they arrive at the Abhayagiri Vihâra, they place it in the Hall of Buddha, where the clergy and laity all assemble in vast crowds and burn incense, and light lamps, and perform every kind of religious ceremony, both night and day, without ceasing. After ninety complete days they again return it to the Vihâra within the city. This chapel is thrown open on the chief holidays for the purpose of religious worship, as the Law (of Buddha) directs. Forty li to the east of the Abhaya Vihâra is a mountain, on which is built a chapel called Po-ti[1] (Bôdhi); there are about 2,000 priests in it. Amongst them is a very distinguished Shaman called Ta-mo-kiu-ti (Dharmakoti or Dharmagupta). The people of this country greatly respect and reverence him. He resides in a cell, where he has lived for about forty years. By the constant practice of benevolence he has been able to tame the serpents and mice, so that they stop together in one habitat, and are not mutully injurious one to the other.

[1] This mountain has been identified by Landresse with the Ling-kia-shan (Lankâgiri) of Hiouen Thsang. But this is impossible, as the latter is situated in the S.E. portion of the island, and this mountain only 40 li to the E. of Anuradhapura. Fah Hian no doubt refers to the celebrated Mahintalá, eight miles due east of Anuradhapura, and which is said to have formed the eastern boundary of the capital.

CHAPTER XXXIX.

SEVEN li to the south of the capital is a chapel called Mâha Vihâra,[1] in which there are 3,000 priests. There was amongst them one very eminent Shaman, who observed the precepts perfectly. The men of the country generally gave him credit for being a Rahat. At the time of his approaching death, the King, having come to enquire after him, followed the custom of the Law, and assembled the priests to ask whether this Bikshu had attained Reason (*i.e.* had arrived at the condition of a Bôdhisatwa). They then, according to their true belief, answered him, "He is a Rahat." After his death, the King immediately examined the Sacred Books, with a view to perform the funeral obsequies according to the rules for such as are Rahats. Accordingly, about 4 or 5 li to the east of the Vihâra, they erected a very great pyre of wood, about 34 feet square, and of the same height. Near the top they placed tiers of sandal wood, aloe, and all kinds of

[1] This celebrated Vihâra was built by Devanampiyatissa about 300 B.C. (Turnour). The Mâha vihâra is enclosed by a wall forming a rectangle of 115 yards by 72. There is a gate and a small entrance lodge, about the middle of the wall, to which some steps lead. The angles of these steps are still in perfect preservation, ... a few priests are still attached to the temple, but they seem poor and their establishments altogether paltry" (Davy).

scented wood. On the four sides they constructed steps by which to ascend it. Then, taking some clean and and very white camlet cloth, they bound it around and above the pyre. They then constructed a funeral carriage, just like the hearses used in this country (China ?), except that there are no dragon-ear handles to it. Then, at the time of the cremation, the King, accompanied by every class of his people, assembled in great numbers, came to the spot provided with flowers and incense for religious offerings. The multitude followed the hearse till it arrived at the place of the funeral ceremony. The King then in his own person offered religious worship with flowers and incense. This being over, the hearse was placed on the pyre, and oil of cinnamon poured over it in all directions. Then they set light to the whole. At the time of kindling the fire, the whole assembly occupied their minds with solemn thoughts. Then removing their upper garments, and taking their wing-like fans, which they use as sun-shades, and approaching as near as they can to the pyre, they flung them into the midst of the fire, in order to assist the cremation. When all was over, they diligently searched for the bones and collected them together, in order to raise a tower over them. Fah Hian did not arrive in time to see this celebrated person alive, but only to witness his funeral obsequies. At this time, the King, being an earnest believer in the law of Buddha, desired to build a new Vihâra for this congregation of priests. First of all he provided for them a sumptuous entertainment; after which, he selected a pair of strong working oxen, and ornamented their horns with gold, silver, and precious things. Then providing himself with a beautifully gilded plough, the King himself ploughed round the four sides of the allotted space; after which, ceding all personal right over the land, houses, or people, within the area thus enclosed, he presented (the whole to the priests). Then he caused to be engraved on a metal plate (the following inscription):—"From this time and for all generations hereafter, let this property be handed down from one (body of priests) to the other, and let no one dare to alienate it, or change (the character of) the grant." When Fah Hian was residing in this country he heard a religious brother from India, seated on a high throne, reciting a sacred book and saying: "The Patra (alms-bowl) of Buddha originally was preserved in the city of Vâisâlî,[1] but now it is in the borders of Gândâra.[2] In somewhat like a hundred years[3] [Fah Hian, at the time of the recital, heard the exact number of years, but he has now forgotten it] it will again be transported to the country of the Western Yu-chi.[4]

[1] As we read in Chap. 24, Buddha gave his Patra or alms-bowl to the Lichharvas of Vâisâlî, who desired to follow him to his death.

[2] As already explained in Chap. 12.

[3] M. Julien has pointed out in his preface to the life of Hiouen Thsang, the mistake in the Chinese Text throughout this passage—the word 'tsien' a thousand, being misprinted for 'kan.'

[4] These are the people of whom we have spoken under Chap. 12, who

After about a hundred years more it will be transported to the country of Khoten.[1] After a similar period it will be transported to Koutché.[2] In about a hundred years more it will once more come back and be taken to the land of Han; after the same period it will return to the land of Lions (Siñhala, Ceylon); after the same period it will return to Mid-India; after which it will be taken up into the Tusita heavens.[3] Then Mitrêya Bôdhisatwa will exclaim with a sigh, 'The alms-dish of Sakya Muni Buddha has come.' Then immediately all the Dêvas will pay religious worship to it with flowers and incense for seven days. After this it will return to Jambudwîpa, and a sea dragon, taking it, will carry it within his palace, awaiting till Mitrêya is about to arrive at complete wisdom, at which time the bowl, again dividing itself into four[4] as it was at first, will re-ascend the Pín-na Mountain.[5] After Mitrêya has arrived at Supreme Wisdom, the four heavenly kings will once more come and respectfully salute him as Buddha, after the same manner as they

were driven to the westward by the Northern Hioungnu, and finally conquered Transoxiana.

[1] But, according to Hiouen Thsang, the alms-bowl was in Persia in his time, which would correspond to the time alluded to in the Text.

[2] This country is that known as Kharachar, lying to the westward of Tourfan, in Chinese Tartary. It was visited by Hiouen Thsang on his outward journey.

[3] That is the heaven where the future Buddha resides.

[4] *Vide* Manual of Buddhism, p. 183.

[5] One of the mountains at the foot of Sumeru, and the residence of the four kings.

have done to the former Buddhas. The thousand Buddhas of this Bhadrakalpa[1] will all of them use this same alms-dish; when the bowl has disappeared, then the law of Buddha will gradually perish; after which the years of man's life will begin to contract until it be no more than five years in duration. At the time of its being ten years in length, rice and butter will disappear from the world, and men will become extremely wicked. The sticks they grasp will then transform themselves into sharp clubs (or, knives and clubs), with which they will attack one another, and wound and kill each other. In the midst of this, men who have acquired religious merit, will escape and seek refuge in the mountains; and when the wicked have finished the work of mutual destruction, they will emerge from their hiding places, and coming forth again, will converse together and say: 'Men of old lived to a very advanced age, but now, because wicked men have indulged without restraint in every transgression of the law, our years have dwindled down to their present short span, even to the space of ten years—now, therefore, let us all practice every kind of good deed, encouraging within ourselves a kind and loving spirit; let us enter on a course of virtue and righteousness.' Thus, as each one practices faith and justice, their years will begin to increase in double ratio till they reach 80,000 years of life. At the time when

[1] That is, the Kalpa in which we live.

Mitrêya is born, when he first begins to declare his doctrine (turn the Wheel of the Law) his earliest converts will be the followers of the bequeathed law of Sakya Buddha, who have forsaken their families, and sought refuge in the three sacred names, and observed the five great commandments, and attended to their religious duties in making continued offerings to the three precious objects of worship. His second and third body of converts shall be those who, by their previous conduct, have put themselves in a condition for salvation."[1] Fah Hian, on hearing this discourse, wished to copy it down, on which the man said, "This is no sacred book, but only what I have learnt by memory, and repeat verbally."

[1] That is, have acquired such merit in previous births as to entitle them to this privilege. The French translation, "are the protegés of Foe," is very loose.

CHAPTER XL.

FAH HIAN resided in this country for two years. Continuing his search (for the sacred books), he obtained a copy of the Vinaya Pitaka according to the school of the Mahisasikas.[1] He also obtained a copy of the Great Âgama[2] (Dirgâgama), and of the Miscellaneous Âgama (Sanyuktâgama), and also a volume of miscellaneous collections from the Pitakas (Sam-

[1] One of the divisions of the great school of the Sarvastîvadas (followers of Râhula), who professed to recognise the true existence of all things in nature.

[2] The four Âgamas, आगम from गम, *i.e.* a means of arriving at knowledge (books of elementary doctrine), contain in an abridged form the various doctrines of the Little Vehicle. They are compilations from the different Sûtras. Their names are as follows:—1. The Ekottarikâgama, *sc.* एकतर + आगम, the numerical Âgama (because the subjects of discussion are arranged in a numerical order, as in a dictionary of terms). 2. The Dîrghâgama (*sc.* दीर्घ + आगम), *i.e.* the Long Agama, in which the order of the universe (cosmogony) is discussed at length, and errors refuted. 3. The Madyamâgama (*sc.* मध्यम + आगम) enters on the discussion of profound subjects connected with philosophy (and, as it appears, principally by way of comparison or parable. Was. § 116). 4. The Sanyuktâgama (संयुक्तागम), which is occupied in treating on miscellaneous rules for religious contemplation (Was. § 115). These Âgamas form the bulwark of the Little Vehicle (Hinayana), and of the Sûtrantika school in particular in opposition to the Vibâshikas. Hence we may understand their popularity in Ceylon, and the agreement of Ceylonese Buddhist dogma with their general doctrine, as the Vibâshika school is distinctively a northern offshoot of the Great Hinayana system.

yukta Pitaka). All these were hitherto entirely unknown in the land of Han. Having obtained these works in the original language[1] (Fan), he forthwith shipped himself on board a great merchant vessel,[2] which carried about two hundred men. Astern of the great ship was a smaller one, as a provision in case of the large vessel being injured or wrecked during the voyage. Having got a fair wind they sailed eastward for two days, when suddenly a tempest (tyfoon) sprung up, and the ship sprang a leak. The merchants then desired to haul up the smaller vessel, but the crew of that ship, fearing that a crowd of men would rush into her and sink her, cut the towing cable and fell off. The merchant men were greatly terrified, expecting their death momentarily. Then dreading lest the leak should gain upon them, they forthwith took their goods and merchandize and cast them overboard. Fah Hian also flung overboard his water-pitcher[3] (koundika) and his washing basin, and also other portions of

[1] That is, in the Pali or Magadhi. The Sanskrit version of the sacred books, common in Nepal, is of a later date than the Pali copies still existing in Ceylon.

[2] It is an interesting fact to know that such large ships traded with Ceylon at this date. If the Saba mentioned by Marignolli be the island of Java, as Meinert supposes (Yule's Cathay, p. 322), then we may understand who the Saba merchants are, alluded to by Fah Hian above (Chap. xxxviii. p. 154), and how their intercourse was kept up with Ceylon in these large merchant ships.

[3] In Chinese, "kwan tchi." The water pitcher and ewer were two articles allowed to the Buddhist monk. Rémusat's translation here is quite at fault.

his property. He was only afraid lest the merchants should fling into the sea his sacred books and images. And so with earnestness of heart[1] he invoked Avâlokitêswara,[2] and paid reverence[3] to the Buddhist saints (the priesthood) of the land of Han—speaking thus: "I, indeed, have wandered far and wide in search of the Law. Oh! would that by your spiritual power, you would turn back the flowing of the water (stop the leak), and cause us to reach some resting place." Nevertheless, the hurricane blew for thirteen days and nights, when they arrived at the shore of a small island,[4] and, on the tide going out, they found the place of the leak; having forthwith stopped it up, they again put to sea on their onward voyage. In this ocean there are many pirates,[5] who, coming on

[1] The phrase "yih sin," one heart, is a very usual one in Buddhist liturgical works; it denotes the union of the soul of the supplicant with the ideal object of worship, what we should call, perhaps, "spiritual worship."

[2] Avâlokitêshwara, the manifested Lord, is invoked by Buddhists in all cases of extreme distress or danger. Avalokitêshwara is generally known in China as "Kwan yin," and is called, in relation to her character, "the Goddess of Mercy."

[3] The phrase here used, "Kwai ming," is equivalent to the Sanskrit expression "Namo," a term of invocation or supplication in prayer. There is a corresponding expression "kwai i," sometimes used.

[4] We have no data for determining the position of this island—the mention of pirates in the following section would point to the islets off the north coast of Sumatra, if the time given had been sufficient, but without further particulars it is impossible to arrive at any satisfactory opinion on the subject.

[5] The pirates who frequent the neighbourhood of Acheen Head are still the terror of merchant vessels becalmed in that neighbourhood.

you suddenly, destroy everything. The sea itself is boundless in extent—it is impossible to know east or west, except by observing the sun, moon, or stars in their motions. If it is dark, rainy weather, the only plan is to steer by the wind without guide. During the darkness of night, one only sees the great waves beating one against the other and shining like fire, whilst shoals of sea monsters of every description (surround the ship). The merchant men were now much perplexed, not knowing towards what land they were steering. The sea was bottomless and no soundings could be found, so that there was not even a rock for anchorage. At length, the weather clearing up, they got their right bearings, and once more shaped a correct course and proceeded onwards. But if (during the bad weather) they had happened to have struck on a hidden rock, then there would have been no way to have escaped alive. Thus they voyaged for ninety days and more, when they arrived at a country called Yo-po-ti[1] (Java). In this country heretics and Brah-

[1] This is the Chinese form of the Sanscrit Yavadwîpa, *i.e.* the land of Yava (यव) or barley. It was so called because the inhabitants of the island lived principally on this grain when the first Indian colonists arrived there. It is rendered phonetically by two Chinese characters having the sound "Chau-wa," corrupted by the addition of one stroke into "Kwa-wa." The meaning of the last characters (if they can be said to have any meaning) is "The sound of the gourd,"—and hence the story of Pére Amiot that the island was so called because of the peculiar tone of voice of the natives. The absurdity of this derivation has been pointed out by M. Pauthier (Marco Polo, 559, *n.*).

mans flourish, but the Law of Buddha is not much known. Stopping here the best portion of five months, Fah Hian again embarked on board another merchant vessel, having also a crew of 200 men or so. They took with them fifty days[1] provisions, and set sail on the 15th day of the fourth month. Fah Hian was very comfortable on board this ship.[2] They shaped a course N.E. for Kwang Chow (Canton province in China). After a month and some days, at the stroke of two in the middle watch of the night, a black squall suddenly came on, accompanied with pelting rain.[3] The merchant men and passengers were all terrified. Fah Hian at this time also, with great earnestness of mind, again entreated Avalokitêswara and all the priesthood of China to exert their Divine power in his favour, and bring them daylight. When the day broke, all the Brahmans, consulting together, said: "It is because we have got this Shaman on board with us that we have no luck, and have incurred this great mischief—come let us land this Bikshu on the first island we meet with,[4] and let us

[1] The voyage from Batavia to Hong Kong (*via* Singapore), with a S.W. monsoon (as was the case with Fah Hian), now occupies on an average twelve days, being somewhat over 2,000 miles.

[2] In consequence evidently of the Danapati or patron whom he met with.

[3] To any one who has voyaged in those seas this account will seem familiar.

[4] They would probably have landed him on the Paracels or the Prata reef, near which they would be at the time. In that case, Fah Hian would probably have been one, out of uncounted numbers, who have perished on those dreary rocks.

not, for the sake of one man, all of us perish." The religious patron (Danapati) of Fah Hian then said: "If you land this Bikshu, you shall also land me with him; and if not, you had better kill me: for if you really put this Shaman on shore (as you threaten), then, when I arrive in China, I will go straight to the King and tell him what you have done. And the King of that country is a firm believer in the Law of Buddha, and greatly honours the Bikshus and priests." The merchantmen on this hesitated, and (in the end) did not dare to land him. The weather continuing very dark, the pilots began to look at one another in mutual distrust.[1] Nearly seventy days had now elapsed. The rice for food, and the water for congee, was nearly all done. They had to use salt water for cooking, whilst they gave out to every man about two pints of fresh water. And now, when this was just exhausted, the merchants held a conversation and said: "The proper time for the voyage to Kwang Chow is about fifty days, but now we have exceeded that time these many days—shall we then undertake the navigation ourselves?" On this, they put the ship on a N.W. course to look for land. After twelve days' continuous sailing, they arrived at the southern coast of Lau Shan[2] which borders on the prefecture of Chang

[1] This passage is obscure.

[2] The mountains of Lau—for there are two—are situated in the southern portion of the Shantung promontory, in the department of Lai-chow. It will be seen from this how far to the north of their designed port the ship had been carried.

Kwang.[1] They then obtained good freshwater and vegetables; and so, after passing through so many dangers, and such a succession of anxious days, they suddenly arrived at this shore. On seeing the Le-ho vegetable (a sort of reed), they were confident that this was, indeed, the land of Han (at which they had arrived). But not seeing any men or traces of life, they scarcely knew what to take for granted. Some said they had not yet arrived at Kwang Chow, others maintained they had passed it. In their uncertainty, therefore, they put off in a little boat, and entered a creek to look for some one to ask what place it was they had arrived at. Just at this moment, two men who had been hunting were returning home; on this the merchants requested Fah Hian to act as interpreter and make inquiries of them. Fah Hian having first tried to inspire them with confidence, then asked them, "What men are you?" They replied, "We are disciples of Buddha."[2] Then he asked, "What do you find in these mountains here, that you should have gone hunting in them? They prevaricated and said, "To-morrow is the 15th[3] day of the 7th month, and we were anxious to catch something to sacrifice to Buddha." Again he asked, "What country is this?" They replied, "This is Tsing Chow,[4] on the borders of the prefecture of Chang

[1] This is the same as the present Ping Tu Chow, situated between Lai Chow and the Lau mountains.

[2] Probably because they said Fah Hian was one.

[3] They had been therefore just three months on their voyage.

[4] Tsing Chow is a departmental city in the province of Shantung, but

Kwang, dependent on the Leou family." Having heard this, the merchants were very glad, and, immediately begging that their goods might be landed, they deputed men to go to Chang Kwang.[1] The Prince Lai Ying, who was a faithful follower of the Law of Buddha, hearing that there was a Shaman on board with sacred books and images, took ship and embarked and came on board (to see Fah Hian). Then, immediately engaging men from the nearest shore, he dispatched the books and sacred figures to be landed and taken forthwith to the seat of his government. After this the merchants returned towards Yang Chow.[2] Meanwhile Leou of Tsing Chow entertained Fah Hian for the whole winter and summer. The summer period of rest being over, Fah Hian dismissed all the doctors of religion (who had been with him). He had been anxious for a long time to get back to Tchang'an. But as the engagements he had entered into were pressing ones, he directed his course first towards the southern capital,[3] where the different doctors edited the sacred books he had brought back.[4]

the district where Fah Hian landed was hardly in this department, unless the ship had altered her position, since she anchored in the department of Lai Chow.

[1] That is Ping Tu.

[2] A large and prosperous town situated on the Grand Canal in the province of Kiangsoo. According to Landresse, however, it at one time included the whole of the province of Kiangnan and part of Honan and Kiangsoo.

[3] That is, Nan King (Nankin).

[4] This is, properly speaking, the end of the narrative.

After Fah Hian left Tchang'an, he was five years in arriving at Mid-India. He resided there during six years, and was three years more before he arrived at Tsing Chow. He had successively passed through thirty different countries. In all the countries of India, after passing the Sandy Desert (of Gobi), the dignified carriage of the priesthood and the surprising influence of religion (amongst the people) cannot be adequately described. But, because our learned doctors had not heard of these things, he was induced, regardless of all personal considerations, to cross the seas, and to encounter every conceivable danger in returning home. Having been preserved therefore by Divine power (by the influences of the Three Honourable Ones), and brought through all dangers safely, he was further induced to commit to writing[1] these records of his travels, desiring that the virtuous of all ages may be informed of them together, as well as himself.

In this year[2] Kea-yin, being the twelfth of the reign of I Hi of the Tsin dynasty, when the star Sheou[3] was just emerging from the summer mansion, Fah Hian, the pilgrim, arrived home. He was detained all the winter in answering the multitude of questions put to him. Whoever enquired of him respecting his travels he always answered obligingly and exactly according

[1] Literally, commit to bamboo slips, on which they used to write before the invention of paper.

[2] That is, in the year 414-15 A.D.

[3] That is, just at the autumnal equinox.

to truth. Of these answers, the summary is found in this book. But when they pressed him to write a full record of all that happened to him from first to last, then he said, "If I were to recall all which has occured to me, then persons of unstable minds would be excited to strive how they might enter on similar dangers and encounter corresponding risks, reckless of their personal safety. For they would argue in this way, 'Here is a man who has escaped all and come back safe and sound;' and so these foolish persons would set about jeopardizing their lives in lands impossible to explore, and to pass through which, not one in ten thousand could hope for." On hearing these remarks, they all said, with a sigh of assent, "This man, in order to preserve the knowledge of old things and new, has himself penetrated to the eastern source of the great doctrine, and is yet alive. He has sought out the Law, and now exhibits it to us. Equally with us, then, shall all those who hereafter attain this knowledge, give him boundless thanks. And those also who assist to diffuse this knowledge, where it has not prevailed, shall acquire incalculable merit; and the chief merit of a sage is this—to neglect those things which are generally esteemed, and esteem those things which are generally neglected."

THE MISSION

OF

HWUI SENG AND SUNG YUN[1]

TO OBTAIN

BUDDHIST BOOKS IN THE WEST.[2]

(518 A.D.)

[*Translated from the 5th Section of the History of the Temples of Lo-Yang (Honan Fu)*].

In the suburb Wan I, to the N.E. of the city of Lo-Yang, was the dwelling of Sung Yun of Tun-Wang,[3] who, in company with the Bikshu Hwui Seng, was sent on an embassy to the western countries by the Empress Dowager (Tai Hau) of the Great Wei dynasty,[4] to ob-

[1] Called by (R.) Sung Yun tse (Fah Hian, cap. viii., note 1); but the word "tse" is no component part of the name. The passage in the original is this:—"In the Wan I suburb (li) is the house (tse) of Sun Yun of Tun-Wang."

[2] Western countries (si yu).

[3] Tun Wang or Sha Chow 40° 12′ N. Lat., 21° 37′ W. Long. from Pekin (Fah Hian, p. 3, note).

[4] At the fall of the Tsin dynasty (420 A.D.), the northern provinces of

tain Buddhist books. Of these they procured altogether 170 volumes, all standard works, belonging to the Great Vehicle.

First of all, having repaired to the capital, they proceeded in a westerly direction 40 days, and arrived at the Chíh Ling (Barren Ridge), which is the western frontier of the country. On this ridge is the fortified outpost of the Wei territory. The Chíh Ling produces no trees or shrubs, and hence its name (Barren). Here is the common resort (cave) of the Rat-Bird. These two animals, being of different species (chung), but the same genus (lui), live and breed together. The Bird is the male, the Rat the female. From their cohabiting in this manner, the name Rat-Bird cave is derived.

Ascending the Chíh Ling and proceeding westward 23 days, having crossed the Drifting Sands, they arrived at the country of the To-kuh-wan.[1] Along the road the cold was very severe, whilst the high winds and the driving snow, and the pelting sand and gravel were so bad, that it was impossible to raise one's eyes without getting them filled. The chief city of the To-kuh-wan is pleasantly situated; and the climate of the neighbourhood is agreeably warm. The written character of this country is the same as that of the Wei

China became the possession of a powerful Tartar tribe, know as the Wei. A native dynasty (the Southern Sung) ruled in the southern provinces, and has been regarded by subsequent writers as the legitimate one (Edkins).

[1] The Eastern Turks.

empire; the rules both of clergy and laity observed by these people are mostly barbarous. From this country, going west 3,500 li, we arrive at the city of Shen-Shen (Leou-Lan, 150 miles S.W. of Tung Wong, now called Makhai. *Vide* Fah Hian, p. 4, *n.*) This city, from its foundation, has been under the rule of the To-kuh-wan; and at present there resides in it a military officer of that country, with a body of troops, who are employed in subjugating the western Tartars.

From Shen-Shen, going west 1640 li, we arrive at the city of Tso-moh (Tche-mo-to-na of H. T.). In this town there are, perhaps, a hundred families resident. The country is not visited with rain, but they irrigate their crops from the streams of water. They know not the use of oxen or ploughs in their husbandry.

In the town is a representation of Buddha, with a Bôdhisatwa—but certainly not executed by any Tartar. On questioning an old man about it, he said, "This was done by Lu-Kwong, who subdued the Tartars." From this city, going westward 1275 li, we arrive at the city of Moh. The flowers and fruits here are just like those of Lo-Yang, but the buildings and the foreign officials are different in appearance.

From the city Moh, going west 22 li, we arrive at the city of Han-Mo.[1] Fifteen li to the south of this city is a large temple, with about 300 priests in it. These priests

[1] This is, probably, the Pi-Mo of Hiouen Thsang (Jul. iii. 243). The figure described in the Text is also alluded to by Hiouen Thsang, and is identified with the Sandal wood image of Oudyâna, King of Kâusambî.

possess a golden full-length figure of Buddha, in height a chang and $\frac{6}{10}$ (about 18 feet). Its appearance is very imposing, and all the characteristic marks of the body are bright and distinct. Its face was placed as usual looking eastward; but the figure, not approving of that, turned about and looked to the west. The old men have the following tradition respecting this figure:— They say that originally it came from the south, transporting itself through the air. The King of Khoten desiring himself to see it for the purpose of paying reverence to it, they attempted to convey it to his city, but in the middle of the route, when they halted at night, the figure suddenly disappeared. On dispatching men to look after it, they found it had returned to its old place. Immediately, therefore, (the King) raised a tower (over it), and appointed 400 attendants to sweep and water (the tower). If any of these servitors receive a hurt of any kind, they apply some of the gold leaf from off this figure to the injured part, and so are directly cured. Men, in after ages, began to build houses around the spot where this image was, (and so the town sprang up). The tower of this image, and the other towers, are ornamented with many thousand flags and streamers of variegated silk. There are perhaps, as many as 10,000 of these, and more than half of them belonging to the Wei country.[1] Over

[1] That is, were presented by sovereigns of the Wei dynasty, or during their reign.

the flags are inscriptions in the square character, recording the several dates when they were presented; the greater number are of the nineteenth year of Tai-Wo, the second year of King Ming (510 A.D.), and the second year of Yen Chang. There was only one flag with the name of the reigning monarch on it, and this was in the time of Yaou Tsun.

From the town of Han-Mo, going west 878 li, we arrive at the country of Khoten. The king of this country wears a golden cap on his head, in shape like the comb of a cock; the appendages of the head-dress hang down behind him two feet, and they are made of taffeta (kün), about five inches wide. On State occasions, for the purpose of imposing effect, there is music performed, consisting of drums, horns, and golden cymbals. The King is also attended by one chief bowman, two spearmen, five halberdiers, and, on his right and left, swordsmen, not exceeding one hundred men. The poorer sort of women here wear trowsers, and ride on horseback just as well as their husbands. They burn their dead, and, collecting the ashes, erect towers over them. In token of mourning, they cut their hair and disfigure their faces, as though with grief. Their hair is cut to a length of four inches, and kept so all round. When the king dies, they do not burn his body, but enclose it in a coffin and carry it far off and bury it in the desert. They found a temple to his memory, and, at proper times, pay religious service to his manes.

The king of Khoten was no believer in the Law of Buddha. A certain foreign merchantman, on a time, brought a Bikshu called Pi-lou-chan (Vâirôchana?) to this neighbourhood and located him under a plum-tree to the south of the city. On this, an informer approached the King and said, "A strange Shaman has come (to your Majesty's dominions) without permission, and is now residing to the south of the city, under the plum-tree." The King, hearing this, was angry, and forthwith went to see Vâirôchana. The Bikshu then addressed the King as follows: "Ju-lai (Tathâgata) has commissioned me to come here to request your Majesty to build for him a perfectly finished pagoda (lit. a pagoda with a surmounting spire), and thus secure to yourself perpetual felicity." The King said, "Let me see Buddha and then I will obey him." Vâirôchana then, sounding a gong,[1] requested (Buddha to appear); on which Buddha commissioned Rahûla to assume his appearance and manifest himself in his true likeness in the air. The King prostrated himself on the ground in adoration, and at once made arrangements for founding a temple under the tree. Then he caused to be carved a figure of Rahûla as he appeared in the air; and, for fear of its perishing, the King afterwards constructed a chapel for its special preservation. At present it is carefully protected by a sort of shade (jar), that covers it; but, notwithstanding this, the shadow of the figure

[1] The expression in the original implies the use of some magical influence to constrain Buddha to send Rahûla.

constantly removes itself outside the building, so that those who behold it can scarcely help becoming converts. In this place (or chapel) are the shoes of a Pratyêka Buddha, which have up to the present time resisted decay. They are made neither of leather or silk,—in fact, it is impossible to determine what the material is. The extreme limits of the kingdom of Khoten reach about 3000 li or so, from east to west.

In the second year of Shan Kwai (519 A.D.) and the 7th month, 29th day, we entered the kingdom of Shih-Ku-Po (Tchakouka) (Yerkiang). The people of that country are mountain dwellers. The five kinds of cereals grow in abundance. In eating these, they make them into cakes. They do not permit the slaughter of animals, and such of them as eat flesh only use that which dies of itself. The spoken language both of clergy and laity is like that of the people of Khoten, but the written character in use is that of the Brahmans. The limits of this country can be traversed in about five days.

During the first decade of the 8th month, we entered the country of Han-Pan-to (Kie-pan-to—Kartchou of H. T.). Still going west six days, we entered on the Tsung Ling mountains; and advancing yet three days to the west, we arrived at the city of Kiueh-Yu; and after three days more, to the Puh-ho-i mountains.[1] This spot is extremely cold. The snow accumulates both by

[1] This phrase Puh-ho-i may also be translated the "Untrustworthy Mountains."

winter and summer. In the midst of the mountain is a lake in which dwells a mischievous dragon. Formerly there was a merchant who halted by the side of the lake. The dragon just then happened to be very cross, and forthwith pronounced a spell and killed the merchant. The King of Pan-to,[1] hearing of it, dispatched an embassy with his own son to the country of Ou-chang,[2] to acquire knowledge of the spells used by the Brahmans. After four years, having procured these secrets, they came back to the King, who again sent them to the lake to enchant the dragon. Having recited the spells, lo! the dragon was changed into a man, who, deeply sensible of his wickedness, approached the King. The King immediately banished him from the Tsung Lung mountains, more than 1000 li from the lake. The king of the present time is of the 13th generation (from these events). From this spot westward the road is one continuous ascent of the most precipitous character; for a thousand li there are overhanging crags, 10,000 fathoms high, towering up to the very heavens. Compared with this road, the ruggedness of the great Pass known as the Mang Mun is as nothing, and the eminences of the celebrated Hian mountains (in Honan) are like level country. After entering the Tsung Ling mountains, step by step, we crept upwards for four days, and then reached the highest part of the range. From this

[1] That is, Kartchou. [2] Oudyâna in N. India.

point as a centre, looking downwards, it seems just as though one was poised in mid-air (and the heavens lay at one's feet). The kingdom of Han-pan-to stretches as far as the crest of these mountains. To the west of the Tsung Ling mountains all the rivers flow to the westward (and enter the sea (Ch. ed.). Men say that this is the middle point of heaven and earth (the roof of the world, Bam-i-Duniah). The people of this region use the water of the rivers for irrigating their lands; and when they were told that in the middle country (China) the fields were watered by the rain, they laughed and said, "How could heaven provide enough for all." To the eastward of the capital of this country (Kartchou?) there is a rápid river[1] (or a river, Mang-tsin; or, a wide-ford river) flowing to the N.E. towards Sha-leh (Sand-curb). The high lands of the Tsung Ling mountains do not produce trees or shrubs. At this time, viz. the eighth month, the air is icy cold, and the north wind carries along with it the drifting snow for 1000 li. At last, in the middle decade of the 9th month, we entered the kingdom of Poh-ho (Bolor?). The mountains here are as lofty and the gorges deep as ever. The king of the country has built a town, where he resides, for the sake of being in the mountains. The people of the country dress hand-

[1] That is, perhaps, the Kará-Sou of Klaproth, which flows into the Tiz-âb, an affluent of the Yerkiang river; or it may be the Si-to river, on which Yarkand stands, and which empties itself into Lake Lob, in the Sandy Desert (Shah-leh?).

somely, only they use some leathern garments. The land is extremely cold—so much so, that the people occupy the caves of the mountains as dwelling places, and the driving wind and snow often compel both men and beasts to herd together. To the south of this country are the great Snowy Mountains, which, in the morning and evening vapors, rise up like gem-spires opposite one.

In the first decade of the 10th month we arrived at the country of the Ye-tha. The lands of this country are abundantly watered by the mountain streams, which fertilize them and flow in front of all the dwellings. They have no walled towns; but they keep order by means of a standing army that constantly moves here and there. These people also use felt garments. The course of the rivers is marked by the verdant shrubs that fringe their banks. In the summer the people seek the cool of the mountains; in the winter they disperse themselves through the villages. They have no written character. Their rules of politeness are very defective. They have no knowledge at all of the movements of the heavenly bodies; and, in the division of the year, they have no intercalary month, or any long and short months; but they merely divide the year into twelve parts, and that is all. They receive tribute from all surrounding nations: on the south as far as Tieh-lo;[1] on the north,

[1] This may possibly be the Hi-mo-ta-la country of Hiouen Thsang, bordering on the great range of the Hindou-Koush.

the entire country of Lae-leh[1] (Lala, or it may be read Chih-leh), eastward to Khoten, and west to Persia—more than forty countries in all. When they come to the court with their presents for the king, there is spread out a large carpet about forty paces square, which they surround, with a sort of rug hung up as a screen. The king puts on his robes of state and takes his seat upon a gilt couch, which is supported by four golden phœnix birds. When the ambassadors of the Great Wei dynasty were presented (that is, Soung Yun and Hwui Seng themselves), (the king), after repeated prostrations,[2] received their letters of instruction. On entering the assembly, one man announces your name and title; then each stranger advances and retires. After the several announcements are over, they break up the assembly. This is the only rule they have; there are no instruments of music visible at all. The royal ladies of the Ye-tha[3] country also wear state robes, which trail on the ground three feet and

[1] The La-la or Lâra people were probably a Northern Scythian tribe, perhaps akin to the Paralatæ of Herodotus.

[2] It is customary among the Chinese to receive royal messages with much ceremony. Amongst the regulations in the work called "Tsing kwei," or "Instructions for the priesthood, for the observance of all fasts and feasts throughout the year," is one for the day of receiving an imperial message, when it is ordered, "that the monks, headed by their superiors, should issue from the monastery and bow their foreheads to the ground three times before receiving the royal mandate." This custom probably prevailed among all Tartar tribes allied to the Wei family.

[3] The Ye-tha were probably the Little Yuchi, or White Huns (C.).

more; they have special train bearers for carrying these lengthy robes. They also wear on their heads a horn, in length eight feet[1] and more, three feet of its length being red coral. This they ornamented with all sorts of gay colours, and such is their head-dress. When the royal ladies go abroad, then they are carried (either in a chariot or other way); when at home, then they seat themselves on a gilded couch, which is made in the shape of a six-tusked white elephant, with four lions (for supporters). As for the rest of the great ladies, they all in like manner cover their heads, using horns, from which hang down veils all round, like precious canopies. Both the rich and poor have their distinctive modes of dress. These people are of all the four tribes of barbarians the most powerful. The majority of them are unbelievers. Most of them worship false gods. They kill living creatures and eat their flesh. They use the seven precious substances, which all the neighbouring countries bring as tribute, and gems in great abundance. It is reckoned that the distance of the country of the Ye-tha from our capital is upwards of 20,000 li.

On the first decade of the 11th month we entered the confines of the country of Po-sse[2] (Persia). This

[1] I see no other way of translating this passage, although it seems puzzling to know how these royal ladies could carry such an ornament as this upon their heads.

[2] The name of Persia or Eastern Persia extended at this time even to the base of the Tsung Ling mountains (*vide* Elphinstone's India).

territory (ground) is very contracted. Seven days further on we come to a people who dwell in the mountains, and are exceedingly impoverished. Both the clergy and laity are rough and unmannered. On seeing their king they pay him no honour; and when the king goes out or comes in, his attendants are very few. This country has a river which formerly was very shallow; but afterwards, the mountains having subsided, the course of the stream was altered and two lakes were formed. A mischievous dragon took up his residence here, and caused many calamities. In the summer he rejoiced to dry up the rain, and in the winter to pile up the snow. Travellers by his influence are subjected to all sorts of inconveniences. The snow is so brilliantly white that they have to cover their eyes, or they would be blinded by it; but if they pay some religious service to the dragon they find less difficulty afterwards.

In the middle decade of the 11th month we entered the country of Shie Mi (Cashmere?). This country is just beyond the Tsung Ling mountains. The aspect of the land is still rugged; the people are very poor; the rugged narrow road is dangerous—a traveller and his horse can hardly pass along it, one at a time. From the country of Po-lu-lai (Bolor) to the country of

The Parthians assumed the Persian name and affected Persian manners, "διασώζουσι καὶ ἀπομιμοῦνται τὰ Περσικὰ ὀυκ ἀξιοῦντες, ἐμοὶ δοκει, Παρθυαῖοι νομίζεσθαι, Πέρσαι δὲ εἶναι προσποιούμενοι," says the Emperor Julian (Or. de Constantin. gest. ii. p. 63; Rawlinson's Herod. i., 534, n.).

Ouchang (Oudyâna) they use iron chains for bridges. These are suspended in the air for the purpose of crossing (over the mountain chasms). On looking downwards no bottom can be perceived; there is nothing to grasp at in case of a slip, but in a moment the body is hurled down 10,000 fathoms. On this account travellers will not cross over, in case of high winds.

On the first decade of the 12th month we entered Ouchang country (Oudyâna). On the north this country borders on the Tsung Ling mountains; on the south it skirts India. The climate is agreeably warm. The territory contains several thousand li. The people and productions are very abundant. The fertility of the soil is equal to that of Lin-tsze (in Shantung) and the climate more equable. This is the place where Pi-lo (Avalôkitêswara?) delivered the child, and where Bôdhisatwa gave his body (to the tigress).[1] Once on a time the whole body of the people left the land, except the clergy, but these availed to protect it. The king of the country religiously observes a vegetable diet; on the great fast days (*vide* Jul. ii. 6, *n.*) he pays adoration to Buddha, both morning and evening, with sound of drum, conch, vîṇâ (a sort of lute), flute and all kinds of wind instruments. After mid-day he devotes himself to the affairs of government. Supposing a man has committed murder, they do not suffer him to be killed; they only banish him to the desert mountains,

[1] This sentence and the following are very obscure.

affording him just food enough to keep him alive (*lit.* a bit and a sup). In investigating doubtful cases,[1]—as, for example, cases of poisoning by accident (*lit.* (death by) administering medicine for the purpose of cleansing the system),—then, after examination, the punishment is adjusted according to the serious or trivial character of attending circumstances. At the proper time, they let the streams overflow the land, by which the soil is rendered soft and fertile. All provisions necessary for man are very abundant, cereals of every kind (*lit.* of 100 sorts) flourish, and the different fruits (*lit.* the five fruits) ripen in great numbers. In the evening the sound of the convent bells may be heard on every side, filling the air with their melody; the earth is covered with flowers of different hues, which succeed each other winter and summer, and are gathered by clergy and laity alike as offerings for Buddha.

The king of the country seeing Sung Yun (enquired respecting him, and) on their saying that the ambassadors of the Great Wei (dynasty) had come to salute him, he courteously received their letters of introduction (this may also be rendered, "hearing that the ambassadors of the Great Wei had come, he bowed down to them and received," etc.). On understanding that the Empress Dowager was devotedly attached to the Law of Buddha, he immediately turned his face to the east,

[1] This passage is translated by (R.) thus: "When any matter is involved in doubt, they appeal to drugs and decide upon the evidence of these" (Fah Hian, c. viii., n. 1).

and, with closed hands and meditative heart, bowed his head (in prayer); then, sending for a man who could interpret the Wei language, he questioned Sung Yun and said, "Are my honourable visitors men from the region of Sun-rising?" Sung Yun answered and said, "Our country is bounded on the east by the great sea; from this the sun rises according to the Divine will (the command of Tathâgata)." The king again asked, "Does that country produce holy men?" Sung Yun then proceeded to enlarge upon the virtues of Confucius and Laou (Tseu) of the Chow dynasty, and then of the silver walls and golden palaces of Fairy Land (Pung loi Shan), and then of the spirits, genii, and sages, who dwell there; in connection with the above he further dilated on the subjects of divination, alchemy and magic, and medicine; descanting on these various subjects and properly distinguishing their several properties, he finished his address. Then the king said, "If these things are really as your worship says, then truly yours is the land of Buddha, and I ought to pray at the end of my life that I may be born in that country."

After this, Sung Yun, with Hwui Seng, left the city for the purpose of inspecting the traces which exist of the teaching (or religion) of Tathâgata. To the east of the river is the place where Buddha dried his clothes. When first Tathâgata came to the country of Ou-chang, he went to convert a dragon king. He, being angry with

Buddha, raised a violent storm with rain. The Sanghâṭi of Buddha was soaked through and through with the wet. After the rain was over, Buddha stopped on a rock, and, with his face to the east, sat down whilst he dried his robe (Kasha). Although many years have elapsed since then, the traces of the stripes of the garment are as visible as if newly done, and not merely the seams and bare outline, but one can see the marks of the very tissue itself, so that in looking at it, it appears as if the garment had not been removed, and, if one were asked to do it, as if the traces might be lifted up (as the garment itself). There are memorial towers erected on the spot where Buddha sat, and also where he dried his robe. To the west of the river is a tank occupied by a Nâga Râja. By the side of the tank is a temple served by fifty priests and more. The Nâga Râja ever and anon assumes supernatural appearances. The king of the country propitiates him with gold and jewels, and other precious offerings, which he casts into the middle of the tank; such of these as afterwards find their way out through a side exit, the priests are permitted to retain. Because the Dragon thus provides for the necessary expenses of this temple (clothes and food), therefore men call it the Nâga Râja temple.

Eighty li to the N. of the royal city there is the trace of the shoe of Buddha on a rock. They have raised a tower to enclose it. The place where the print of the shoe is left on the rock, is as if the foot had trodden on soft mud. Its length is undetermined, as at one time it is long, and at another time short. They have now founded a temple on the spot, capable of accommodating seventy priests and more. Twenty paces to the south of the tower is a spring of water issuing from a rock. It was here Buddha once came to cleanse (his person), on which occasion he bit off a piece of his tooth-stick (Dantakâshṭa) (Jul. iii. 49 and ii. 55), and planted it in the ground; it immediately took root, and is at present a great tree, which the Tartars call Po-lou.[1] To the north of the city is the To-lo[2] temple, in which there are very numerous appliances for the worship of Buddha. The pagoda is high. The priests' chambers are ranged in order round the temple (or tower). There are sixty full-length golden figures (herein). The king, whenever he convenes (or convening yearly) a great assembly, collects the priests in this temple. On these occasions the Shamans within the country flock together in great crowds. Sung Yung and Hwui Seng, remarking the strict rules and eminent piety (extreme austerities) of those Bikshus, and from a sense that the example of these priests singularly conduced to increase (their own) religious feelings, remitted two servants for the use of the convent to prepare the religious offerings and to water and sweep the temple. From the royal city, going S.E. over a mountainous

1 The Pilu tree (Salvadora Persica).

2 To-lo, a contraction (probably) of Cho-lo-tou-lo, *i.e.* Salâtoura.

district, eight days' journey, we come to the place where Tathâgata, practising austerities, gave up his body to feed a starving tiger. It is a high mountain, with scarped precipices and towering peaks that pierce the clouds. The fortunate tree[1] and the Ling chi grow here in abundance, whilst the groves and fountains (or the forest rivulets), the docile stags and the variegated hues of the flowers, all delight the eye. Sung Yun and Hwui Seng devoted a portion of their travelling funds to erect a pagoda on the crest of the hill, and they inscribed on a stone, in the square character, an account of the great merits of the Wei dynasty. This mountain possesses a temple called "collected bones,"[2] with 300 priests and more. One hundred and odd li to the south of the royal city is the place where Buddha (Julai), formerly residing in the Ma-hiu country, peeled off his skin for the purpose of writing upon it, and extracted (broke off) a bone of his body for the purpose writing with it. Asôka Râja raised a pagoda on this spot for the purpose of enclosing these sacred relics. It is about ten chang high (120 feet). On the spot where he broke off his bone, the marrow run out and covered the surface of a rock, which yet retains the colour of it, and is unctuous as though it had only recently been done.

[1] Probably the tree known in the south as the "Calpa Wurksha," or the tree that gives all that is desired. R. translates it the tree "Kalpa daru."

[2] R. gives this "collected gold," but I know not on what authority.

To the S.W. of the royal city, 500 li, is the Shen-chi[1] hill (Sudatta) (or, the hill of (the Prince) Sudatta). The sweet waters and delicious fruits (of this place) are spoken of in the Sacred Books (the Sûtras and Vyâkaranas). The grottoes of this mountain are agreeably warm; the trees and shrubs retain a perpetual verdure. At the time when the pilgrims arrived (Ta'i Tshau), the gentle breeze which fanned the air, the songs of the birds, the trees in their spring-tide beauty, the butterflies that fluttered over the numerous flowers,—all this caused Sung Yun, as he gazed on this lovely scenery in a distant land, to revert to home thoughts; and so melancholy were his reflections, that he brought on a severe attack of illness; after a month, however, he obtained some charms of the Brahmans, which gave him ease.

To the S.E. of the crest of the hill Shen-chi, is a rock-cave of the Prince,[2] with two chambers to it. Ten paces in front of this cave is a great square stone on which it is said the Prince was accustomed to sit; above this Asôka raised a memorial tower.

[1] Shen-chi, "illustrious resolution," evidently a mistake for "shen-chi," "illustrious charity."

[2] That is, of the Prince Sudatta or the Bountiful Prince. The whole of the history alluded to in the text may be found in Spence Hardy's Manual of Buddhism, under the Wessantara Jâtaka, p. 116. The account states that Wessantara (the Prince alluded to in the text, called "the Bountiful," because of his extreme charity) gave to the King of Kâlinga a white elephant that had the power to compel rain to fall. On this the subjects of the Prince's father (who was called Sanda) forced him to banish the prince, with his wife (Madridéwi) and his two children, to the rock Wankagiri, where the events alluded to in the text occurred.

One li to the south of the tower is the place of the Pansala (leafy hut) of the Prince. One li N.E. of the tower, fifty paces down the mountain, is the place where the son and daughter of the Prince persisted in circumambulating a tree (in order to escape from the Brahman who had begged them from their father as slaves). On this the Brahman beat them with rods till the blood flowed down and moistened the earth. This tree still exists, and the ground, stained with blood, now produces a sweet fountain of water. Three li to the west of the cave is the place where the heavenly king Sekra, assuming the appearance of a lion sitting coiled up in the road, concealed Man-këa.[1] On the stone are yet traces of his hair and claws. The spot also where Adjitakouta[2] (O-tcheou-to-kiu) and his disciples nourished the Father and Mother (*i.e.* the Prince and Princess). All these have memorial towers. In this mountain formerly were the beds of 500 Arhats ranged N. and S. in a double row. Their seats also were placed opposite one to another. There is now a great temple here with about 200 priests. To the north of the fountain which supplied the Prince with water is a temple. A herd of wild asses frequent this spot for grazing. No one drives them here, but they resort here of their own accord. Daily at early

[1] This may possibly allude to Madri-dewi, but the whole passage is obscure.

[2] Called Acchuta in the Singhalese accounts. He was an ascetic who resided in the neighbourhood of the hill.

morn they arrive—they take their food at noon, and so they protect the temple. These are spirits who protect the tower (protecting-tower-spirits), commissioned for this purpose by the Rishi Uh-po (Oupa? conf. Oupagupta, defended by Oupa). In this temple there formerly dwelt a Shami (Samanêra), who, being constantly occupied in sifting ashes (belonging to the convent), fell into a state of fixed composure (Samâdhi). The Karmadana of the convent had his funeral obsequies performed, thinking he was dead, and not observing that his skin continued unchanged. After his burial, the Rishi Oupa continued to take the office of the Samenêra in the place of sifting the ashes. On this the king of the country founded a chapel to the Rishi, and placed in it a figure of him as he appeared, and ornamented it with much gold leaf.

Close to the peak of this hill is a temple of Po-kin (Bhagaván?), built by the Yakshas. There are about 80 priests in it. They say that the Rahats and Yakshas continually come to offer religious services, to water and sweep the temple, and to gather wood for it. Ordinary priests are not allowed to occupy this temple (or, "as to the usual body of lay servants, the Bikshus do not allow them to dwell in the temple"). The Shaman To Yung, of the Great Wei dynasty, came to this temple to pay religious worship; but having done so, he departed, without daring to take up his quarters there. During the middle decade of the 4th month of the reign Ching Kwong (520 A.D.), we entered the kingdom of Gandhára. This country closely resembles the territory of Ou-chang. It was formerly called the country of Ye-po-lo.[1] This is the country which the Ye-thas[2] destroyed and afterwards set up Lae-lih to be king over the country; since which events two generations have passed. The disposition of this king was cruel and vindictive, and he practised the most barbarous atrocities. He did not believe the Law of Buddha, but loved to worship demons. The people of the country belonged entirely to the Brahman caste; they had a great respect for the Law of Buddha, and loved to read the Sacred Books, when suddenly this king came into power, who was strongly opposed to anything of the sort, and entirely self-reliant. Trusting to his own strength, he had entered on a war with the country of Ki-pin (Cophene)[3] respecting the boundaries of their kingdom, and his troops had been already engaged in it for three years.

The King has 700 war elephants, each of which carries ten men armed with sword and spear, whilst the elephants are armed with swords attached to

[1] Referring, in all probability, to the Dragon Apalâla, whose fountain to the N.E. of Moungali (the capital of Ou-chang) gave rise to the river Subhavastu or Swêti, that flows through this territory.

[2] Alluding to the conquest of Kitolo, the king of the Little Yu-chi (or Ye-thas) at the beginning of the 5th century. This king conquered Gândhâra, and made Peshâwar his capital.

[3] Then in the possession of the Great Yuchi, whose capital was Kabul.

their trunks, with which to contend when at close quarters. The King continually abode on the frontier and never returned (to his kingdom), in consequence of which the seniors had to labour and the common people were oppressed. Sung Yun repaired to the royal camp to deliver his credentials. The King[1] was very rough with him, and failed to salute him. He sat still whilst receiving the letters. Sung Yung perceived that these remote barbarians were unfit for exercising public duties, and that their arrogancy refused to be checked. The King now sent for interpreters, and addressed Sung Yun as follows:—"Has your worship not suffered much inconvenience in traversing all these countries and encountering so many dangers on the road." Sung Yun replied, "We have been sent by our royal mistress to search for works of the great translation through distant regions. It is true the difficulties of the road are great, yet we dare not complain or say we are fatigued; but your majesty and your forces as you sojourn here on the frontier of your kingdom, enduring all the changes of heat and cold, are you not also nearly worn out?" The King, replying, said: "It is impossible to submit to such a little country as this, and I am sorry that you should ask such a question." Sung Yun, on first speaking

[1] This king was probably the one called Onowei, who reigned under the title "So-lin-teu-pim-teu-fa Khan," or, "the Prince who seizes and holds firmly." We are told that he refused homage to the Wei Tartars, alluding probably to the circumstance recorded in this account of Sung-Yun (C.).

with the King (thought), "this barbarian is unable to discharge with courtesy his official duties,—he sits still whilst receiving diplomatic papers, and is wrapped up in himself;" but, on second thoughts, reflecting that he also had the feelings of a man, he determined to reprove his conduct and said, "Mountains are high and low—rivers are great and small—amongst men also there are distinctions, some being noble and others ignoble. The sovereign of the Ye-tha, and also of Ou-chang, when they received our credentials, did so respectfully; but your Majesty alone has paid us no respect." The King, replying, said, "When I see the King of the Wei, then I will pay my respects; but to receive and read his letters whilst seated, is surely no such outrageous occurrence. When men receive a letter from father or mother, they don't rise from their seats to read it. The Great Wei sovereign is to me (for the nonce) both father and mother, and so, without being unreasonable, I will read the letters you bring me, still sitting down." Sung Yun then took his departure without any official salutation. He took up his quarters in a temple in which the religious services were very poor. At this time the country of Po-tai[1] sent two young lions to the King of Gandhâra as a present. Sung Yun had an opportunity of seeing them; he noticed their fiery temper and courageous

[1] Perhaps the same as the Fa-ti (Betik) of Hiouen Thsang, 400 li to the west of Bokhara (Jul. iii. p. 282).

mien. The pictures of these animals common in China are not at all good resemblances of them.

After this, going west five days, they arrived at the place where Tathâgata made an offering of his head for the sake of a man—where there is both a tower and temple, with about twenty priests. Going west three days, we arrive at the great river Sin-tou. On the west bank of this river is the place where Tathâgata took the form of (or became) a great fish called Ma-kie (Magara), and came out of the river, and for twelve years supported the people with his flesh. On this spot is raised a memorial tower. On the rock are still to be seen the traces of the scales of the fish.

Again going west thirteen days' journey, we arrived at the city of Fo-sha-fu.[1] The river valley (in which this city is built) is a rich loamy soil. The city walls are constructed with double gates. There are very many groves (around the city), whilst fountains of water enrich the soil; and, as for the rest, there are costly jewels and gems in abundance. Both clergy and laity are honest and virtuous. Within this city there is an heretical temple[2] of ancient date called "Sang-teh" (Sânti?). All religious

[1] The Varousha (Po-lou-sha) of Hiouen Thsang.

[2] In this passage I take the word "Fan" (all) to be a misprint for "Fan" (Brahman), in which case the expression "Wei fan" would mean "heretical Brahmans." If this be not the correct translation of the passage, then it may perhaps be rendered thus: "Within and without this city there are very many old temples, which are named "Sang-teh" (sanḍi, union or assembly?).

persons frequent it and highly venerate it. To the north of the city, one li, is the temple of the White Elephant Palace.[1] Within the temple all is devoted to the service of Buddha. There are here stone images highly adorned and very beautiful, very many in number, and covered with gold sufficient to dazzle the eyes. Before the temple and belonging to it is a tree called the White Elephant Tree, from which, in fact, this temple took its origin and name. Its leaves and flowers are like those of the Chinese Date tree, and its fruit begins to ripen in the winter quarter. The tradition common amongst the old people is this: "That when this tree is destroyed, then the Law of Buddha will also perish." Within the temple is a picture of the Prince[2] and his wife with their children, begging of a Brahman. The Tartar (conquerors of the country), seeing this picture, were so moved that they could not refrain from tears.

Again going west one day's journey, we arrive at the place where Tathâgata gave his eyes in charity. Here also is a tower and a temple. On a stone of the temple is the impress of the foot of Kasyâpa Buddha. Again going west one day we crossed a deep river,[3] more than 300 paces broad. Sixty li S.W. of this we arrive at the capital of the country of Gandhâra.[4] Seven li to the S.E.

[1] This is probably the Pilousâra Stoupa of Hiouen Thsang (Jul. ii. 54).
[2] That is, of the Bountiful Prince (Wessantara) referred to before.
[3] The Indus.
[4] That is, Peshâwar.

of this city there is a Tsioh-li Feou-thou[1] (a pagoda called Tsioh-li). [The record of To-Yung says: "Four li to the east of the city."] Investigating the origin of this tower, we find that when Tathâgata was in the world he was passing once through this country with his disciples on his mission of instruction; on which occasion, when delivering a discourse on the east side of the city, he said, "Three hundred years after my Nirvâṇa, there will be a king of this country called Ka-ni-si-ka (Kanishka). On this spot he will raise a pagoda (Feou-thou). Accordingly, 300 years after that event, there was a king of this country, so called. On one occasion, when going out to the east of the city, he saw four children engaged in making a Buddhist tower out of dung; they had raised it about three feet high, when suddenly they disappeared. [The record states, "One of the children, raising himself in the air and turning towards the king, repeated a verse (Gâtha).] The king surprised at this miraculous event, immediately erected a tower for the purpose of enclosing (the small pagoda), but gradually the small tower grew higher and higher, and at last went outside and removed itself 400 feet off, and there stationed itself. Then the king proceeded to widen the foundation of the great tower 300 paces and more.[2] [The record of To-Yung says 390 paces.] To crown all, he placed a roof-pole upright and even.

[1] Tsioh-li means a sparrow—possibly it may be a corruption of She-li (Sarîras), alluding to the relics contained in this celebrated pagoda.

[2] Hiouen Thsang says it was a li and a half in circumference.

[The record of To-Yung says it was 35 feet high.] Throughout the building he used ornamental wood; he constructed stairs to lead to the top. The roof consisted of every kind of wood. Altogether there were thirteen stories; above which there was an iron pillar, 3 feet high,[1] with thirteen gilded circlets. Altogether the height from the ground was 700 feet. [To-Yung says the iron pillar was 88$\frac{8}{10}$ feet (high), with fifteen encircling discs, and 63$\frac{2}{10}$ changs from the ground (743 feet).] This meritorious work being finished, the dung pagoda, as at first, remained three paces south of the great tower. The Brahman, not believing that it was really made of dung, dug a hole in it to see. Although years have elapsed since these events, this tower has not corrupted; and although they have tried to fill up the hole with scented earth, they have not been able to do so. It is now enclosed with a protecting canopy. The Tsioh-li pagoda, since its erection, has been three times destroyed by lightning, but the kings of the country have each time restored it. The old men say, "When this pagoda is finally destroyed by lightning, then the Law of Buddha also will perish." The records of To-Yung says, "When the king had finished all the work except getting the iron pillar up to the top, he found that he could not raise this heavy weight. He proceeded, therefore, to erect at the four corners a lofty

[1] Most likely there is a mistake in the text, as the height of the iron pillar should be 30 feet.

stage; he expended in the work large treasures, and then he, with all his court and princes ascending on to it, burnt incense and scattered flowers, and, with their hearts, called on the gods to help them; then, with one turn of the windlass, they raised the weight and so succeeded in elevating it to its place. The Tartars say, therefore, that the four heavenly kings lent their aid in this work, and that, if they had not done so, no human strength would have been of any avail. Within the pagoda there is contained every sort of Buddhist utensil; here are gold and jewelled (vessels) of a thousand forms and vast variety—to name which even would be no easy task; at sunrise the gilded discs of the vane are lit up with dazzling glory, whilst the gentle breeze of morning causes the precious bells (that are suspended from the roof) to tinkle with a pleasing sound. Of all the pagodas of the western world, this one is by far the first (in size and importance). At the first completion of this tower they used true pearls in making the net-work-covering over the top; but after some years, the king, reflecting on the enormous value of this ornamental work, thought thus with himself: "After my decease (funeral) I fear some invader may carry it off"—or "supposing the pagoda should fall, there will be no one with means sufficient to re-build it;"—on which he removed the pearl work and placed it in a copper vase, which he removed to the N.W. of the pagoda 100 paces, and buried it in the earth. Above the spot he planted a tree, which is called Po-tai (Bôdhi), the branches of which, spreading out on each side, with their thick foliage, completely shade the spot from the sun. Underneath the tree on each side there are sitting figures (of Buddha) of the same height, viz. a chang and a half (17 feet). There are always four dragons in attendance to protect these jewels; if a man (only in his heart) covets them, calamities immediately befall him. There is also a stone tablet erected on the spot, and engraved on it are these words of direction: "Hereafter, if this tower is destroyed, after long search, the virtuous man may find here pearls (of value sufficient) to help him restore it."

Fifty paces to the south of the Tsioh-li pagoda there is a stone tower, in shape perfectly round, and two chang high (27 feet). There are many spiritual portents gathered from this building; so that men, by touching it, can find out if they are lucky or unlucky. If they are lucky, then by touching it the golden bells will tinkle; but if unlucky, then, though a man should violently push the tower, no sound would be given out. Hwui Seng, having travelled far from his country and fearing that he might not have a fortunate return, paid worship to this sacred tower, and sought a sign from it. On this, he did but touch it with his finger and immediately the bells rang out. Obtaining this omen, he comforted his heart. And the result proved the truth of the augury. When Hwui Seng first went up to the capital, the Empress had conferred upon him a thousand streamers of a hundred feet in length and of the five colours, and five hundred figured (mats ?) of scented grass. The princes, dukes and nobility had given him two thousand flags. Hwui Seng, in his journey from Khoten to Gândhâra,—wherever there was a disposition to Buddhism,—had freely distributed these in charity; so that when he arrived here, he had only left one flag of 100 feet in length, given him by the Empress. This he decided to offer as a present to the tower of Sivika Raja, whilst Sung Yun gave two slaves to the Tsioh-li pagoda, in perpetuity, to sweep it and water it. Hwui Seng, out of the little funds he had left, employed a skillful artist to depict on copper the Tsioh-li pagoda and also the four principal pagodas of Sakya Mouni.

After this, going N.W. seven days' journey, they crossed a great river (Indus), and arrived at the place where Tathâgata, when he was Sivika Râja,[1] delivered the dove; here there is a temple and a tower also. There was formerly here a large storehouse of Sivika Râja, which was burnt down. The grain which was in it was parched with the heat, and is still to be found in the neighbourhood (of the ruins). If a man takes but a single grain of this, he never suffers from fever; the people of the country also take it to prevent the power of the sun hurting them.

[1] *Vide* Jul. ii. 137.

The records of To-Yung say, "At Na-ka-lo-ho[1] there is a skull bone of Buddha, four inches round, of a yellowish-white colour, hollow underneath, sufficient to receive a man's finger; to the touch it is soft as wax.

We then visited the Ki-ka-lam[2] temple. This contains the robe (kasha) of Buddha in thirteen pieces. In measurement this garment is as long as it is broad (or, when measured, it is sometimes long and sometimes broad). Here also is the staff of Buddha, in length a chang and seven-tenths (about 18 feet), in a wooden case, which is covered with gold leaf. The weight of this staff is very uncertain; sometimes it is so heavy that a hundred men cannot raise it, and at other times it is so light that one man can lift it. In the city of Nagrâk is a tooth of Buddha and also some of his hair—both of which are contained in precious caskets; morning and evening religious offerings are made to them.

We next arrive at the cave of Gopâla, where is the shadow of Buddha. Entering the mountain cavern fifteen feet, and looking for a long time (or, at a long distance) at the western side of it opposite the door, then at length the figure, with all its characteristic marks, appears; on going nearer to look at it, it gradually grows fainter and then disappears. On

[1] Nagarahâra.

[2] The Khakkharam Temple, or the Temple of the Religious Staff (*vide* Fah Hian, cap. xiii.).

touching the place where it was with the hand, there is nothing but the bare wall. Gradually retreating, the figure begins to come in view again, and foremost is conspicuous that peculiar mark between the eye-brows (ourna), which is so rare among men. Before the cave is a square stone, on which is a trace of Buddha's foot.

One hundred paces S.W. of the cave is the place where Buddha washed his robe. One li to the north of the cave is the stone cell of Mogalan; to the north of which is a mountain, at the foot of which the great Buddha, with his own hand made a pagoda, ten chang high (115 feet). They say that when this tower sinks down and enters the earth, then the Law of Buddha will perish. There are, moreover, seven towers here; to the south of which is a stone with an inscription on it; they say, Buddha himself wrote it. The foreign letters are distinctly legible even to the present time.

Hwui Seng abode in the country of Ou-chang two years. The customs of the clergy and the laity of the western foreigners (Tartars) are, to a great extent, similar (with ours); the minor differences we cannot fully detail. When it came to the second month of the second year of Ching-un (521 A.D.) he began to return.

The foregoing account is principally drawn from the private records of To-Yung and Sung Yun. The details given by Hwui Seng were never wholly recorded.

STEPHEN AUSTIN, PRINTER, HERTFORD.

ERRATA.

Title Page, *for* "Amithâba" *read* "Amitâbha."
Page xxvi., *for* "517 A.D." *read* "517 B.C."
" lvii. n., *for* "âtma" *read* "âtman."
" lxiv., line 23, *for* "incurred" *read* "occurred."
" 7, for 1 read 2, and for 2 read 1, in the notes.
" 8, n. 2, *for* "du" *read* "de."
" 14, n. 1, *for* "Meridan" *read* "Meridian."
" 19, line 2, *for* "size" *read* "the size."
" 19, n. 3, *for* "Far kai lih to" *read* "Fah kai lih to."
" 20, place 1 and 2 at the head of the notes.
" 22, n. 4, *for* "did" *read* "died."
" 25, n. 1, *for* "70 feet" *read* "19 feet."
" 26, n. 1, *for* "East" (line 2) *read* "West," *and for* "West" (line 3) *read* "East."
" 32, n. 1, *for* "Τα'ξιλα" *read* "Τάξιλα."
" 40, n. 3, line 6, *for* "of" *read* "or."
" 48, line 6, *omit* "ten."
" 79, line 11, *for* "the Chandâla woman" *read* "the woman Sundara," or, "the Beauty."
" 128, line 24, *for* "with" *read* "within."
" 142, n. 2, *for* "Chap. xxvi." *read* "Chap. xxvii."
" " n. 3, line 10, *omit* "do."
" 174, line 16, *for* "the Eastern source of the great doctrine" *read* "the source of the Eastern diffusion of the great doctrine."
" 178, line 18 and following, *substitute* "they apply some gold leaf to the part of the figure corresponding to the place of their hurt or pain."
" 186, line 4, *for* "ornamented" *read* "ornament."
" " line 9, *read* "which is made of ivory from elephants of the Chhadanta Lake (Hodgson, 186)."
" 192, line 11, *after* To-lo *add* "(Târa Devi)" *and omit* note 2.
" 197, line 3, *for* "it was formerly called" *read* "its native name is Nieh-po-lo (? Nilâba)."
" 197, line 8, *for* "of this king" *read* "of the reigning king," and in the lines following this, to the end of clause, *substitute* verbs of the *present* tense.
" 203, line 12, *for* "Brahman" *read* "Brahmans."

NOTE.

The following contractions are used throughout this work :—

Jul. I. II. III.—The Life of Hiouen-Thsang and the 1st and 2nd Vol. of the Si-yu-ki, by M. Stanislas Julien.

V. St. M.—Vivien St. Martin's addenda to Hiouen-Thsang.

M. B.—The Manual of Buddhism, by Spence Hardy.

E. M.—Eastern Monachism, by Spence Hardy.

C.—The Archæological Surveys of India.

P.—Pauthiers's Marco Polo.

R.—Rémusat's Fo-koue-ki.

I. B.—Introduction to Indian Buddhism, by Burnouf.

THE figures stamped upon the covers of this work are—(1.) (On the obverse) a copy of the sandal wood figure of Buddha, made by King Oudâyana. This figure is photographed from a large scroll brought by Colonel Barnard, R.M.A., from one of the Lama Temples, near Pekin. It is the best traditional likeness of Buddha, and has a history attached to it in China dating from the first century A.D. (2.) (On the reverse) a copy of a figure of Manes or Mani—the founder of the Manichæan sect—taken from a well-known work called the Confessional of Kwan-yin. He is regarded by the Chinese as one Manifestation of Iswara, *i.e.* God (Avalokitêshwara).